What others are saying
about Frank Schaeffer's
PATIENCE WITH GOD

12/10

"Frank Schaeffer is a patient writer but a passionate one too. This beautiful, argumentative, and even funny book is popular theology at its best, an explanation of tradition and its absence from a writer who knows better than most that God—whether you do or don't believe—is always a brilliant story."

—JEFF SHARLET, *New York Times*
bestselling author of *The Family*

"Ever feel straitjacketed by the Church? Convinced that God can't be put in a box? You've got to read Frank Schaeffer's explanation of why you're not alone, and how contradictions can be a paradox to be celebrated. You'll be intellectually challenged and spiritually heartened by his life story and lessons learned."

—RICHARD CIZIK, President, The New Evangelicals,
Fellow, The Open Society Institute

"*Patience With God* does more than celebrate the gift of paradox—it's a feast for those hungering for something truly greater than themselves and their own ideas."

—CHARLES E. MOORE, editor, *Provocations:*
The Spiritual Writings of Kierkegaard

"With remarkable skill Schaeffer exposes the flaws of fundamentalists and atheists alike, only to reveal the true meaning of faith."

—PATRICIA FERNÁNDEZ-KELLY, Princeton University

"*Patience With God* gives us voice, it validates our experiences, it starts a conversation—one that has been needed for a long, long time."

—JOHN F. DEFELICE, University of Maine at Presque Isle

"*Patience with God* presents an alternative that we would do well not to ignore. It is an appeal for sanity, compassion, tolerance, and authentic spirituality."

—REVEREND ANTONY HUGHES, St. Mary
Orthodox Church, Cambridge, Massachusetts

PATIENCE WITH GOD

Patience

With

God

Faith for People Who Don't Like Religion (*or* Atheism)

by

FRANK SCHAEFFER

DA CAPO PRESS
A Member of the Perseus Books Group

Designed by Brent Wilcox
Set in 11 point Sabon by the Perseus Books Group

Library of Congress Cataloging-in-Publication Data
Schaeffer, Frank.
    Patience with God : faith for people who don't like religion (or
atheism) / by Frank Schaeffer. — 1st Da Capo Press ed.
        p.   cm.
    ISBN 978-0-306-81854-7 (alk. paper)
    ISBN 978-0-306-81922-3
    1. Faith.   2. Schaeffer, Frank.   3. Christianity and atheism.
4. Fundamentalism.   I. Title.
    BV4637.S3263 2009
    261.2'1—dc22

                                                        2009026242

First Da Capo Press edition 2009
First paperback edition 2010

Published by Da Capo Press
A Member of the Perseus Books Group
www.dacapopress.com

Da Capo Press books are available at special discounts for bulk purchases
in the U.S. by corporations, institutions, and other organizations. For
more information, please contact the Special Markets Department at the
Perseus Books Group, 2300 Chestnut Street, Suite 200, Philadelphia, PA
19103, or call (800) 810-4145, ext. 5000, or e-mail
special.markets@perseusbooks.com.

10 9 8 7 6 5 4 3 2 1

*To
my granddaughter
Lucy*

*and to her mother
Becky*

CONTENTS

PROLOGUE *Why This Book May Not Be What You Expect* XI

PART I
Where Extremes Meet

1 How the New Atheists Poison Atheism 3

2 How Many Ways Are There to Say, "There Is No God!"? 15

3 Why Does Dawkins Oppose Faith with Lapel Pins? 27

4 Determinism Religious and Secular Is the Ultimate Insanity Defense 43

5 Dennett Says Religion Evolved the Way Folk Music Did 59

6 Hitchens Poisons Hitchens 71

7 The Only Thing Evangelicals Will Never Forgive Is Not Hating the "Other" 89

8 Spaceship Jesus Will Come Back and Whisk Us Away 109

PART II

Patience With Each Other, Patience With God

9   So Naked Before a Just and Angry God   125

10   There Is More in Man Than the Mere Breath of
     His Body   143

11   That "Truth Button" Should Humble Everyone   165

12   How Do Spiritual Catalysts Work?   175

13   "Shedding over Every Daily Task the Light of Love"   185

14   He Never Left a Trace That He'd Been There   201

15   Much More Miraculous Than a Good Cup of Coffee   211

16   "First and Last Alike Receive Your Reward"   221

ACKNOWLEDGMENTS   229

Why This Book
May Not Be What You Expect

So let others admire and extol him who claims to be able to
comprehend Christianity. . . . I regard it then as a plain duty
to admit that one neither can nor shall comprehend it.

The Sickness Unto Death, Søren Kierkegaard

When I place my five-month-old granddaughter Lucy on a blanket
on my kitchen table, and I help her stretch by rubbing her feet, legs,
and arms in what my wife Genie calls "Lucy's Grandpa spa," everything fades away—bills, the economy, who got elected, even the
background "sound track" of my impending doom, that ticking
clock of aging, never too far below the surface these days. Lucy loves
stretching after her naps. She smiles and looks into my eyes with
such contentment that I feel transported to a place beyond time and
reckoning where nothing exists but my hunger to reward this little
girl's love.

I find myself praying, "Lord, may none but loving arms ever hold
her." That prayer has nothing to do with theology. I'd pray it
whether I believed there is a God or not, for the same reason that
on a lovely spring morning when I'm looking at the view of the river
that flows past our home I sometimes exclaim, "That's beautiful!"
out loud, even when I'm alone.

Genie and I offered my son John and his wife Becky a place to live while they got on their feet financially. It has been a long haul since John unexpectedly volunteered to serve in the Marines right out of high school, was deployed to war several times, returned home, concluded his time of service, went to the University of Chicago, married Becky, graduated from U of C with honors, had Lucy, and started a new job. This is the son I was on my knees praying for while he was being shot at. He came home! My son's baby daughter Lucy is in my arms! Life is sweet! When I hold Lucy, belief in God seems natural.

Why do I write about faith and/or include religion and religious people in so many of my books? What's it to me if I disagree with the New Atheists *and* with religious fundamentalists? First, one writes about the life one has experienced. I've lived religion. Second, I don't like to be forced to choose between lousy alternatives. Third, I think that I keep writing about faith because my faith needs affirmation.

One person running around shouting "Jesus saves!" or throwing stones at the Devil while circling a large black rock, or proposing that science is *the* alternative to religion sometimes appears crazy, even to himself or herself. Fill a church with a thousand people moaning, "Lord have mercy," or pack a million pilgrims on their hajj around that rock, or fill a classroom with students applauding someone's declaration of atheism, and each member of the group can say to himself or herself, "So many of us can't be wrong! There must be something to this!"

Speaking of God, there are thousands of books hanging around in my house worrying me. In those books are tens of millions of words. None of those words (including these) explain why the greatest pleasure that I experience during any given day is when I lose myself in the small yet overwhelming presence of my granddaughter. Caring for Lucy feels as if I'm diving through warm, crystal clear water above some shimmering Mediterranean reef. Body temperature and water match. Everything is stunningly beautiful. I disappear. The usual selfish "me" that is the sum total of my genes and/or God/Mom/Dad/whatever–induced worries, is temporarily forgotten.

The experience evokes the fondest of childhood memories, of being once again truly carefree, as I was when my family traveled by train each year from our home in Switzerland to Portofino, Italy, where we vacationed, where sand and sea, freedom to wander, and the blood-warm water and languid pace of life left such a lasting impression of joy that the childhood memory of "my" Italy defines happiness for me fifty years later. So it is with Lucy; I stop worrying when I hold her, and simply *am*.

Thanking someone for Lucy seems natural to me. I pray even though I'm a "faith person" who often wishes he weren't. I'm sick of religion for the same reason that I'm tired of my body, how it's getting old, how every morning when I wake up, the dreary realization crashes in: I'm still me. Sick of being me or not, I still brush my teeth, take a daily vitamin, stick to my low-dose aspirin regimen, drink red wine because I like it *and* it's better for me than white wine, and get colonoscopies from time to time. I still go to church, too, regardless of the fact that I get dumb hate emails signed "in Christ," blasting me for everything from my support of President Obama to my having fled my evangelical/fundamentalist roots and the Republican Party.

This is a book for those of us who *have* faith in God in the same way we might *have* the flu, less a choice than a state of being in spite of doubt, in spite of feeling wounded by past religious contagion, in spite of our declared agnosticism or even atheism, in spite of the sorts of idiots like me who are attracted to or, more accurately, bred to, religion and run around defending and /or criticizing it.

This book is part of a conversation, not a sermon. I've written it the way faith in God, and everything else, happens, to me. *Happens* is the right word. In Hollywood when I used to work as a movie director, the producers always wanted an "arc" to the story. The worse the script was, and the more formulaic, the more obvious the arc. There was a beginning, a middle and an end; good guys and bad guys; first, second, and third "acts" leading to the conclusion. But faith in

God, and great movies made by the greatest directors (of whom I certainly was never one) such as Bob Altman and Federico Fellini, don't string along like cars of a train or come in tidy packages. They *are* a slice of life, not a story *about* life.

My only promise is that I'm trying to tell the truth about my slice of life as I see it, even when the best I can do is to say that I don't know the answers. So there are ideas here but also stories memoir and memory of what shaped the person writing down the ideas. That means we jump from ideas to stories that could be from a novel about the person writing the essay. Don't be surprised by these twists and turns. This is how conversations go. This is what life, rather than false "arcs," is like.

In Part I, the first chapters are a critique of the New Atheists. The next chapters are a critique of the religious fundamentalists. Then in Part II, I write about my experiences related to faith or lack of faith in God, and the evolving nature of what I describe as the catalysts that may take us to whatever the next stages of our personal and communal spiritual evolution may be.

Bob Altman said of his movie directing that "accidents are what push the 'truth button.'" I've tried not to edit out those accidents, even in the parts of this book that tend to essay style. In other words, this book is for those of us who are stuck feeling that there is more to life than meets the eye, whatever we call ourselves or say we believe. Or put it this way: If an angel showed up outside my office window and explained "everything" to me, I'd simultaneously question my sanity, be scared as hell, *and* feel mightily relieved, because believing in invisible things is tough.

I'm not the only person wrestling with issues of meaning, religion, and purpose. You will find a small sample here of the several thousands of emails from my readers who have been responding to my writing, radio, and TV interviews and lectures about religion, politics, and society. Their emails, including the following note, inspired me to write this book. (I've omitted names to protect privacy and have indicated trims by ellipses. And each email represents many similar to it.)

Hello, Mr. Schaeffer. I watched your Princeton lecture. I found it interesting, but I learned nothing of your new religious beliefs, except that you enjoy Greek Orthodox liturgy. I presume you still avow some form of Christianity.

I do still avow some form of Christianity in spite of my doubts, the attack on faith by the New Atheists, and the "certainties" of the religious fundamentalists who claim their way is the only truth, which is another way to attack faith because it drives people away from experiencing God. I believe that the ideological opposites I'll be talking about—atheism and fundamentalist religion—often share the same fallacy: truth claims that reek of false certainties. I also believe that there is an alternative that actually matches the way life is *lived* rather than how we usually talk about belief. I call that alternative "hopeful uncertainty."

My hopeful uncertainty will either resonate with you eliciting a "me too" and "been there" or not. I am not trying to make converts. If what I write resonates, it will be because we've shared certain experiences, for instance your own childhood stories and your own love for a friend, lover, or a husband or wife, children, and grandchildren, not because I convince you of anything. I offer no proofs. There are none. When talking about the unknowable, pretending to have the facts is about as useful as winning a medal from the Wizard of Oz. In this game—the meaning game—it's all about intuition, hope, and the experience of life, a letting go of all concepts, words, and theologies because they can only be metaphors and hinder our experience of the truth as it is—not as we desire, believe, or hope it might or should be, but as it *is*.

Before continuing I have several disclosures to make. To begin with, I have a vested interest in keeping faith in God relevant. Also, I'll be talking about religion but concentrating on Christianity. That is the tradition I know a little about, having been raised by evangelical/fundamentalist American missionaries.

As a young man in the early 1970s I did a really stupid thing and stopped painting, drawing, and sculpting, thus truncating what was becoming a promising art career. I'd had successful shows in New York, Geneva, and London by the time I was twenty-two. I got greedy for a faster track with a steadier income, and I became my parents' (Francis and Edith Schaeffer) sidekick. I then became a leader in my own right on the big-time evangelical/fundamentalist circuit after we Schaeffers got famous—famous within the evangelical/fundamentalist ghetto, that is.

By the early 1980s, at the height of my involvement in the evangelical/fundamentalist religious right, I was invited to preach from Jerry Falwell's pulpit, appeared many times on *The 700 Club* with Pat Robertson, and met privately with many of the top Republican leadership of the day. In the midst of these heady experiences I began to change my mind about what I believed, and not just about religion but about politics too.

By the mid-1980s I began the process of escaping my family's literal-minded religion and the political causes that had become indistinguishable from it. I went to Hollywood, directed four indifferent-to-pretty-terrible R-rated feature films, quit the movie business, and then started to write novels in the early 1990s. I received encouragement from the critics and my readers. I've been a "secular" full-time writer of both fiction and nonfiction ever since.

Although I'm no longer proselytizing, I've profitably (in every sense of that word) mined the divine mother lode of my background through my Calvin Becker trilogy of semi-autobiographical novels *Portofino*, *Zermatt*, and *Saving Grandma* and also in *Baby Jack* (where God shows up as an African American Marine drill instructor on Parris Island), not to mention my memoir *Crazy for God*. As my religion-preoccupied writing demonstrates, one can run from a religion but can never entirely escape.

I not only grew up in the fevered atmosphere of an American religious commune—L'Abri Fellowship (located in Switzerland of all places)—but at age ten I was sent to an evangelical British boys boarding school called Great Walstead, where I encountered an easygoing and refreshingly new to me, Anglican-derived faith that embodied a level of religious tolerance I wasn't familiar with. Later in life the memory of that encounter shaped my sense that there might be better alternatives to the strict fundamentalism I was raised on. It may also be one reason why, much, much later when in midlife, I discovered that sacrament-based liturgical worship was a comfortable fit for me and I joined the Greek Orthodox Church.

So please note, as I conclude this disclosure, that my only "qualification" for meditating on faith in God is no more than the better part of a lifetime spent thinking about faith and reading about religion (and a few other things) and then living among, and then fleeing, the faithful. I'm with Danish philosopher Søren Kierkegaard when he says of Christianity that "one neither can nor shall comprehend it."

Kierkegaard's view was closer to many of the early Church Fathers—in other words, to the first leaders in the early Christian Church (during the first to sixth centuries) than it is to today's fundamentalists. Until I was on my way out of my evangelical/fundamentalist subculture and actually read a little church history and some of the writings from the earliest Christians, I assumed that older is always stricter. In the case of the Christian religion, this is not so. It's mostly the later eras of Christianity that produced the most rules-based approach to faith, something like the transition from the sixties and early seventies to the "Reagan eighties," as hippies got haircuts and put on suits and turned out to be more middle-class and "bourgeois" than their parents.

So for people who think that Christianity was strict, literalistic and fundamentalist and filled with nothing but rules and regulations from the beginning and that a more "mystical," "tolerant," "progressive," or "liberal" approach to faith is a lax modern phenomenon, the writings of some of the most important early Christian figures are a startling wake-up call. For instance, one fourth-century ascetic—Evagrius Ponticus—was a revered spiritual leader. He led by example rather than by official standing because he was not a bishop. Writing in *The Gnostikos*, he made this anti-fundamentalist statement: "Do not define the Deity: for it is only of things which are made or are composite that there can be definitions."

Speaking of "the Deity," I have a love-hate relationship with God—well, actually not with God (as Evagrius said, who knows anything about that?) but with the people who have tried to define God in ways that the more tolerant earlier Christians didn't. My love-hate relationship is with fundamentalists who say they believe in God and with people who are so sure there is no God that they've turned atheism into just another brow-beating religion. That means I have a love-hate relationship with myself, because I find both sides of the faith/no faith debate coexisting within me. Those "sides" are expressed well by juxtaposing the following emails from two men with very different viewpoints:

> Frank: Any religious faith is nothing more than an adult fairy-tale. . . . Now I admit that I may be wrong . . . you may enjoy Orthodox liturgy for its own sake. . . . Still, I find it perplexing. . . . My question to you is: Why do you, a very smart person, continue to hold to a fairy-tale?
>
> *Respectfully, T.*

Just as I was about to try and come to the defense of the "fairy-tale," I received an email from an Orthodox priest. Unlike a lot of the emails I get, at least this one was signed—but for current purposes, let's just call the sender Father X.

The email questioned my Christianity because I supported a pro-choice candidate like Obama. Since Fr. X believed that Obama represented everything Christianity does not stand for, where did I get off calling myself a Christian? Not to mention that I blogged on the *Huffington Post*, that internet portal to damnation.

OK—comes with the territory. But here's the kicker. The sender signed what was a very insulting note: *In Christ, Father X.*

(*Rant starts here:*) When I got this email I thought it might be a joke, because my long experience with Orthodox priests and bishops has been almost uniformly positive. I googled the name and found that this man was an actual priest. Father X badgered me for several weeks since I chose not to answer him. Then I began to receive emails that Fr. X had been sent a copy of, as had a growing list of others whose names showed up from then on in my email letterbox. It seemed that Father X had "introduced" me to his far right friends.

Abortion was their big issue, as were Obama's "communism." Several people accused me of "supporting the Antichrist." Nearly all of them told me I was due for a severe punishment from God.

None of these prolific email writers seemed to bother to read my replies, to which I attached articles I'd written for the *Huffington Post* explaining in some detail why I was both pro-life *and* pro-Obama, given that I believed that his social programs might help reduce the numbers of abortions, just as he said that he hoped they would, and that, conversely, the Republicans had been cynically using the "life issue" to drum up votes while cutting funding for health care, contraceptives, sex education, and child care. Of course I could have been wrong about all my political ideas on the subject, but I certainly hadn't become a "leading abortionist," as three of my email correspondents said I had.

I can only imagine the steady diet of junk ideology that must have been spewing from right-wing websites, evangelical/fundamentalist leaders, talk radio, and bizarre newsletters into the heads of these email writers to have pushed them—including a priest no less, supposedly a confessor, shepherd, and comforter—to put politics ahead of faith and berate a *complete stranger* and question his faith on the basis of who that stranger voted for and what websites he writes for and because of a disagreement over *tactics* regarding how best to reduce the number of abortions.

The Religious Right has seduced millions of Americans with titillating hatred and lies: The earth was created in six days and is *not* warming; Obama is a secret Muslim (perhaps even the Antichrist!) and wants women to have more abortions; gays are trying to take over America; the United Nations (and/or Obama and/or the president of the European Union) is the Antichrist; an unregulated market economy is Christian; guns keep people safe; taxing the rich is "communism"; capital punishment is good; immigrants are the enemy; national health care is "communist." Some or all these paranoid fantasies are accepted as truth by a whole substratum of "Christians" determined to judge their country as "fallen away from God." They believe America is "doomed" because they don't agree with their fellow citizens' politics or because, as their signs routinely proclaim, "God Hates Fags!" They call people like me "abortionists" because I and others say that maybe the best way to reduce abortion is to keep it legal but to also help women escape poverty, educate young people, and provide contraception rather than trying to reverse *Roe v. Wade* (realistically an impossibility, on which pro-lifers have wasted almost forty years of effort and untold tens of millions of dollars).

Appeals to facts get nowhere with these folks because they don't trust any sources but their own and listen only to what emanates from an alternative right-wing universe. Thus arguments become circular. The more impartial the source, the more suspect it becomes. Propaganda, fulminating (and fundraising), and hatred of gays, women, our government, big-city folks, black people, the educated "elite," everything-not-like-us-Real-Americans supplant compassion and even common sense. And one is guilty by association. Write for the "wrong" people "these people," in the words of Fr. X or vote for the "wrong" president, or make the "wrong" call on a practical way to reduce abortions, and it's off to the stake.

The late Neil Postman, author, New York University professor, and prophet, predicted how and why people such as today's members of the evangelical/fundamentalist movement and other right wingers would be living in a dream world cut off from reality. Postman is best known for his 1985 book about television, *Amusing Ourselves to Death*, in which he wrote

> Television is altering the meaning of 'being informed' by creating a species of information that might properly be called disinformation. Disinformation does not mean false information. . . . What Orwell feared were those who would ban books. What Huxley

feared was that there would be no reason to ban a book, for there would be no one who wanted to read one. . . . Orwell feared that the truth would be concealed from us. Huxley feared the truth would be drowned in a sea of irrelevance. Orwell feared we would become a captive culture. Huxley feared we would become a trivial culture, preoccupied with some equivalent of the feelies, the orgy porgy, and the centrifugal bumble puppy.

Postman is not the only person to have accurately predicted where we are headed and the sort of society that our disjointed news-media-as-entertainment, texting as "writing," blogging as "news" would produce. *RoboCop* (1987) was a mediocre (and nastily sadistic) little movie, but director Paul Verhoeven got one thing right: the "news" shows on TV in his futuristic dystopia. His parody of glib, cheerful trivia clips as news has come horribly true, even more so with the advent of the ideologically divided Web, wherein people have their "information" filtered by like-minded ideologues and rarely encounter views they disagree with. As Postman predicted, Huxley's prophetic vision came to pass: We *are* "a trivial culture, preoccupied with some equivalent of the feelies."

We have become a nation of not terribly bright children who essentially have a collective learning disability manifested by an inability to concentrate or defer gratification, to hold one thought long enough to see it through to a conclusion, or to contemplate making real sacrifices for the sake of long-term benefits. The Father Xs of this world are one result.

Just in case you think that Father X's excesses let atheists off the hook—and also to capture a little of the tone of the atheist/religion debate these days—here is another email I got from a reader objecting to an article I wrote criticizing the New Atheists. (Misspellings in the original)

Sir, You had an insolence . . . to call the brightest people of our time "the fundamentalist Atheists." These people: Hitchens,

Dawkins, Harris are the great Heroes of our time. . . . These heroes are withstanding to the thousands and thousands of years of corrupted, filthy religious fanaticism. . . . We would avoid many, many deceases if not for religion. Religion is the opium for the masses. It was said by a smart man. I completely agree with this comment. You are, Sir, brainwashing people and are filling your deep pockets with the dirty money using people's stupidity. Shame on you!

Sincerely
Y

No, I didn't make that up. Though I *was* tempted to forward Y's email to Fr. X, feeling that these men would understand each other quite well!

(*End of rant!*)

Okay, about that "fairy-tale" of religion. I discovered from the emails I've been inundated with since my memoir was published that there are more of us perplexed former (or currently) religiously inclined or religiously raised folks on a journey from past certainties to points unknown than I'd been aware of. We want to have faith in God in spite of our bad experiences with religion, oppressive family relationships, and/or doubts and questions. We too worry that we've been hoodwinked by a fairy tale. I hope that this book will provide a meeting place for those of us who count ourselves among the scattered members of what I'll call the Church of Hopeful Uncertainty in the same way that this man's email helped me feel less alone.

Frank: Growing up, I attended a private Christian school which was started by a very conservative religious right church connected with Bob Jones University. . . . I have studied to be a preacher, and seem to have no desire to be one but have no experience to do anything else. . . . Truth be told, I have more questions than answers. . . . I have broken through the false, religious right, closed minded doctrine of hate that was my past. However, I have not found any answers from the religious left. The left is good at saying what the right has done wrong but not at giving me anything to hold on to.

Thank you, K.

This book is a search for that "something" to hold on to. I don't know if my up-and-down, hot-then-cold-then-hot-again faith in God persists because I was conditioned by my parents to see everything in spiritual terms or if faith is a choice. Either way, whatever I believe or feel, or *think* I feel or *think* I believe, it's flawed at best. Like most people, I've changed my mind before about the so-called Big Questions and will again. Opinion is a snapshot in time.

Because I belong to the Greek Orthodox Church, there are parts of this book that reflect my personal experience with one form of liturgical worship. In those Orthodox-oriented parts my aim is to offer an example of *one approach*, knowing that other people take other religious paths (or none) and find spiritual comfort. And I certainly do not speak for the Orthodox Church. Nor has being in the Orthodox Church answered all my questions. Far from it. And I know that some of what I say here may be a departure from what some Orthodox (especially to the political right) think is true. But I believe that my journey is worth describing because my life experiences have led me to believe that there are better choices than being asked to decide between atheistic cosmic nothingness and fundamentalist heavenly pantomimes.

PART I

Where Extremes Meet

CHAPTER 1

How the New Atheists
Poison Atheism

He who became unhappy in love, and therefore became a poet, blissfully extols the happiness of love so he became a poet of religiousness, he understands obscurely that it is required of him to let this torment go.

The Sickness Unto Death, Søren Kierkegaard

At a time when Islamist extremists strap bombs to themselves and blow up women and children; when America has just come staggering out of the searing thirty-year-plus embrace of the reactionary, dumb-as-mud Religious Right; and when some people are bullying, harassing, and persecuting gay men and women in the name of religion, it's understandable that the sort of decent people most of us would want for neighbors run from religion. There is a problem, though, for those who flee religion expecting to find sanity in unbelief: The madness never was about religion, let alone caused by faith in God. It was and is about how we evolved and what we evolved into.

In other words, Pogo, the Walt Kelly possum cartoon character, was right: "We have met the enemy and he is us!" If only making ourselves happy, kind, and tolerant were as simple as giving up religious faith. If that's all it took, the Soviet Union under Stalin and China under Mao would have been such nice places to live, and for that matter, our secularized Ivy League universities would be filled with saints, instead of back-stabbing intellectuals ready to destroy each other over who gets tenure.

Like it or not, we humans are flawed spiritual creatures peering from biological brains. By "spiritual" I mean self-contemplating and/or self-loathing. I think that our spirituality is best defined as our awareness of our own consciousness. Rats, mice, amoebas, and planets aren't self-contemplating and/or self-loathing. We're different. So there is a tension between what we *are*, material beings living in a material universe, and how we *feel* about ourselves. We feel that we are more than the sum of our parts. We try and bridge this spirit/body gap. We look to religion, science, faith, psychology whatever to answer the question: Why are we self-observing, or, to put it another way, who am I?

Here is an important question: Who, exactly, is doing the observing? Why do we have a sense of a "self" that stands apart from, or thinks it stands apart from, the biological machines we are? Who is this person living within me asking questions about *me*? Joseph LeDoux, a neuroscientist and a professor at New York University, has explored the self in a number of books, including *The Emotional Brain* and *Synaptic Self: How Our Brains Become Who We Are*. LeDoux came up with a theory: It's the neural pathways, the synaptic relationships in our brains, that make us who we are.

I don't know enough about neuroscience to have an opinion about whether LeDoux is correct. He makes sense to me, but the point here isn't the science of consciousness, but rather that we humans try to understand how and why consciousness resides in our material bodies. We want to believe in something to help us explain our self-contemplating natures. One thing we can count on: Everyone has faith in something, even if it is faith in having no faith. And as this woman wrote to me, our faiths are not static, they evolve:

Frank: I was a preacher's kid raised in Virginia in the 60's. . . . From a young age, I openly questioned and rebelled. . . . Thankfully in my 40s I found Buddhism and am finding peace and a filter to look at Christian precepts that, heretofore, were so tinny in sound and virtually meaningless. . . . Today, my partner and I are caring for my 85 yr old mother who has Alzheimer's. . . . This too is a spiritual growing experience. . . . Over time it has allowed me the opportunity to "dis-identify" with her anger and anxiety [and] . . . see them as less personal to me.

Sincerely, F.

The question is: Will our faith in God, or something nonreligious, be practiced with the humility and tolerance discovered by F, or will it breed Father X's unfortunate "certainties"? How do we find peace? Perhaps the choice isn't between chaos and resolution. Maybe there is another alternative: accepting irresolution. Maybe faith that doesn't evolve is not living faith because all living things change.

"Logic" is beside the point because we can't look *at* ourselves, only *through* ourselves. We're stuck *inside* the painting we're trying to critique *and* paint at the same time—in other words, our lives. A scientist like LeDoux is trapped trying to figure out what is going on inside his head while *using his head* to do the figuring. So let's admit the problem Charles Darwin identified in his *Autobiography.* "Can the mind of man, which has, as I fully believe, been developed from a mind as low as that possessed by the lowest animal, be trusted when it draws such grand conclusions?"

In the prologue I wrote about my faith needing affirmation. I'm not the only person writing books and thereby seeking allies and/or trying to encourage fellow travelers. There have been many best-selling books recently published proselytizing for or against faith in God. I'll be discussing a few of these books and their authors in a bit more detail (not necessarily in this order), because they illustrate larger issues. (You don't have to have read any of these works to understand what I'll be saying about the questions they raise.)

As a token of the tens of thousands of books pushing the evangelical/fundamentalist worldview, I'll look at Rick Warren's *A Purpose Driven Life* and Jerry Jenkins and Tim LaHaye's *Left Behind* series of novels presenting their version of a Jesus-solves-everything born-again message. On the flip side are the New Atheists' books. These include Sam Harris's *The End of Faith*, Daniel Dennett's *Breaking the Spell*, Richard Dawkins's *The God Delusion*, and Christopher Hitchens's *God Is Not Great*. There are many other evangelical/fundamentalist and New Atheist books, and more are being published almost daily, but they tend to repeat the ideas set forth in the ones I've chosen to focus on.

Some of the New Atheists make insulting claims about religion. For instance, Dennett coined a self-referential term for atheists, "Bright," that, by inference, leaves the rest of us, who believe in God, as "Dim." And Harris doesn't stop with labels. In his book he suggests that some religious people may need to be killed because of their dangerous beliefs.

I suspect, although I can't prove, that the timing of the New Atheists' crusade against religion has less to do with religion per se and more to do with a post-9/11 reaction against militant Islam. Then there's the politics. The context of the heating up of the New Atheist movement also has to do with the justifiable anger felt by reasonable people everywhere at the horrible way George W. Bush led the United States. An unnecessary war in Iraq, legalized torture, an unregulated market economy (which proved ruinous), a badly managed war in Afghanistan, little-to-no action to repair the earth's environment, an unforgivably slow response to the devastation of Hurricane Katrina, presidential sniping at evolution being taught in schools, an affirmation of the most mindless sort of "born-again" faith, a campaign against sex education, ties to the apocalyptic "End Times" evangelical/fundamentalist cult that many suspect skewed Bush's Middle East politics toward the State of Israel (in a way that was harmful to all concerned)—this and more was the context of the New Atheist reaction. Bush was the born-again's born-again, the evangelical's president par excellence. His voter base was the American evangelical movement. Bush's idea of governance (or should I say non-governance) was clearly shaped by his religion.

I agree with the New Atheists: It is time for religion to go—intolerant, politicized ugly religion as we know it, that is. I agree with religious people, too: Atheism has killed many more millions of people, specifically in the name of godless ideologies, than all religions combined ever killed in the name of God or any gods. Or put it this way: The atheist yells, "Crusades!" The religious believer counters, "Stalin!" The atheist says, "Faith in science!" The believer answers, "Faith in God!" Are we stuck trading catchphrases like school children taunting each other on the playground, or is there a better way to discuss what boils down to just two issues: the quest for meaning in our lives and the search for an answer concerning the origin of everything?

Although they usually seem to lack the self-criticism gene, and I do not agree with a lot that the New Atheists have written or said, nevertheless I think that they are doing us a service by offering their harsh critiques of religion. The problem I have with the "solution" offered by the more radical of the New Atheists—which is to get rid of religion—is that we are spiritual beings with or without their permission, no matter what we (or they) say we are. The New Atheists have proved this by turning their movement into a quasi-religion with priests, prophets and gurus, followers, and even church services.

It seems to me that the various New Atheist priests, prophets, and gurus have one thing in common: They are old-fashioned literalists. The tone of their books strikes me as stuck in a premodern time warp. They return in spirit to the era before postmodernism when people from the intellectuals behind the Bauhaus architecture and art movement to literal interpreters of Marxism were given to pronouncing grand theories that set out to explain everything, be it everything about art, politics, philosophy, history, or architecture.

The term *postmodernism* as used here describes an aesthetic, artistic worldview that is characterized by a distrust of ideology. I think it also applies to the "certainties" on both sides in the religion vs. atheist debate. The New Atheists pit religion's literalistic truth claims against their own literalistic truth claims. In that sense the New Atheists turn out to be secular fundamentalists arguing with religious fundamentalists.

To me the secular and religious contenders seem to miss the reality of our actual condition: We are specks on a tiny planet and our concept of truth, time, and space is related to our limited perspective. It strikes me that postmodernism possesses a healthy sense of skepticism when it comes to grand theories. Truth is, if not only "in the eye of the beholder," nevertheless always seen through an opaque filter. And whatever solutions we embrace had better be on a human scale and reflect something of the paradoxes we encounter in real life.

Consider how Richard Dawkins proposes his alternative to God regarding his idea of how we got here. As we shall see, he talks about the billions and billions perhaps trillions of solar systems increasing the probability of life originating, and he speaks in terms that evoke a kind of Russian roulette. Because everything must have happened at least once in an infinite universe, maybe that explains, well, everything. The problem is that these are just words. They could just as well be used to argue the probability of the existence of God in a limitless universe where everything must have happened at least once somewhere—say, for instance, a virgin birth.

Words were invented by people to describe what they perceive to be "true" from what amounts to an ant's roadside eye-view of passing cosmic traffic. Dawkins *knows* no more about the vast, forever-beyond-our-reach totality of the universe than I do about God. He thinks, hopes, surmises, does a bit of reading, uses words as metaphors to describe his ideas about things (which is all words are), grows old, and dies. So do we all.

No one *knows* anything about the Big Questions, and what we "know" about our minuscule place in the universe, and even of our own lives, is spectacularly limited. In other words, humility is in order, or, as the biblical writer of First Corinthians puts it: "And if anyone thinks he knows anything, he knows nothing yet as he ought to know."

Before moving on I'll define the terms *fundamentalist, evangelical/ fundamentalist* and *New Atheist* as used here. My definition of *fundamentalism*, religious or otherwise, is the impulse to find *The* answer, a way to shut down the question-asking part of one's brain. Fundamentalists don't like question marks. Fundamentalists reject both Christian humility and postmodern paradox. In that sense an atheist too may be a fundamentalist. And a fundamentalist wants to convince others to convert to what fundamentalists are *sure* they *know*.

I also use the term *evangelical/fundamentalist*. I do this as a way of drawing a distinction between the tolerant traditions within the Protestant evangelical community (embodied in groups such as the Mennonites, Quakers, predominantly black denominations such as the Progressive National Baptist Convention, the African Methodist Episcopal Church, and ministries like the Salvation Army and the Sojourners—this last led by theologian and social activist Jim Wallis) and the all-too-common conservative, right-wing, politicized "Christianity" of the evangelical/fundamentalist establishment.

The term *New Atheist* is just a flash-in-the-pan media invention. Nevertheless, I think it denotes a useful distinction from an older form of atheism. The word *new* sets the New Atheists apart as especially aggressive, political, and evangelistic. The "new" part is more about tactics and tone than substance.

To put the New Atheism in context, let's take a quick look at the older atheism. British philosopher and mathematician Bertrand Russell, a twentieth-century atheist, wrote in *Why I Am Not a Christian and Other Essays on Religion and Related Subjects*, "Religion is based, I think, primarily and mainly upon fear. It is partly the terror of the unknown. . . . A good world needs knowledge, kindliness, and courage; it does not need a regretful hankering after the past or a fettering of the free intelligence by the words uttered long ago by ignorant men."

Most New Atheists are no more anti-religious than the atheists such as Russell who denounced faith as "regretful hankering after the past,"—they're just louder. And for all their in-your-face "attitude," the New Atheists are positively polite compared to the religious fundamentalists. Incidentally, if some of the earlier atheists (what I guess we should call the Old, *Old* Atheists), such as Baruch Spinoza and David Hume, were more polite than today's New Atheists, they had good reason to be: fear of bigoted religious believers ready to kill people who challenged their ideas.

Unlike today's New Atheists, who have an army of adoring groupies following their every move, the Old, Old Atheists paid a steep price for their beliefs. Take Spinoza, a Jew born in Amsterdam in 1632 and trained in Talmudic scholarship. Spinoza understood his predicament as someone flying in the face of religious convention at a time when people were sometimes hanged or burned for doing just that. He wore a ring engraved with the word *caute*, meaning "cautiously." Spinoza's beliefs evolved from traditional Judaism to pantheism, then to a sort of paneverythingism that holds that God is everywhere and everything and therefore, in the traditional sense, nowhere. Spinoza also became what today we'd call a determinist and said that everything that happens occurs through "necessity."

The Jewish minority, fearing persecution by the Christian majority on charges of atheism, offered Spinoza 1000 florins to keep his mouth shut. He refused. He was called to a rabbinical court and excommunicated. The *Ethics* and most of Spinoza's other pantheistic/atheist works were published only after his death. His manuscripts had been hidden by friends.

Another big name in the Old, Old Atheist pantheon was Scottish philosopher, economist, and historian David Hume. Only a few years before Hume began writing in the eighteenth century, a teenager named Thomas Aikenhead was hanged for "blasphemy" in Hume's hometown of Edinburgh. Aikenhead had called religion nonsense.

Hume wasn't threatened with death but nevertheless expressed his atheistic views in essays such as *Of Superstition and Religion* in a nondirect manner, using dialogue to cast his speculating in the guarded form of questions asked by others. Hume didn't acknowledge authorship of *A Treatise of Human Nature*, (one of his most overt atheistic statements), but it was widely known to be his. He also attenuated the criticisms of religion in the *Treatise* in relation to Bishop Butler, to curry favor. His *Dialogues on Natural Religion* was posthumously published.

The style of the New Atheists' books has less in common with Hume's indirect introspection or Spinoza's pantheism/sort-of-atheism than with the crusading fundamentalism of today's right-wing American evangelical/fundamentalist leaders. The New Atheists, like their evangelical/fundamentalist counterparts, aren't on an intellectual journey. They are already at their destination, all i's dotted and all t's crossed. Everything they encounter is run through a fixed ideological grid. To them there are the good guys—smart atheists leaving appropriate comments on their websites—and the bad guys—dumb religious believers who must be answered with the correct arguments handily provided in the lists of debate points found on Dawkins's and other atheists' websites on how to deal with the other. The arguments tend to take on the tone of the pious denouncing the sinful. As Harris writes in *The End of Faith*, believers are a threat, enemies of happiness, actually, downright evil:

> As long as it is acceptable for a person to believe that he knows how God wants everyone on earth to live, we will continue to murder one another on account of our myths. . . . It is time we recognized that all reasonable men and women have a common enemy. It is an enemy so near to us, and so deceptive, that we keep its counsel even as it threatens to destroy the very possibility of human happiness. Our enemy is nothing other than faith itself.

Harris says that some Islamic states may not ever be reformed because so many Muslims are "utterly deranged by their religious faith." He concludes, "Some propositions are so dangerous that it may even be ethical to kill people for believing them."

In the December 29, 2008, issue of *The Guardian*, journalist Andrew Brown summed up what makes the New Atheists tick. He pointed out that the New Atheism is largely a political rather than an intellectual or scientific movement:

> In some ways it can be understood as the canary in the coalmine of American power and exceptionalism. Before the [financial] crash [of 2008–09], when it was possible to believe that globalised capitalism would go on making us richer and more liberal forever . . . the new atheism was one of the few ways to express disbelief and fear and loathing in the way the world was going. Religion became a synecdoche for everything that might go wrong, so that belief in the evil qualities of Faith was not so very different from belief in the evils of witchcraft.

According to Brown, the New Atheists believe religious faith is primarily a matter of false belief and that the cure for faith is science. Science will lead people into the "clear sunlit uplands of reason," and in this struggle, "religion is doomed."

Whether we are embracing the life of the spirit or running from it, most of us seem to affirm or reject faith too vehemently to claim we just don't care. The impulse to shut down debate with the other side hasn't changed much since those Scottish Calvinists hanged Aikenhead. His executioners would have appreciated a line in one email I got threatening that "No child of God gets out of here without the proper discipline," and they would have cried "Amen!" to Harris's chilling line "Some propositions are so dangerous that it may even be ethical to kill people for believing them."

The New Atheists have been so shrill in their attempts to put us Dims in our place that even some other atheists find them abrasive. These critics of the New Atheists might be called *New* New Atheists. They have come forward to also proclaim atheism yet to denounce the New Atheists in a way that to me is reminiscent of the contortions my family went through as we became members of ever "purer" churches through one separation after another, until the "Truth" more or less boiled down to just our family!

For instance, in *The Little Book of Atheist Spirituality* the French philosopher André Comte-Sponville tries to present a moral foundation for the life of unbelief. Comte-Sponville says that his "way of being an atheist" was influenced by the Catholicism of his youth. He acknowledges the positive aspects of faith. And then there is Ronald Aronson, a philosopher teaching at Wayne State University, and author of *Living Without God*. Aronson's book is somewhat of an answer to the atheist polemics of Dawkins, Hitchens, Harris, et al.

Aronson first laid out a critique of the New Atheists in a June 2007 review of their books that was published in *The Nation*:

> Where does the work of the New Atheists leave us? . . . Living without God means turning toward something. To flourish we need coherent secular popular philosophies that effectively answer life's vital questions. Enlightenment optimism once supplied unbelievers with hope for a better world, whether this was based on Marxism, science, education or democracy. After Progress, after Marxism, is it any wonder atheism fell on hard times? Restoring secular confidence will take much positive work as well as the fierce attacks on religion by our atheist champions.

In the *Nation* article Aronson also criticized *The End of Faith* for its "intolerance" and "zealotry." He advocated "the most urgent need" for secularists to embrace "a coherent popular philosophy that answers vital questions about how to live one's life." A "new atheism must absorb the experience of the 20th century and the issues of the 21st," he said. "It must answer questions about living without God, face issues concerning forces beyond our control as well as our own responsibility, find a satisfying way of thinking about what we may know and what we cannot know, affirm a secular basis for morality, point to ways of coming to terms with death and explore what hope might mean today."

Then, in his book *Living Without God*, Aronson fleshed out his New Atheist critique:

> To live comfortably without God today means doing what has not yet been done—namely, rethinking the secular worldview after the eclipse of modern optimism. . . . Religion is not really the issue, but rather the incompleteness or tentativeness, the thinness or emptiness, of today's atheism, agnosticism and secularism. Living without God means turning toward something.

It might also mean that we should look for a less drastic alternative to fundamentalist faith in God than a fundamentalist faith in no God. Perhaps both atheists and religious fundamentalists have been looking through the wrong end of the same worn-out telescope.

CHAPTER 2

How Many Ways Are There to Say, "There Is No God!"?

I ask: what does it mean when we continue to behave as though all were as it should be, calling ourselves Christians according to the New Testament, when the ideals of the New Testament have gone out of life? The tremendous disproportion which this state of affairs represents has, moreover, been perceived by many.

Journals, Søren Kierkegaard

Most of our heated chatter about meaning is something like children talking loudly as they walk down a dark, scary road. The fact that we need to talk so loudly—even threaten to call down the wrath of God on our opponents and/or say that they should be killed—is more significant than anything we're saying.

Because of our limitless capacity for brooding over our distressingly short lives, there's always room for a little more speculating about faith, life, meaning, and religion. Just ask St. Paul, Spinoza, Billy Graham, Sam Harris, or me. Speculating about the unknowable and/or arguing with or threatening and insulting those with contrary ideas, has provided a good living for proselytizers and grand inquisitors from St. Constantine to Voltaire, from pastor Rick Warren to Bill Maher and Richard Dawkins.

> Frank: I grew up Methodist and remained so until I was 60 years old. I always participated in my church but never knew much about the theology of mainline [more liberal] Christianity. . . . I have done a lot of reading . . . and am now a Unitarian. . . . One of the great ironies of our life is that we have three children, all married and on their own, however, all of them have become much more conservative [than me] religiously speaking. . . . Fortunately we have worked around this and solved the problem by not discussing religion.
>
> *J.*

What does it say about our various faiths that belief has to be reinforced by others and/or ignored to keep the peace? What does it say about the nature of faith in God that when a believer—say, a former evangelical/fundamentalist like me—questions his or her faith or changes it, there are otherwise seemingly sane people so threatened that they take the time to call down God's judgment on the questioner?

I think it comes down to the fact that most of us take comfort in safety in numbers. So the man or woman whose defection depletes the number of the faithful is resented, shunned, even killed either literally, as in the case of Muslim "apostates," or figuratively, as in the character assassination with which backsliders are "dealt" by evangelical/fundamentalists defending their turf.

Evangelical/fundamentalists aren't the only clan clinging to group-think. Why do atheists write books and other atheists read them, if not to reinforce each other's faith in no faith? I mean, how many ways are there to say, "There is no God!"?

Speaking of the need to reinforce one's faith, Bill Maher's 2008 movie *Religulous* provided the atheist version of a church-going experience and altar call. *Religulous* was a blunt (and funny) stripped-down example of the you're-in-or-out New Atheist method. When I was watching *Religulous* in an Upper West Side theater in New York City, it seemed to me that the laughter and shouted comments were just another version of "Amen!" and "Preach it brother!" There were even several screams of "Yes!" after Maher "nailed" this or that particularly asinine religious person. I assume that these cries of joyful affirmation emanated from the more spirit-filled atheists in the audience!

Maher's documentary built on the foundation laid by Harris in *The End of Faith*. Harris began his book with a scene of a young Islamic terrorist in Jerusalem smiling enigmatically as he commits suicide by blowing up a bus full of innocent people. In *Religulous* Maher also included many images of look-how-crazy-God-makes-everyone violence. The Harris/Maher message was as clear as it was intolerant: The world would be better off without religious people.

Maher's movie struck me as similar to Sacha Baron Cohen's wonderfully mean-spirited and wickedly (if uncomfortably) hilarious *Borat*. Both movies hit easy religious targets. However, Cohen is an equal opportunity insulter, and he went after everyone from feminists to socialites and movie stars, religious or not. Maher reserved his ridicule—with one brief exception when he interviewed a scientist who is an evangelical—for the dumbest religious believers he could find.

In a series of interviews, Maher set up pastors, imams, evangelists, political leaders, and assorted flakes and actors (these last at a religious theme park) to look their worst. Maher's questions were those one might expect from a literal-minded, fairly dim-witted ten-year-old stuck in Sunday school who was trying to annoy his teacher into throwing him out. The questions ranged from "How can you believe in a talking snake?" to "How could Jonah have lived in a fish?" to "How can God hear the prayers of everyone *at once*?" (To which one answer might be, if Google can do it, why not God?)

When approaching the biblical narrative through his handpicked interviewees (and how he edited their comments), Maher didn't seem to "get" allegory, let alone literary imagination or the results of religious faith in ordinary people's lives—for instance, the fact that religion has provided a means, place, and tradition of forgiveness, charity, and mercy for generations of believers. He also seemed to think that religion, and Christianity in particular, is only about literal belief in the various biblical stories. It's not. It never has been.

Yes, there have been literalists and fundamentalists shaping religion through a hard-edged fundamentalist "thread" running through Jewish and Christian history. Yes, many Jews and Christians following this literal-minded thread have done terrible things. Yes, the Jewish and Christian faiths are full of such people today. What Maher ignored is that there has been a *parallel tradition*, another thread, running alongside the literalistic tendency he caricatures.

The open and questioning thread weaves another and more tolerant and nuanced color into the tapestry of faith. This too has been there from the beginning of the Jewish and Christian traditions. It represents the compassionate, mystical approach to faith in God— in other words, enlightenment.

The word *enlightenment* has become commonplace in the parlance of secular circles, but I would rather not hand it over wholesale without a debate. Enlightenment is not necessarily only a secular version of redemption. In all the major religious traditions, enlightenment is the state of being said to be a "place" from which one is able to see things as they really are, not as we believe them to be, want them to be, or hope they will be. In some Orthodox Christian reckonings, the spiritual life is divided into three stages: purification, enlightenment, and theosis (or "deification" or "divinization"— the process of being united with God). Only in the first stage do we have any control. The last two stages are Divine Gifts bestowed as we are ready.

Back to my threads. Sometimes the competing threads—enlightened verses dogmatic, the mystical versus theological—have even been found in the same people. Individuals may veer one way, then another, are sometimes compassionate and at other times judgmental, merciful and vengeful, literalistic and then nuanced. My father was one such person: compassionate personally, harsh in his early theology. And if you asked me, "What was Francis Schaeffer about?" the only true answer would be for me to ask you what stage of his life, thinking, and work you were talking about. There were several "Francis Schaeffers." By the way, that's true of me too, and, I think, of many people.

To ignore the open and questioning tradition and to dwell only on the fundamentalist thread is disingenuous, or in Maher's case more likely simply ignorant. It's as if Maher had made a documentary on medicine and concentrated solely on the experiments done on duped prisoners, criminal back-alley abortion doctors, eugenics scientists inventing racist "solutions" for society, and so on, while ignoring Jonas Salk and his discovery of polio vaccine or the early African American leaders in nursing, such as the outstanding Mary Eliza Mahoney, who was the first black professional nurse in America.

If Maher applied his *Religulous* approach to Shakespeare's *Macbeth*, he would have been interviewing actors and asking, "How can Macbeth *really* see a ghost? What sort of idiot believes in ghosts?"

Nuanced interpretations of religious faith within the Christian tradition are not inventions of modern-era higher critical or biblical criticism studies that have their origins in the context of the rationalism of the seventeenth and eighteenth centuries. Rather, some of these subtle and complex approaches hark back to the beginning of the Christian era. In the writings of the Church Fathers in the third to sixth centuries one finds an allegorical, non-literal, what today's evangelical/fundamentalists would denounce as "liberal" or "touchy-feely," even "relativistic," approaches to faith and the Scriptures.

This is to say that if Maher had taken deconstructing religion seriously, he would have at least tried to address the *actual tradition* that some of the early Christian leaders passed on, a tradition that is still alive and well today in parts of the Christian community. But instead he interviewed the rube element of the American evangelical/ fundamentalist communities and zeroed in on people who wouldn't know a Church Father if one bit them in the ass.

Ironically, the same historical representatives of the Christian faith that Maher chose to ignore (or has never heard of) are the Church Fathers that evangelical/fundamentalists also ignore for their own ideological reasons. They ignore them (or even denounce them) because the very existence of the early representatives of a more enlightened thread of Christianity undermines the evangelical/fundamentalist claim that somehow only fundamentalism represents the original ancient Christian faith. It does not.

One man whom evangelical/fundamentalists would rather ignore as too "liberal" and who was nevertheless very big deal in the early church was St. Clement. In the third century, Clement became the leader of the Alexandrian School, the center of the highest level of academic learning in the Christian world at that time. Clement included lots of quotations from the Old Testament in his (not to be confused with St. Paul's) *Letter to the Corinthians*. Clement said that the literal meaning of Scripture is just a "starting point . . . suitable for the mass of Christians" but that there is always a "deeper meaning."

Instead of being what today we'd call a literalist spouting off about how the Bible is "inerrant," Clement used the Bible to illustrate all sorts of ideas. Clement didn't go on and on about how all the details of various stories were true, without error, or were science or history, but used the stories to extrapolate wisdom about everyday life.

Clement was not alone. St. Ignatius, the second-century bishop of Antioch writing about First Corinthians, took Paul's words out of context in a way that today's American evangelical/fundamentalists would denounce as heretical. He applied Paul's words to his contemporary personal situation as though they were abstractions he could fit into other forms and derive subtle hidden meanings from. Today's evangelical/fundamentalists would have fired him from their seminaries in a heartbeat.

Even Mr. Big himself, big in the Church's history—St. Augustine—promoted what today's fundamentalists would denounce as a "relativistic" approach to the Scriptures. He said that the Bible should be interpreted several ways: as "literal" (some stories might be true), as "allegorical" (made-up stories to illustrate a point), as "moral" (to give us direction on how to live), and as "analogical" (some Bible stories obviously did not happen but are a way of telling a made-up story to make a larger point).

Another one of the important founders of the Church was St. Basil the Great, a bishop in the fourth century. Besides becoming a leader in founding monastic communities, starting orphanages and hospitals, writing a version of the Divine Liturgy, giving away his family inheritance to help the poor, setting up soup kitchens, fighting against the Roman practice of infanticide, *and defending the use of secular medicine*, Basil said that Scripture and tradition are "equal in value, strength, and validity" and have the "same power where piety is concerned."

Talk about an idea that drives evangelical/fundamentalists nuts! As for the New Atheists, they don't much care for people such as Basil either. How do you prepare answers to an oral and therefore *evolving* tradition that this leading Christian placed on an equal footing with the Bible? You might have to actually have a conversation with believers in a tradition like Basil's, rather than just trading scripted zingers. That would require thought, because the people you'd be debating might be open to change, to adding to their tradition as time passed, to elevating the human and scientific contribution to the *living of faith* to equal standing with that faith's scriptures.

During a talk to a gathering of Harvard alumni (in his capacity as a professor of philosophy and theology at the Harvard Divinity School) David Lamberth nicely summed up the underlying problem with the New Atheist argument:

The [New Atheists] see religion most fundamentally in terms of belief, and this is, in large part, a key to where they fail. . . . All these
authors appear to think . . . that adherence to religion depends on
beliefs in a given system . . . [but] religion, in its broad and multi-
faceted character as a human social phenomenon, is not only much
more than belief, but is not necessarily founded primarily on it.

Besides ignoring what historical Christianity actually *is* and *was*,
Maher also seemed unaware that there are intelligent contemporaries of his who are deeply religious and who have spent lifetimes
thinking about faith in God in ways that are far from the absolutist
verities of the (mostly) North American evangelical/fundamentalism
Maher set up to knock down. For instance, Maher ignored many
brilliant intellectuals, writers, and artists who are practicing Christians that he might have talked to, such as the late John Updike.
(Updike was alive and well when the movie was being made.)
Maher might also have interviewed then Senator, now President,
Obama.

Had Maher interviewed Obama, he could have asked him about
Obama's 2006 lecture on religion and public policy, delivered at the
"Call to Renewal" event sponsored by the evangelical Sojourners
group. On that occasion, Obama described his own faith in Christ
and also spoke about how he converted. He talked about how faith
should or should not impact policy making. Obama also castigated
some elements of the secular community for being short-sighted in
their anti-religious views. As he said, "At worst, there are some liberals who dismiss religion in the public square as inherently irrational or intolerant, insisting on a caricature of religious Americans
that paints them as fanatical, or thinking that the very word 'Christian' describes one's political opponents, not people of faith."

Obama continued:

I speak with some experience on this matter. I was not raised in a
particularly religious household. . . . It wasn't until after college,

when I went to Chicago to work as a community organizer for a group of Christian churches, that I confronted my own spiritual dilemma . . . It was because of these newfound understandings that I was finally able to walk down the aisle of Trinity United Church of Christ on 95th Street in the Southside of Chicago one day and affirm my Christian faith. . . .

That's a path that has been shared by millions upon millions of Americans—evangelicals, Catholics, Protestants, Jews and Muslims alike; some since birth, others at certain turning points in their lives. It is not something they set apart from the rest of their beliefs and values. In fact, it is often what drives their beliefs and their values. And that is why that, if we truly hope to speak to people where they're at—to communicate our hopes and values in a way that's relevant to their own—then as progressives, we cannot abandon the field of religious discourse.

Or Maher might have asked Updike why he included smart and conflicted people of religious faith as characters in his books, or how the writings of Kierkegaard had inspired Updike's religious thinking. It's not as if Updike's faith was hidden. (His last book, *Endpoint and Other Poems*, published posthumously in 2009, includes beautiful reflections on religious faith written literally on his deathbed.)

Updike's Christian belief is well known. As *Religion and Ethics Newsweekly*, a publication of the Corporation for Public Broadcasting, noted,

At a talk on religion in his work Thursday evening, Nov. 18, 2008 . . . Updike told the audience that his Christian faith had "solidified in ways less important to me than when I was 30, when the existential predicament was realer to me than now. . . . I worked a lot of it through and arrived at a sort of safe harbor in my life. . . ." Responding to a question submitted from the audience on whether orthodox Christian theology's invocation to accept

God's will runs counter to progressive politics, Updike concluded, "Yes, I think to a certain degree it mitigates against trying to change the world, instead trying to find a peaceful, satisfactory place within the world that exists. It is consoling to think that if not every detail is the will of God, there is a kind of will bigger than your own."

Maher also ignored the inconvenient bits of the history of the twentieth century, not to mention the present. Unlike the New, *New* Atheist Aronson who, as we've seen, wrote, "New atheism must absorb the experience of the 20th century and the issues of the 21st," Maher ducked inconvenient facts. Maher never mentioned the violent side of the recent experiment in secularism: the blood-drenched twentieth century and the inhumane barbarity of today's Chinese rulers, or, say, the greed and bloody brutality of the Castro family.

Mao, Hitler, Stalin, Castro, Pol Pot, the scientists who recently led the eugenics movement, and the like did not oppress their people and/or liquidate them in the name of God. The bloodiest of all historical periods is not that of the Spanish Inquisition or the Crusades, or even that of today's Islamic terrorism, but the recent and ongoing history of secularism run amok. "Rational" science has not been blameless either.

People have slaughtered each other in the name of Christ and Muhammad, and Hindus have been killing Christians and Muslims, and vice versa. But people have also—and recently in exponentially greater numbers—been slaughtered in the name of nationalism (World War I), secular political ideology (the Gulag), tribal rivalry (Rwanda), a master race informed by the secular "science" of eugenics (Nazi Germany), consumerism (America's Middle Eastern oil wars), and state atheism (China's continuing pogroms against believers from all religions and forced and brutal late-term abortion programs). Science has also created the plethora of earth-destroying and often unnecessary products and provided science-based ways to sell them to consumers.

Maher's attempt to put religious belief in its place only reinforces the fact that for most people, one belief system is always replaced by another. In an act of unintended self-parody at the end of his movie, Maher preaches a fiery sermon against religion, even begging "moderate religious believers" to abandon their faiths and convert to his point of view. Like some old-time evangelist, Maher wants to save us from his version of hell via his version of a born-again experience. It's Maher's way or the Apocalypse. Where have I heard that before?

CHAPTER 3

Why Does Dawkins Oppose Faith with Lapel Pins?

Christianity takes a prodigious giant-stride . . . into the ab-surd—there Christianity begins.

The Sickness Unto Death, Søren Kierkegaard

One doesn't have to buy Richard Dawkins's books because he's found a way to offer his wisdom to passersby. Just hang around New Atheist gatherings and you may read Dawkins's writings on T-shirts worn by his disciples or emblazoning their sweat shirts, tote bags, and bumper stickers.

Here are some samples taken from Dawkins's official website of the means and methods for spreading the Dawkins's gospel and/or for collecting his life's work. What follows is just as I found it on the Dawkins site in the spring of 2009. And this sampling represents a mere fraction of what would, if downloaded, run to hundreds of pages of products, tips for atheist living, resources, further thoughts posted on bulletin boards, and so on.

NEW! *The God Delusion* T-ShirtProduct 5/7 $20.00

sizes m, l, xl and 2xl are in backorder, and will be shipped as soon as they come back in stock (approx. 2 weeks).

The God Delusion T-Shirt with what is perhaps the book's most famous quote: *"The God of the Old Testament is arguably the most unpleasant character in all fiction: jealous and proud of it; a petty, unjust, unforgiving control-freak; a vindictive, bloodthirsty ethnic cleanser; a misogynistic, homophobic, racist, infanticidal, genocidal, filicidal, pestilential, megalomaniacal, sadomasochistic, capriciously malevolent bully."*

Richard Dawkins, *The God Delusion*

White text on slate grey t-shirt. 100% cotton, American Apparel. Made in the U.S.A. These sizes may run a little smaller than some are accustomed to.

Add to Cart:

If T-shirts aren't what you fancy by way of proudly displaying "perhaps the book's most famous quote," there are many other fine products. For instance, you may purchase the "Scarlet A Lapel Pin" (I'm not making this up.) And if you don't know what *that* is, you may "watch [as] Richard Dawkins explains his Scarlet A lapel pin during an interview, just click *Here*."

According to the atheist product catalogue, the Scarlet A Pin is a "Red A with silver edging and back," and it costs $5. The customer reviews published on Dawkins's site are glowing. The pin gets Five Stars from just about everyone.

Oliver gives the pin Five Stars! and writes, "Brilliant badge. Sublime concept. Let's get in their faces. Thank God for Dawkins!" Rich also gives the pin Five Stars! and says, "Excellent. Worn it for a couple of months now; four conversations followed I have to order two more." Another satisfied customer writes, "I love it, but you should really consider offering a Scarlet A necklace." The next reviewer gives it only four stars, but moving on, Yvonne gives the pin Five Stars! and says, "It looked awesome on my black bag." Luke gives the pin Five Stars! too and notes, "Great product. I actually turned mine into a pendant by bending the pin and attaching a wire loop." Then we get back into four star territory: "This is great, but I would much rather have it as a necklace."

The comment that most interested me was the one from Rich: "Worn it for a couple of months now; four conversations followed." That really brought back the memories.

When I was a young child, and to my eternal mortification, Mom used to carry something called the Gospel Walnut. It was a hollowed-out actual walnut shell filled with ribbons of different colors sewn together into one thin, shoestring-like, yard-long band: black for sin, red for Jesus's blood, then white for how clean your heart would be after it got washed of sin. You cranked it out with a little handle attached to the walnut shell, and the ribbon would seem to emerge from the nut magically. The point of doing this was to invite questions from strangers, which it did. This would lead to what Rich said the A Pin he wears leads to: conversations. In other words, both the Gospel Walnut and the Scarlet A Pin offer a chance to witness to potential converts.

If my experience as a child is any guide (regarding the just-kill-me-now embarrassment I felt as Mom accosted strangers on trains and buses with her magic nut), we can expect that the mortified children of Dawkins's atheist pin-wearing missionaries will someday become zealous evangelicals, Muslims, or Druids—anything but atheists, that is. Who knows, the children raised by Dawkins's groupies may well be the foundation of the next Great Awakening.

Anyway, Oliver was also onto something with his "Let's get in their faces" comment. That too induced flashbacks. It reminded me vividly of how we evangelical/fundamentalists regarded those who weren't "saved." "They" were always *they* to us, and "we," the born-agains, were as saved as they were "lost."

So Dawkins, it turns out, is my mother, circa 1959! Hi Mom!

Just in case the dedicated Dawkins follower watched only the edited version of *The Enemies of Reason*, now there is *The Uncut Interviews*, a "full length version" to add to your "cart" before "proceeding to checkout." (All major credit cards are accepted.)

The Enemies of Reason + Enemies of Reason: The Uncut Interviews$40.00 $33.00 Save: 18% off Buy together and save $7.00!

During the filming of Channel 4's *The Enemies of Reason*, Richard Dawkins conducted several extended interviews which were cut down for the program's final broadcast. . . . Explore the issues in more depth . . . . There are two ways of looking at the world through faith and superstition or through the rigors of logic, observation and evidence in other words, through reason. Reason and a respect for evidence are precious commodities, the source of human progress and our safeguard against fundamentalists and those who profit from obscuring the truth. Yet, today, society appears to be retreating from reason. . . . Richard Dawkins confronts what he sees as an epidemic of irrational, superstitious thinking. He explains the dangers the pick and mix of knowledge and nonsense poses in the internet age, and passionately re-states the case for reason and science.

Run Time: 96 minutes—1 DVD

Dawkins will "safeguard [us] against fundamentalists and those who profit from obscuring the truth" by selling us the *uncut* version. And when the Dear Leader is not picking the "most famous" of his quotes for his T-shirts, or designing atheist conversation-starting witnessing jewelry, Dawkins also writes books that contain grand zingers: "Atheism is the only logical belief once one accepts evolution." And "Religion is incompatible with science."

But what Dawkins says he's most proud of is the part of his website called "Convert's Corner" where, as he told Bill Maher in an interview on Maher's TV show in 2008, "You can go and read *all the testimonies* of people who have been converted!" Then he said, "When *I'm* on *my* deathbed I'll have a tape recorder switched on because people like me are victims of malicious stories after they're dead of people saying they had a deathbed conversion when they didn't." Maher looked a bit puzzled, so Dawkins explained that he suspects creationists may already be plotting to do this to him and pointed out that "they now claim Darwin had a deathbed conversion."

When Maher asked Dawkins about *The God Delusion*, Dawkins said little about the book's content but exclaimed, "*It's sold a million and a half copies!*" Then Maher, like an enthusiastic puppy scampering around a big dog, yelped, "And *now* it's in paperback, it will be *even more* available!" Maher paused to take a breath then added, "I'm your biggest fan!" Then Dawkins, slipping into his rock star mode, explained that he has so many fans because "I think people are getting a bit fed up with other people thrusting their imaginary friends down their throats."

Prompted by Maher, Dawkins also explained one of his other ideas. "There is a scale of One to Seven of atheism," said Dawkins, "but I'm only a Six on my scale." Dawkins laid out the details of the Atheism Sincerity Scale. "A One is a complete believer in God and a Seven is a total disbeliever."

Something was bothering Maher, and he asked, "Why are *you* only a Six? Why aren't *you* a Seven?"

Dawkins didn't miss a beat; "As a *scientist* I can't *definitely commit* to anything, including that there are no fairies!" Big laugh and cheers from both Maher and his audience. Dawkins added, "I can't say I *know* there are no pink unicorns either, so maybe I'm a Six Point Nine is reasonable!"

Louder cheers from the audience, and I think I actually heard Maher squeal.

This intellectually rigorous Dawkins/Maher exchange put me in mind of one of my favorite scenes in the movie *This Is Spinal Tap* that also had to do with numbers. It didn't seem much of a stretch to picture Maher in the role of the rockumentary interviewer Marty DiBergi (Rob Reiner) and to imagine Dawkins doing a splendid interpretation of Nigel Tufnel (Christopher Guest as lead and rhythm guitar, backing and lead vocals) discussing the band's extra powerful *very special* amplifier.

NIGEL TUFNEL: The numbers all go to eleven. Look, right across the board, eleven, eleven, eleven, and . . .

MARTY DIBERGI: Oh, I see. And most amps go up to ten?

NIGEL TUFNEL: Exactly.

MARTY DIBERGI: Does that mean it's louder? Is it any louder?

NIGEL TUFNEL: Well, it's one louder, isn't it? It's not ten. You see, most blokes, you know, will be playing at ten. You're on ten here, all the way up, all the way up, all the way up, you're on ten on your guitar. Where can you go from there? Where?

MARTY DIBERGI: I don't know.

NIGEL TUFNEL: Nowhere. Exactly! What we do is, if we need that extra push over the cliff, you know what we do?

MARTY DIBERGI: Put it up to eleven?

NIGEL TUFNEL: Eleven. Exactly! One louder!

Apart from the sales figures (and what I'll always think of as the Atheist One-to-Seven Dawkins/*Tap* moment), then, what is *The God Delusion* about? For one thing, it seems to mainly be about Dawkins's website. I've never read a book in which the author works his website addresses into the actual text—not to mention the front and back matter—half a dozen times. But according to Dawkins his book really isn't a book, so perhaps literary customs don't apply. As he puts it, *The God Delusion* is a "consciousness-raising" tool. "Atheists" he writes, "as well as theists unconsciously observe society's convention that we must be especially polite and respectful to faith." He wants to change all that.

In the preface to the paperback edition, Dawkins responds to the criticism that he is just as much of a proselytizing fundamentalist as those he criticizes. Dawkins answers, "No, please, it is all too easy to mistake passion that can change its mind for fundamentalism, which never will . . . it is impossible to overstress the difference between such a passionate commitment to biblical fundamentals and the true scientist's equally passionate commitment to evidence." As a scientist Dawkins claims that by definition his passion can't be like other, lesser people's passions, because as a *scientist* he is above such things. Maybe the same can be said for his entrepreneurial passion, which might, in ordinary people, be mistaken for televangelist-style hucksterism but, because he is a scientist, is no doubt just research carried on by other means.

Even Dawkins's compassion seems strangely self-serving. Take the story Dawkins includes in his book about an atheist doctor who wrote to him describing the moving atheist ceremony at his young atheist son's funeral. Dawkins uses the story to point out that atheists can be comforted by their beliefs at the big moments—death, for instance—just as religious people are comforted by religion. However, Dawkins also works in the address of his website, by just happening to mention that the grateful bereaved doctor asked the mourners at his son's funeral to make donations to Dawkins's foundation's website—once again listed in the context of the father's letter.

On the first page of the preface to *The God Delusion*, Dawkins asks us to imagine a world without religion and tells us that without religion, the World Trade Center would be standing, John Lennon would be alive, there would've been no Crusades and no witch hunts, no partition of India, no Palestinian/Israeli conflict. He then tells us that what he objects to most about religion is the way it captures children.

"I want everybody to flinch," Dawkins writes, "whenever we hear a phrase such as 'Catholic child' or 'Muslim child.' Speak of a child of Catholic parents if you like; but if you hear anybody speak of a 'Catholic child,' stop them and politely point out that children are too young to know where they stand on such issues, just as they are too young to know where they stand on economics and politics." Given that a few pages earlier in the book Dawkins tells us the story of the atheist doctor and his devoutly atheist child, I wonder whether Dawkins wrote to that father asking him if he'd given his son the chance to make up his mind about religion by regularly taking him to attend church services. For that matter does Dawkins object to babies being given passports before they get to choose their country?

Just in case not all past or present scientists have gotten Dawkins's consciousness-raising memo re their God delusions, Dawkins notes that "Great scientists of our time who sound religious usually turn out not to be so when you examine their beliefs more deeply." He makes a particular point of saying that Einstein was horribly misunderstood when it comes to the impression that he had any sort of religious sensibility. Dawkins writes, "Let me sum up [Einstein's] religion in [a] quotation from Einstein himself: 'To sense that behind anything that can be experienced there is a something that our mind cannot grasp and this beauty and sublimity reaches us only indirectly and as a feeble reflection, this is religiousness. In this sense I am religious.'" Dawkins then says of the Einstein quote, "In this sense I too am religious, with the reservation that 'cannot grasp' does not have to mean 'forever ungraspable.'" Dawkins adds, "My title, *The God Delusion*, does not refer to the God of Einstein and the other enlightened scientists. . . . That is why I needed to get Einsteinian religion out of the way to begin with: it has a proven capacity to confuse."

It takes a lot of hard work by Dawkins to make sure we're never confused and to prove that the big-name scientists have all been atheists, or at least *not* believers of the kind he doesn't approve of. "Newton did indeed claim to be religious. So did almost everybody until significantly I think the nineteenth-century . . . great scientists

who professed religion become harder to find in the 20th-century. . . .
I suspect that most of the more recent ones are religious only in the
Einsteinian sense which, I argued . . . is a misuse of the word."
Dawkins notes that today he knows of only three scientists in Britain
who claim to be religious. And as for those scientists in the past who
claimed to be religious, Dawkins says that because everyone had to
say nice things about religion in those days, they probably weren't
religious anyway, just pretending to be.

Cleaning up of the historical record is an obsession with
Dawkins. Not only the present and future must go his way, but the
past too. He finds himself compelled to make sure that we know
that "The deist God of Voltaire and Thomas Paine . . . [is not] the
Old Testament psychotic delinquent . . . the deist God of the 18th-
century Enlightenment is an altogether grander being: worthy of his
cosmic creation." Dawkins says that (1) Voltaire and Thomas Paine
and Einstein would *actually* be on his side whatever they said, if they
had only had the foresight and moral courage to be a little clearer,
and that (2), the Fathers of the Enlightenment, who may have believed in God, believed in a God that somehow would also be on
Dawkins's side and that their God is not to be confused with the
God Dawkins doesn't like.

It turns out that the deism of the founders of the American republic was also *actually* mostly atheistic, if properly understood.
Dawkins asks how these enlightened men founded a country that
became so religious? "Precisely because America is largely secular,
religion has become free enterprise . . . what works for soap flakes
works for God, and the result is something approaching religious
mania amongst today's less educated classes . . . the Founding Fathers would have been horrified."

What's to be *done* about America's "less educated classes" who
love soap flakes *and* religion? One answer is to organize speaking
tours featuring Dawkins. In his "An Atheist's Call to Arms," a talk
he gave in California in 2002, Dawkins opened his show with a blast
of music from *Aida* and volunteered, by way of explanation, that

he'd "chosen this triumphant music for my funeral." He will feel triumphant he said . . . then corrected himself quickly since, well, he won't be *feeling* anything at his funeral, but, you know, if he *could* feel, he'd be feeling so good, "at being given the opportunity to understand something about why I was here before I was here."

The audience seemed somewhat bemused, so Dawkins asked, "Can you understand my quaint English accent?" Big laugh from the audience anxious to prove that although they might not quite get what Dawkins meant by playing and then "explaining" his funerary music as the opening to his remarks, nevertheless, *they* weren't members of the less educated classes. So, oh "Yes! Yes!" they called out amid warm laughter, we *can* understand English accents! They're like *soooo* cool!

But, as in so many operatic plots, after the laughter must come the tears! Once the opera selection had played, Dawkins turned to the business at hand and sternly waded into the main point of his talk. "In this country you can't be too careful," Dawkins said; "it's fair to say that American biologists are in *a state of war!* The *war* is *so worrying* that *I* have to say something about it."

In *The God Delusion*, Dawkins paints a similarly sinister picture of the ongoing conspiracy against atheists in America, citing as proof (though he laments that the reporter who heard the president say this didn't use a tape recorder) a story about President George Bush Sr. saying, "No, I don't know that atheists should be considered as citizens, nor should they be considered patriots. This is one nation under God." (My family got to know President and Barbara Bush quite well and this story seems very unlikely, given Bush's rather liberal religious views.)

Dawkins claims that America is in the grip of oppressive religion, to the extent that even the police organize purges against atheists. He explains how the police persecuted an atheist street protestor, or so Dawkins has heard. As he points out in his book, "Anecdotes of . . . prejudice [in America] against atheists abound." Dawkins relates one such anecdote about a cop who was ready to beat up someone who organized a peaceful demonstration to warn people about a fraudulent faith healer. Dawkins supplies us with the cop's dialogue: "'To hell with you, buddy. No policeman wants to protect a goddamned atheist. I hope somebody bloodies you up good.'"

When not regaling us with anti-atheist cop dialogue, Dawkins explains, as if to not very bright infants, that

> Constructing models is something the human brain is very good at. When we are asleep it is called dreaming; when we are awake we call it imagination or, when it is exceptionally vivid, hallucination. As Chapter Ten will show, children who have "imaginary friends" sometimes see them clearly, exactly as if they were real. If we are gullible, we don't recognize hallucination . . . for what it is and we claim to have seen or heard a ghost; or an angel; or God or especially if we happen to be young, female and Catholic the Virgin Mary.

Oh those young *female* Catholics!

A few chapters into *The God Delusion* Dawkins gets to his main, and only, point: that the Darwinian biological theory of evolution should be applied to explain *the entire universe*. Dawkins starts his argument by saying, "A deep understanding of Darwinianism teaches us to be wary of the easy assumption that design is the only alternative to chance." Dawkins then grasps at and pushes his own easy assumptions. But first he tells us how and why he will be making his argument: "Feminism shows us the power of consciousness raising, and I want to borrow the technique for natural selection."

Dawkins borrows from the science of biological natural selection too and adapts Darwin's theory of the evolution of life forms into the speculative field of the creation of everything—in other words, cosmology. Dawkins tells us that his solution to understanding how we all got here is what he calls "the Goldilocks zone," as with the three bears and the porridge: The conditions for life had to be "just right."

To find the Goldilocks zone is to discover that with the billions, actually trillions, of planets and perhaps innumerable "other universes" chances are that somewhere conditions would be "just right" for life to evolve. "We live on a planet that is friendly to our kind of life," Dawkins writes; "there are billions of planets in the universe. . . . Now it is time to take the anthropic principle back to an earlier stage, from biology back to cosmology. . . . Some physicists are known to be religious . . . predictably, they seize upon the improbability of the physical constants . . . in their more or less narrow Goldilocks zones, and suggest that there must be a cosmic intelligence deliberately [doing] the tuning [to get the porridge 'just right']. I have already dismissed all such suggestions as raising bigger problems than they solve."

"I have already dismissed. . . ." So that settles that, God is out. "Goldilocks zones" are in. Narrow-minded physicists, who, unlike Dawkins-the-biologist, deal with cosmology as part of their field of study, are out, or rather "already dismissed."

Dawkins borrows Daniel Dennett's phrase about what Dennett calls "the trickle down" theory of creation. Dawkins explains it as "the idea that it takes a big fancy smart thing to make a lesser thing." This, said Dennett (and Dawkins quotes him), is why people believe in God as creator. But Dawkins goes the next step. Given the improbability, verging on impossibility, of the convergence of factors needed to make and sustain life, Dawkins has his own trickle down theory of a Big Fancy Smart Thing (the huge universe) to make lesser things, in other words: us.

What simplistic evangelical/fundamentalist theology tries to explain about creation, using God as the magical Big Thing, Dawkins does with brain-melting Big Numbers wrapped in meant-to-obfuscate and meant-to-intimidate science jargon. The problem is that neither religious fundamentalists nor Dawkins can explain any of what they claim they are explaining. Why? Because they are deep into the realm that Einstein was talking about: the realm "that our mind cannot grasp and this beauty and sublimity reaches us only indirectly and as a feeble reflection, this is religiousness."

It turns out that Dawkins agrees with creationists who say that it's nutty to credit pure chance as responsible for the design of something as complex as life. But Dawkins says that whatever that something is it can't be God, because "Then you would have to ask, who created the creator?"

Instead of God, Dawkins says he's discovered "the anthropic principle." So Dawkins has invented a theology with a scientific-sounding name. He even has doctrines, what he calls the "six fundamental constants of nature," which for him fill in the "gaps." Believers could say that God chose these six "laws" to encourage the evolution of life, but Dawkins won't buy this, because God can't be explained by Dawkins. Apparently the origin of life, however, *can* be explained by Dawkins. Dawkins says that the chance that a God exists who was able to figure Dawkins's six rules out, and thus create the "just right" conditions for life, is as improbable as these rules being "created" by chance.

So after *all that* we're back where we started! There is no reason to have a God because in our limitless universe (or universes) anything is statistically possible, except for there being a God. Why? Because Dawkins says so. Dawkins's "anthropic principle" turns out to be Dawkins. Dawkins's Big Idea seems closer *The Hitchhiker's Guide to the Galaxy* than to science.

As Robert Stewart (a professor of philosophy) wrote about Dawkins's book when reviewing it on the *Evolutionary Philosophy* website,

> Dawkins' claim about differing probabilities appears very naive. Whatever explanation you give for the existence of our universe, whether you believe that the ultimate source of all reality is a mindless cosmic machine, an infinite cosmic chaos, or a purposeful creative force; they are all logically impossible. Without a shred of evidence to support it, the only difference between cosmological evolution and any other kind of creation myth is that it is cleverly shrouded in scientific words. Dawkins does this a lot throughout

his book. He takes questionable concepts and shrouds them in scientific words in order to give them the look of scientific legitimacy.
Intelligent design theorists use the same tactic.

Once Dawkins has made his case for his Goldilocks cosmology,
he pads the remaining hundred pages or so of his book with a numb-
ingly repetitive attack on the creationist movement and all the other
things he doesn't like about religion and religious people, from the
"dark side of absolutism" and the sanctity of human life, to priests
molesting children and, of course, Pastor Ted Haggard's malfeasance,
Oral Roberts's fakery etc., etc. It all seems a long way from science.

For those who become impatient with reading Dawkins's complete works in bits and pieces off assorted merchandise, and who
want to buy "the" Dawkins book, I recommend *The Selfish Gene*.
The big noise has been about *The God Delusion*, but *The Selfish
Gene* is where Dawkins as a serious Oxford professor—back in 1976,
before he won the talk show lottery and went into the clothing
trade—provided some interesting conjecture about biological evolution. Dawkins invented the term *selfish gene* as a way of saying
that evolution is acting on our genes and that selection of popu-
lations doesn't override selection based on genes. He says that our
genes are selfish in the sense that they seem to manipulate us their
hosts to their own ends, often with goals.

These "goals" aren't necessarily going to make us happy. Our
genes delude us with emotions we take at face value, but in reality
these emotions are a charade. We're fooled into doing what's good
for our genes (and not necessarily good for us) by feeling love, fear,
hate, and loathing in ways that push us to procreate, defend our
children, and stay alive long enough for our genes to move on into
and through the next generation. To Dawkins, love and altruism are
at least partly explained as crafty genetic ruses, based on a biological trick perpetuated by blind chance.

In *The Selfish Gene* Dawkins makes a dispassionate scientific
observation that may not have his later atheistic spiritual fervor,

but he seems to come to a sort of spiritual conclusion in terms of human strategies of cooperation that are in line with what he would regard as our gene-driven behavior. In other words, he tries to come up with an answer (and perhaps a reason) for altruism and cooperation, and thus a society not entirely based on genetic-inspired selfishness.

Although the thought is descriptive, it has prescriptive overtones, I think.

> An evolutionary stable strategy is defined as strategy which, if most members of a population adopt it, cannot be bettered by an alternative strategy. . . . Another way of putting it is to say that the best strategy for an individual depends on what the majority of the population are doing. Since the rest of the population consists of individuals, each one trying to maximize his own success, the only strategy that persists will be one which, once evolved, cannot be bettered by any deviant individual.

In other words: our genes "say" be nice and cooperate on behalf of the needs of the many. It's too bad that Dawkins couldn't live by this genetic theory of cooperation in a way that might have motivated him to find harmony with religious believers and (for instance) jointly advocate the sort of ecological agenda we all need to agree on to save our planet. But like all fundamentalists, Dawkins would rather be proved correct "theologically" than compromise in order to win a larger, more important (and real) battle. In that sense Dawkins's book title, *The God Delusion*, seems to describe a disorder that the author suffers from himself.

CHAPTER 4

Determinism Religious and Secular Is the Ultimate Insanity Defense

Man is a synthesis of the infinite and the finite, of the temporal and the eternal, of freedom and necessity; in short it is a synthesis. A synthesis is a relation between two factors. So regarded, man is not yet a self.

The Sickness Unto Death, Søren Kierkegaard

I agree with the atheists who say that an ethical life doesn't require belief in God. We judge an atheist and a religious person by the same standard: what they do, rather than what they say they believe. Atheists can live as moral a life as any religious person. Where atheists have a problem is in pinning down a definition of what morality *is*.

Religious people have that same problem. Because religions and factions within religions don't agree, we're all in the same boat. So there is no reason to pull a New Atheist tantrum, or preach a proselytizing evangelical/fundamentalist sermon and try to lord it over one another. There is no "they." There is only us. Life is too short to know, so religion's most basic lesson—humility—is not just a good idea but also logical. And humility is, I think, also the most basic lesson taught by science, which, by definition, illumines the vastness of our ignorance.

If I'm to pass some sort of exam on what it "means to be a Christian," theology and belief aren't relevant to the test. What is relevant is what Genie and my children can tell you about what I'm like to live with, and whether my years spent on a sacramental path have made me less of a self-centered idiot. That is what faith in God is *about*, just as that is what being a moral atheist is *about*.

If you want to know about the truth qualities of Dawkins's or Maher's or Hitchens's philosophical/moral claims, it's relevant to take into consideration what their wives, girlfriends, maids in hotels, taxi drivers, agents and editors, or even people who stood in line to get a book signed might have to say. What is it like to live with these icons of reason, meet them, or work for them? It's relevant to ask because the New Atheism isn't just about non-belief in God. The leaders of this movement make loud, repeated, and bold claims about atheism being better and more moral, more ethical, and a vastly improved alternative to religion. If we are to dismiss Christianity partly because of the likes of Oral Roberts, Ted Haggard, and their shenanigans (not to mention child-molesting Roman Catholic priests) it is just as legitimate to ask about the characters of the people pointing out religious people's many moral faults.

The discussion between reasonable atheists and reasonable religious people might better focus not just on what it means to be a good person but also on how to become one, rather than just on competing truth claims about the abstract Big Questions, let alone swapping horror stories. For instance, is it being a good Muslim to stone to death a girl who was raped? Is it being a good Christian to slap your wife silly because the Bible "says" she is to submit to you? Is it being a good atheist to beat Tibetan monks to death because they reject the enforced secular education policies of China's government?

Do life, history, common sense, culture, the needs of our small fragile planet, religion, and science hold clues to what the word *good* means? Do we all have blind spots, such as, say being someone who claims he'll save us from religion turning his career into just another religion and gathering goofy followers who collect Scarlet A pins and exclaim "Thank Dawkins" instead of "Thank God"?

We all face the same questions and demons. Genes may push me to love, but why does it hurt so much to contemplate the idea that my love for my family might be a chemically induced delusion? Why do we all struggle against the idea of meaninglessness? Surely our all-knowing and powerful genes could make us seamlessly accept our fate. Foxes and rabbits, snakes and birds are also slaves to their genes. They aren't worrying about meaning or starting wars on the basis of religious ideology.

Wouldn't evolution work better if there weren't so many people doing irrational things driven by angst to despair? Our genes certainly seem to have screwed up a few philosophers and artists, some of whom became so despairing (over the atheistic proposition that life holds no transcendent meaning) that they committed suicide or tried to. Gauguin tried to kill himself after painting his bleak *Whence? What? Whither?* about which he wrote, "I have finished a philosophical work on this theme comparable to the gospel . . . Fate how cruel thou art, and always vanquished, I revolt."

In his 1991 essay "Viruses of the Mind," Dawkins says his "memetic theory" explains why religion exists. He says it's like a computer virus. Dawkins wants to inoculate us sufferers from the religion virus. He calls for anti-virus intellectual programs to cure us of our religious illness. He believes we need his help because, "Like computer viruses, successful mind viruses will tend to be hard for their victims to detect . . . and [they] may even vigorously deny it." Or, as David St. Hubbins (lead guitar of *Spinal Tap*) said about

other hard-to-detect facts, "Dozens of people spontaneously combust each year. It's just not really widely reported."

Dawkins gives the reader signs to look out for related to those
about to spontaneously combust with religious delusions. These signs
include, "Some deep inner conviction that something is true." He describes the religious person as a "faith-sufferer." And yet another
symptom is believing that "'Mystery,' *per se*, is a good thing."

The points that Dawkins raises sound less like science and more
like a high school debate wherein one debater has learned the trick
of mentioning his opponent's beliefs first in order to strip them of
their power, not by proving anything about them but just by mentioning them in a disparaging way that puts the other person on the
defensive. Refer to "mystery" with a sneer so that you strip the word
of its power to remind people that there are indeed mysteries. Mention inner conviction snidely and you've made the way most people
actually function, by ill-thought-out but nevertheless deep inner convictions about what is right and wrong, seem childish. It's a cheap
diversion—of the same kind that some men use when they throw
around the word *hysterical* while discussing a woman's ideas—but
it achieves nothing other than to affix the label "stupid" to the ways
in which most people—including most atheists—actually work out
their problems in real life: we combine reason with emotion.

The truth is that logic has little to nothing to do with the way we
think. We're lucky this is so. If logic ruled us, no one would fall in
love, write a novel, go skydiving, or help an old lady across the street.

There is another way to look at people's inner convictions and
their intuition—that the words *mystery* and *faith* do describe something hard to pin down but true: If people have strong inner convictions, might that not be a symptom of God's revelation to human
beings? Dawkins would probably answer that he is arguing for truth
over falsehood, but it's just his word against religion when it comes
down to it. One man's virus is another man's faith.

To me Dawkins's zeal echoes the paternalistic Victorian "civiliz-
ing" missionary impulse that sent the white man to "darkest

Africa." His mission field is "darkest America" and those "Catholic females," not to mention the "less educated" American classes. Why do his genes make Dawkins want to be a secular missionary to the ignorant religious tribes and motivate him to send his apostles amongst us, organized into local clubs and armed with debate points? Does anyone in his movement have enough of a sense of humor left (after all the hours spent in v-e-r-y s-e-r-i-o-u-s debate) to see that there is a bit of irony in Dawkins-the-rational using *exactly* the same kinds of religious witnessing tools (remember the Gospel Walnut) that my missionary parents used in the 1950s? (Mom and Dad had the good sense to realize that witnessing tools are trite, and they abandoned them, much to my pre-teen relief.)

How the atheist call to convert to atheist faith squares with our being conditioned by our genes is not explained. Are atheists *less* conditioned? Do they have *better* genes? If an atheist and a religious believer marry, are their children likely to have *agnostic* genes?

Dawkins and company preach with moralistic passion but also make the argument that there is no ultimate meaning to be passionate about because it's really their genes doing the talking. Of course, some Christians believe the same sort of thing when they follow the sixteenth-century French Protestant reformer John Calvin.

Calvinism is also a form of deterministic fatalism. It's not quite right to say that Calvin thinks people were created for damnation, because that leaves out the relevance of "The Fall" to the whole process. Elected to eternal damnation is the correct term, but it depends on something called "foreknowledge" by God of what would happen. So the "out" for the Calvinists is that they can say that humans are created as *possibly* meriting damnation, but are not created *for* damnation. However one parses his theology, Calvin believed that his monster "god" had determined everything, including who will be saved or lost. This means that Calvinists (no matter how much they try to worm out of this conclusion) actually must believe that their "god" created some people in order to damn them. That idea puts Calvin's followers in a strange position.

My father was a Calvinist until later in life, when he had the good sense to give up the stricter Calvinistic ideas of his youth. As a young child I knew that we Calvinists were supposed to evangelize everyone to get them saved but, at the same time, we also believed that God had *already* decided everything. My novel *Zermatt* takes my young alter-ego protagonist, the aptly named Calvin Becker, on a bizarre mental journey while he's trying to unravel the mind-bending idea of predestination and foreknowledge in light of his emerging sexuality (and a horny waitress hitting up on him). God predestined everything, so is God *making* my protagonist masturbate? "Did God make me do it?" Calvin wants to know, while trying to square the idea of moral choice with being trapped in the web of God's foreknowledge.

Believe me, when one has been raised on Calvinist theology, it can, as we put it in the sixties, "mess with your head." I imagine that somewhere out there, some kid being raised by Dawkins's groupies is also worrying about whether he's in love with his girlfriend or whether it's just his genes talking, and if so, why aren't *her* genes sending her the *right message* about wanting to have sex?!

How curious that the Calvinist wing of the Protestant religion finds its soul mate in the atheist's determinism. Both get rid of free will theoretically while demanding that their followers *choose* to go out and save the world with correct thinking. And both lace their demands with guilt. God hates you if you disagree with correct theology, and/or Dawkins dismisses you as "less educated" if you question his ideas. God will get even for eternity, Dawkins with his next paperback.

But if we're just the product of brain chemistry or of God's omnipotent will, or of what we learned in our evolutionary ancestral home, and/or of genetics, then all our ideas about free will are also part of what we can't help or change. From whence does the determinist Dawkins derive a morally freighted, even imperial-sounding "You should"? Or, more bluntly, where do Dawkins and the Calvinists get off telling the rest of us what to believe when both insist we're in the grip of powerful cosmic factors beyond our control?

With the notable exception of Daniel Dennett (whose work we'll look at in Chapter 5), the New Atheists seem to underestimate, or even ignore, the mitigating influence of the religion "virus." We don't hear much from the New Atheists about the fact that hospitals as we know them developed in the fourth century and are inextricably related to monastic and other Christian groups (as Andrew Crislip points out in his book *From Monastery to Hospital*). Nor do the New Atheists say much about William Wilberforce and other evangelicals like him, who, while in the grip of "some deep inner conviction that something is true" fought successfully to abolish the slave trade on the basis of their specifically evangelical religious beliefs.

It was Nelson Mandela's and Desmond Tutu's Christian faith that led them to pursue reconciliation rather than vengeance in South Africa. And many atheists enjoy religious music by Bach, applaud biblically informed plays by Shakespeare, love paintings made by virus-infected believers such as Rembrandt, and/or call 911 when hit by a car, expecting that ambulance services, first established by religious people on the principle that humans are little lower than the angels and therefore worth saving, will show up!

Even Dawkins calls himself a "cultural Christian," which is a pleasantly frank (and, for him, an unusually honest) acknowledgment of the fact that a moral/ethical (or, in his case, an aesthetic and nostalgic) viral infection may be comforting. As the BBC reported in December of 2007 on its homepage, "Prof Dawkins, who has frequently spoken out against creationism and religious fundamentalism, [said], 'I'm not one of those who wants to stop Christian traditions. This is historically a Christian country. I'm a cultural Christian in the same way many of my friends call themselves cultural Jews or cultural Muslims. So, yes, I like singing carols along with everybody else. I'm not one of those who wants to purge our society of our Christian history.'"

Most of the time, atheists won't admit that they're borrowing ethical and/or aesthetic cultural traditions from religion. I've read the work of just two recent atheist thinkers—philosopher Richard Rorty and ethicist Peter Singer—who seem to have tried to avoid all the assumptions of religious moral norms in their writing. Most atheists cop out, as Sam Harris does in his book *The End of Faith*. He finishes his slam on religion with a feeble religious-sounding sophomoric whine. He says that he knows we all need meaning. So hey, how about we embrace a sort of secularized Eastern mysticism to help get us through the night, you know, being that hard-edged secular *Truth* is, well, absolutely true and all, but it hurts our feelings, being as it's sort of like, you know, *depressing*.

What Harris doesn't do is reexamine his atheistic ideas based on the fact that if he's right, and in a raw, pure and absolutist form, atheism is unpalatable to most people, then that might be an indication that there is something to all this "religion stuff" besides feeling better. Maybe, if wanting meaning *is* the way people *are*, and we are *part of nature*, then those feelings, however they express themselves, might indicate something true *about the reality of nature* and the way it actually *is*, rather than just signaling an emotional need for religious therapy. Or as author (and brilliant writer on evolutionary psychology) Robert Wright puts it in his book *The Evolution of God*, "If history naturally pushes people toward moral improvement, toward moral truth, and their God, as they conceive their God, grows accordingly, becoming morally richer, then maybe this growth is evidence of some higher purpose, and maybe—conceivably—the source of that purpose is worthy of the name divinity."

As I said, one atheist who tried to bite the bullet in a way that Harris lacked the testicular fortitude to do was Richard Rorty. Rorty argued that we make up morality. He believed that bright people are "ironists" who understand that we know nothing except our own "vocabularies." He said that morality is merely "the language games of one's time."

Rorty was the grandson of Walter Rauschenbusch, a theologian, a Baptist minister, and a leader in what was called the Social Gospel movement in the late nineteenth and early twentieth centuries. So Rorty's nihilism is nihilism with a twist of religious awareness. Rorty is clear about his legacy from the Social Gospel/theological liberalism of his grandfather. Maybe that's why he brings a bare-knuckle honesty to his work that, by comparison, makes Harris seem positively wimpy. In *Rorty and His Critics*, Rorty writes

> The fundamentalist parents of our fundamentalist students think that the entire "American liberal establishment" is engaged in a conspiracy. The parents have a point. . . . [W]e do our best to convince these students of the benefits of secularization. We assign first-person accounts of growing up homosexual to our homophobic students for the same reasons that German schoolteachers in the postwar period assigned *The Diary of Anne Frank.* . . . So we are going to go right on trying to discredit you in the eyes of your children, trying to strip your fundamentalist religious community of dignity, trying to make your views seem silly rather than discussable. I am just as provincial . . . as the Nazi teachers who made their students read *Der Stürmer*; the only difference is that I serve a better cause.

Rorty was honest enough to admit that he had problems with selling his idea of an individually invented moral vocabulary, because no society raises children "to make them continually dubious," as he said. So he wrote that "ironists" like himself should keep their views secret or at least separate their "public and private vocabularies." In other words, Rorty admitted that his ideas had to be lied about in order to succeed, because the way people *actually are* does not correspond to his stark atheist philosophy.

Then there is the Princeton University professor, atheist, and bioethicist Peter Singer. Singer also has tried to invent an ethic with no nostalgic nod to religion, especially not toward Judaism or

Christianity's sanctity-of-life beliefs. He has said that some defective children should be destroyed during a trial period after their births. Similar to his argument for abortion, Singer argues in his *Practical Ethics*, (2nd edition, 1993) that newborns lack the characteristics of personhood—"rationality, autonomy, and self-consciousness"— and that therefore "killing a newborn baby is never equivalent to killing a person, that is, a being who wants to go on living." In Germany, his positions have been compared to the Nazis', and his lectures have been disrupted all over the world by groups representing the handicapped.

According to my friend Angela Creager (she's one of Singer's colleagues and a professor of the history of science at Princeton), Singer is a kind man moved by compassion. Nevertheless, he seems not to understand how his ideas strike others for instance, people with disabilities. Singer gets upset when commentators compare his proposals to Nazism, because his family lost people in the Holocaust. Singer's objections don't seem reasonable to me. As Michael Burleigh, a leading historian of the Third Reich, has pointed out in the context of a commentary on Singer's work, eliminating defectives in *pre*-Nazi Germany was *exactly* what opened the door to the Holocaust. In his book *Confronting the Nazi Past*, Burleigh writes, "Singer omits to mention that one of the essential elements of [Nazi] propaganda was the denial of personality to their victims." He adds that Singer is "displaying remarkable naiveté" when he suggests that the choices that would have to be made in evaluating a prospective defective for elimination would be in trustworthy hands if doctors were in charge. Burleigh notes that the Nazi euthanasia program was led by scientists and psychiatrists, people drawn from the best-educated and most "civilized" ranks of a sophisticated secular medical class not too different from the academic class Singer himself belongs to.

Atheists say that morality isn't derived only from religion. I think they're right. But they seem to have problems when deciding the limits of what is permissible under the rules of their "invented vocabulary" of morality *à la* Rorty and Singer. Maybe the point is that religion is derived *from* morality.

I'm guessing that morality predates religion. We all act as if that's the case. We don't have long theological debates about, say, incest or wife abuse as though the jury is still out on what is wrong or that our sense of the matter depends on Bible verses. We evolved ideas that make life easier and less chaotic, as in: I don't want to be clubbed in my sleep so let's all agree that clubbing people in their sleep is wrong! Those ideas—including parents not taking kindly to "experts" telling them what they should do about their "defective" child—might be a reflection of the character of God. If there is no God, or if He doesn't care about us, then our common morality is still the result of practical, reality-based needs, which also "teach" that a good life depends on the "Do unto others . . . " ethic. Either way, morality is a lot more than an individual's invented vocabulary. Either way, Singer's ethic seems monstrous to many people for the same reason that George W. Bush's torturing prisoners in the name of national security was a threat to us all.

How individuals are treated affects everyone. Ideas such as Singer's and George W. Bush's have consequences. There may indeed be babies born who'd be "better off" killed or prisoners who "deserve" to be water-boarded or punched and exposed to hunger, cold, and snarling dogs. But the rest of us aren't better off when morality becomes a function of expediency, be that in the name of national security or of "sensibly" getting rid of the need for all those expensive handicapped ramps by getting rid of the handicapped themselves, at birth.

Who decides who's next? Do you trust an academic ethicist like Singer to make life-and-death judgments when he's so far removed from reality that he gets hurt feelings when his seminars are picketed by people in wheelchairs (the very sorts of human beings that Singer says might have been better off being killed at birth)? Should a Darth Vader figure like former vice president Dick Cheney be kept handy to decide when torture is "okay"? Is national security worth preserving if it entails turning our country into a police state?

Do atheists really believe that morality doesn't exist just because it can't be put under a microscope? Do any atheists claim that (and, far more tellingly, live as if) moral propositions have no objective value? If Singer finds himself on a planet where handicapped people are the norm and he is a minority of one, will he gladly entrust himself to a panel of experts to decide his fate as—in that context—an "abnormal" person? If Rorty had not been paid the royalties generated by the sale of his books, would he have failed to take his publishers to court had his editor argued that in the "invented moral vocabulary" of publishing, they'd just changed the rules of accounting? For that matter, when Singer gets his feelings hurt by outraged handicapped people who compare him to the Nazis, isn't that a tacit admission that there is a right way and a wrong way to treat people, including Australian ethicist/ Princeton professors who feel that their benign intensions are being misunderstood?

And what if the New Atheist agenda succeeded beyond Dawkins and his followers' wildest dreams? Would everything work out perfectly? For instance, what would happen to the environmentalist movement? The appeal of the environmentalist movement is handily compatible with the idea of stewardship. Maybe that appeal works because a sense of stewardship and a sense of the sacred in Nature are intrinsic to *our* natures, a part of the divine revelation we are gradually developing a capacity to experience. Watch any TV program on the wonders of life on earth. Even if there is no religious content the tone is reverential, and a sense of the sacred permeates the hushed narration. Why?

A lot more motivation can be inspired by maintaining that one may do God's will by conserving the earth than by telling people that their lives mean nothing in an ultimate sense, that they are slaves to their genes, conditioning, and evolutionary quirks, but, oh, by the way, they should sacrifice their comforts to save the planet for equally meaningless and deluded future generations that they'll never meet. Or, as atheist apologist Princeton University professor and molecular biologist Lee M. Silver writes in *Challenging Nature: The Clash of Science and Spirituality at the New Frontier of Life*, about the question of life having meaning and therefore a point: "I have yet to hear a good answer, other than there is no point."

Now that will really fire people up to make sacrifices!

It seems to me the New Atheists have it wrong. If you deprive people of the solace of faith in a moral system of meaningful connection with something bigger than themselves, and bigger than mere connection to many other "meaningless" people, you aren't just stripping away window dressing but demolishing the supporting structure of a happy life. As I said, I think that Harris tacitly admits this by appending his squishy ending to his otherwise hardnosed book. Atheists too depend on some form of spirituality for happiness. Why else do you think that Dawkins's zeal can only be described as religious, and his followers as disciples? Maybe it's because the need for meaning won't be denied, even by people who gather to do just that.

Even one of the most church-hating fathers of the Enlightenment, Voltaire, to whom Christianity was an "infamy," found the influence of faith, and of Christianity in particular, useful: "I want my attorney, my tailor, my servants, even my wife to believe in God," he wrote, because "then I shall be robbed and cuckolded less often."

If atheists visiting the Metropolitan Museum of Art refused to visit any exhibitions containing religious works or any works created by artists who had a deep personal religious faith, they'd find their stay brief. They'd be stuck looking at a rotting shark in a tank of formaldehyde, maybe a Picasso or two. (Actually, I'm not sure about that. Picasso's early communism had religious overtones to the point where Picasso once said, "I am a communist and my painting is communist painting.") The rest of us would enjoy the other 99 percent of the exhibits, not to mention just about every concert given on any night in New York City, from Vivaldi to Duke Ellington.

In a lecture on BBC 3 in the spring of 2009, composer James McMillan drew attention to the fact that many poets and composers of the modern era have taken a religious stance, from T. S. Eliot, W. H. Auden, and John Betjeman to John Tavener, György Ligeti, and many others. This is a point not lost on atheists. In fact, one atheist website is full of defensive comments promoting art by atheists, as though atheist artists are a special-needs case whose work should be exhibited in a dedicated venue something like the Special Olympics. "Atheists are as creative as religious people!" proclaims the site. The site also promises to help atheists "network and promote, sell and display our atheist work."

My beef with the New Atheists *and* with religious fundamentalists is that their ideas just don't seem aesthetically pleasing or imbued with the poetry that I experience in real life. Ideas *about* life are too small. Life trumps description—just as what some severely handicapped people actually grow up to do (and be) trumps sage theories on just whose life is "worthy to be lived." Is Dawkins correct when he says religious people appeal to mystery as a cop-out? Are unnamed things meaningless? Do we have to *understand* something in order to experience it? Is scientific prediction of outcomes not still just prediction? Enter Lucy!

I play music to Lucy even though she doesn't know what music is. It is a mystery to her. I read that babies' brains develop better, or do something good anyway, when they hear classical music. Lucy seems to favor Italian opera, Beethoven's Sixth, Handel's Messiah, and Glen Gould playing Bach's "Goldberg Variations." My son Francis (whom in our family we call Fact Boy, given his voracious reading habits and encyclopedic store of general knowledge) told me that when children hear various languages spoken from birth, their brains develop differently, and later they can speak those languages or at least learn foreign languages more easily. So, just in case, I do these "scientifically improving things" for Lucy before she understands anything about them. What I'm *really* doing, though, is basking in the glow of my beautiful little granddaughter, while feeling much the same as a lizard lying on a warm rock in the sun.

If the love I have for Lucy is love, not just a chemical ruse, then it is completely selfless *and* completely selfish—both pleasure and pain. Selfless because I'll do anything for Lucy: be drooled on without complaint, develop a stiff neck carrying her for hours, change a particularly ruinous diaper, do dishes laboriously with one hand as I hold her in my other arm because she loves watching real activities. Selfish because being with her makes me deliriously happy.

There are also other times of inner stillness when I'm so completely absorbed by what I'm doing that everything else seems like a rude intrusion. That sometimes happens when I write or paint. But when I find stillness of spirit through the love of someone precious to me, it's an entirely different experience from the stillness I enjoy when concentrating on any useful activity. It is also what I find in the stillness of prayer.

When writing novels or painting small oils (of the marsh and what grows in my garden), I'm mining what's inside me, and that's a finite source limited by what I know and have experienced and what I can see and do. When I find I'm captivated by loving another person, say Lucy, the experience takes on the aura of infinity. All those millions of words in the books on so many shelves in my old dusty house can't approach the reality of an actual moment of loving communion.

Words may "explain" how our genes are driving Lucy and me to bond for reasons of species propagation, tribe cohesion, and genetic survival; how our evolutionary ancestral home, where tribes first formed, has made Lucy and me the way we are; how altruism is just a genetic survival mechanism; and so forth. Other books on the same shelves drone on about theology, meaning, philosophy, and the "nature of God." None, be they Dawkins's atheist sermons or religious tomes by men such as Thomas Aquinas, capture the empathy between Lucy and me, let alone describe one second of the actual reality.

Even after having read *The Selfish Gene*, and Mr. Silver's pronouncement that there is no point to life, and John Calvin's "explanation" that God has already decided everything (including whom I love), I still bring Genie a cup of coffee in bed. I still say "I love you" to her and believe that those words have a deeper meaning than my genes fooling my brain. I still say "I love you" to Lucy, too, even before she can understand those words. I believe those words represent a choice. I also believe they embody a mystery that I'm not ashamed to enjoy rather than try to explain.

CHAPTER 5

Dennett Says Religion Evolved the Way Folk Music Did

One sees now how . . . extraordinarily stupid it is to defend Christianity, how little knowledge of men this betrays, and how truly, even though it be unconsciously, it is working in collusion with the enemy, by making of Christianity a miserable something or another which in the end has to be rescued by a defense.

Fear and Trembling, Søren Kierkegaard

On the first page of *Breaking the Spell—Religion as a Natural Phenomenon*, Daniel Dennett writes, "I may have missed my target." Dennett strikes me as somebody actually looking for answers. He is an atheist, but no fundamentalist. One reason I find Dennett so appealing is his decency. His humility, wit, and empathy speak volumes to me and lends a solid gravity to his wisdom. It certainly proves you don't need to believe in God to come across as just the sort of person anyone would like to have for a friend.

Dennett is a philosopher whose science research is related to evolutionary biology. He is also director of the Center for Cognitive Studies at Tufts University. Dennett deserves better friends than his fellow contributors to the emerging New Atheist canon. Maybe he knows this, because he puts a little distance between Dawkins and himself. In *Breaking the Spell* Dennett levels a subtle rebuke at Dawkins, even though he doesn't name him: "Biologists are often accused of gene-centrism—thinking that everything in biology is explained by the action of genes. And some biologists do indeed go overboard in their infatuation with genes. They should be reminded that Mother Nature is not a gene centrist!" Dennett also wrote a review of Dawkins's *The God Delusion* for *Free Inquiry*, saying that he and Dawkins agree about many ideas, "but on one central issue we are not (yet) of one mind: Dawkins is quite sure that the world would be a better place if religion were hastened to extinction and I am still agnostic about that."

We've never met but I've watched Dennett debate, have read him, and have heard him interviewed. He seems fair and knowledgeable about religion, acknowledging that all religions have a toxic component and yet that they also have a good side. Dennett has even proposed that a course on religions should be taught—worldwide— as a compulsory part of education both private and public, secular and religious. He wants this done because, as he correctly says, "All toxic parts of religion depend on the enforced ignorance of the young." Dennett also looks forward to the day that the Vatican becomes "a museum of Roman Catholic religion" and "Mecca becomes Disney's Magic Kingdom of Allah." He said that in a debate (held at Tufts University in 2008) with the right-wing author Dinesh D'Souza. It's also a somewhat tongue-in-cheek point Dennett makes in his book.

The essential idea put forward in *Breaking the Spell* is that humans are like ants whose brains have been infected by a parasite. We're like an ant who climbs again and again to the top of a stalk of grass, driven to do that by a parasite lodged in its brain. Dennett asks, "Does anything like this ever happen with human beings? Yes indeed. We often find human beings setting aside their personal interests, their health, their chances to have children, and devoting their entire lives to furthering the interests of an *idea* that has lodged in their brains."

Dennett admits that "The comparison of the Word of God to lancet fluke [parasite] is unsettling." And he asks, "How are ideas . . . spread from mind to mind, surviving translation between different languages, hitchhiking on songs and icons and . . . rituals, coming together in unlikely combinations in particular people's heads, where they give rise to yet further new 'creations' bearing family resemblances to the ideas that inspired them?"

Dennett believes that the answer is that religions evolved as a response to our fears and as an explanation to ourselves of what we don't understand. These explanations became more and more sophisticated until they emerged as religions, a few of which have survived and become established. "Some of the features of our minds are endowments we share with much simpler creatures, and others are specific to our lineage. . . . These features sometimes overshoot, sometimes have curious byproducts . . . [and] some of these patterns look rather like religions."

Nevertheless, Dennett believes that religion can be a wonderful thing for many people. Unlike the other New Atheists, Dennett realizes that the consequences of his work attempting to debunk religion might damage individuals and societies. As he puts it, breaking the spell that religion casts over people could be something like letting your cell phone ring at a concert. "I don't want to be that person," he writes. He continues, "The problem is there are good spells and there are bad spells . . . and it may be the best way to break these bad spells is to introduce the spellbound to a good spell."

Dennett is open to the idea that one possibility for breaking the spell of bad religion is to look for a "good gospel." He says that good intentions are not enough. "If we learned anything in the twentieth century, we learned that . . . we made some colossal mistakes with the best of intentions. In the early decades of the century, communism seemed to many millions of thoughtful, well-intentioned people to be a beautiful and even obvious solution to the terrible unfairness that all can see, but they were wrong."

Dennett recognizes the perils of secularism in a way that the other leading New Atheists writers don't, or rather won't. He also acknowledges the limits of his (and all) knowledge and asks, "Who is right? I don't know. Neither do the billions of people with their passionate religious convictions. Neither do those atheists who are sure the world would be a much better place if all religion went extinct." Dennett seems to understand that we're all in the same situation: "Even atheists and agnostics can have sacred values," he writes, "values that are simply not up for re-evaluation at all. . . . [M]y sacred values are obvious and quite ecumenical: democracy, justice, life, love, and truth."

Dennett is critical of the blind spot atheists discussing religion bring to their theories: "We don't just walk up to religious phenomena and study them point-blank as if they were fossils . . . Researchers tend to either be respectful [and] deferential [or] hostile, invasive, and contemptuous." Dennett is honest. "People who want to study religion," he writes, "usually have an ax to grind. . . . [T]his tends to infect their methods with bias."

Why did he write his book? Dennett answers, "I, for one, fear that if we don't subject religion to . . . scrutiny now, and work together for whatever revisions and reforms are called for, we will pass on the legacy of ever more toxic forms of religion to our descendents." Post 9/11, post the impact of the Religious Right on American life and politics, who can argue with that?

Dennett asks, "How can we [stop religion] from being used to shelter the lunatic excesses?" The solution he says, would be to make religion less of a "sacred cow" and more of what he calls "a 'worthy alternative.'" Dennett says, "Until the priests and rabbis and imams and their flocks explicitly condemn *by name* the dangerous individuals and congregations within their ranks, they are *all* complicit."

Amen!

Dennett points out that religions evolve. Perhaps he means this as a criticism of religion, but for me it's a hopeful sign. I'm glad that religion changes as we do. Perhaps someday it—and we—will grow up. My quibble with Dennett's view, that somehow religious evolution is a problem for religion, is that individual religions aren't the point. What is the point is the question raised by the existence of *any* religion: in other words our longing for meaning.

Because every plant, four-legged creature, and human, fish, and bird has evolved from single-celled organisms, our evolutionary journey is clearly toward complexity. And what religion is, is the expression of a dimension of complex consciousness. From my point of view, that is a reason to be hopeful about the fact that we human animals, in the course of our evolution, were brought—and will be brought—to a better place by the gradual understanding of a larger reality. Thus the gradual revelation by God comes to us *through* us. Whom else does Dennett think it would come through?

And why, just because religious belief evolves in and through us—or is, as Dennett puts it, invented by us—does that mean that what we invent is any less true? Maybe we aren't inventing but rather discovering. No one invented electricity. It was discovered. It existed before we evolved sufficiently to recognize its potential.

Dennett says, "I look around and I'm so glad to be alive!" He "gets" the spiritual wonder of life. I just think Dennett is using a needlessly limited vocabulary to express his spirituality. Nevertheless, Dennett comes up with one of the best definitions of what religion is. He writes of "keeping that awestruck vision of the world ready to hand while dealing with the demands of daily living."

In his debate with D'Souza, Dennett said, "I wish that there was someone I could properly express my gratitude to for all this wonderful stuff. But there isn't anybody to be the appropriate recipient of my gratitude, so what I do instead is just thank goodness." And he added, "There is moral goodness too. There is the goodness of human morality. It all evolved. This is a hard idea for people to understand."

It seems to me that Dennett's desire to express gratitude is in itself a sort of witness to the fact that there might be a someone there to whom gratitude is due. Why would the human animal have such a weird and completely novel impulse to express gratitude unless it was an echo of a greater reality, yet to be fully discovered?

Dennett believes there is an inversion of reason, where *unknowing* becomes the only explanation. That's what I believe too, and his is one of the best articulations I've read of that idea. This is another point where Dennett and Dawkins seem to disagree, in that Dennett's "inversion of reason" might well be dismissed as a mystery-type cop-out by Dawkins when it is applied to faith in God.

I don't think we need a creator to explain anything, such as design and order. What I do believe we need, and will eventually find, is that there is spiritual meaning that exists objectively, apart from us, and comes from God (or from what we call "God"). And that that meaning, for now, is best expressed by the words "Love your neighbor" and "Thank you."

If Dennett fails, it's where many brilliant scholars have failed: He seems to lack imagination when it comes to what lies outside of what he studies. It's a sort of beautiful failure similar to the failure of the painter Georges Seurat.

Seurat was influenced by two scientists, Chevreul and Rood, who wrote on optical effects and perception. So Seurat invented a technique of painting—all those lovely little dots of color in his paintings such as *A Sunday Afternoon on the Island of La Grande Jatte*—that he believed was more scientific than any previous art. His method reflected what some nineteenth-century scientists regarded as *the* way we see. Seurat's style conformed to their theory, but the paintings turned out to be just another phase of impressionism, lovely and yet oddly limited by subjecting art to a science-based *theory* of art. It was a bad fit, I think. Art has truths to offer, but perhaps being an illustration of the science of how we see isn't one of them.

That is my problem with Dennett. My sense is that he's stuck in a moment of time that will someday look as lovely as Seurat's pointillist paintings, but also just as needlessly limited. Dennett's generous spirit would be better served transcending his self-imposed limits. The art in what Dennett says will outlast his science, I think, because science is always partly yesterday's news. Whereas there are truths of the spirit that are what they are forever. Beauty and love expressed in art, poetry, and religion are among the things that last.

I believe that Dennett is right when he tells us that free will and intentionality are explained by Darwinian science. It isn't that I disagree with Dennett (or Darwin), it's that I feel Dennett doesn't go far enough. To use the Seurat metaphor again, I long for Dennett to step outside his idea of what he must say to be a scientist/philosopher in good standing with like-minded academics and try on another style of perception. Or put it this way: I'd like to be a parasite (very briefly!) inhabiting Dennett's brain and able to experience what is beyond his ability to describe when he watches the sky lighten at dawn from the deck of his sailboat. My sense is that he would be experiencing the sacred.

As Dennett said in his debate at Tufts, "We're stuck telling each other how to live our lives and how to live morally." And that fact that we are *all* stuck doing this makes us very different from everything else we know in nature. It also makes the "we and they" way in which some atheists and religious people are dismissing each other childish.

The truth at the heart of why religion exists is that moral/metaphysical/spiritual/aesthetic experiences are part of our lives. Moral/metaphysical/spiritual/aesthetic experiences are part of Dennett's life too. If they weren't, he wouldn't bother using an art form—writing—in an attempt to refute the power of religion by trying to explain its biological origins. And he writes beautifully, which takes skill and effort. Dennett's aesthetic qualities seem spiritual to me.

Explaining the theoretical biological origin of spirituality has no more impact on our need for, and enjoyment of, religious experiences than explaining that water is "only H2O" strips water of its actual meaning. We *know* what water *is*. But it's also fun to jump into and play in, good to drink, beautiful to look at, exciting to sail on, capable of putting one to sleep with the sound of lapping waves, useful for baptizing babies in, responsible for inspiring Turner to paint, and *wet*—even after one knows that there is no such thing as "wet" or "dry" because wet is merely a set of sensations that we call "wetness" caused by a configuration of molecules that are neither dry nor wet. So here's one answer to the question "What is water?" It might also be a partial answer to Dennett's claim that he doesn't know whom to thank: Lucy *loves* her bath!

Lucy loving her bath and smiling while she kicks and splashes all the water out of the baby tub is also "why" water exists. The pleasure we take in a baby's pleasure might be a hint of what our meaning is too: the pleasure of God enjoying our pleasure at existing in the midst of, as Dennett calls it, "all this wonderful stuff."

While I am bathing Lucy, the gulf between my understanding of what is going on between us as Lucy smiles at me and my heart melts, and what is actually happening, is larger than the gulf between Lucy's preverbal state and my "sophistication" as a fifty-six-year-old writer. And as for the meaning of water, molecules are the least of it; the big story is my joy at watching Lucy's joy.

The essence of Lucy's and my times together depends on something different from ideas about what it all means. It is what it *is* with or without anyone's descriptions, let alone anyone's approval. I look into Lucy's eyes as she looks into mine, and there is an amazing exchange of whatever we call it or don't call it. I watch her seeing everything for the first time. I hold her in the crook of my left arm as I paint on a blank canvas with my right hand. When holding Lucy, I paint fast and sloppy so that the drama of the spreading colors will hold her attention. Lucy has never seen a blank canvas miraculously turn blue and green and yellow. Lucy—thank God!—

has never seen a TV either, so she is discovering the world and her relationship to it in real time.

To Lucy, watching paint being applied is a miracle. She literally holds her breath. And I hold mine too, because seeing the intense freshness of her experiencing the act of painting overwhelms my jaded, seen-it-all outlook. Lucy's gift to me is her wonderment. I could be presented with a thousand options, and not one activity or reward could lure me away from tasting the sweetness of "being" five months old again and waking up to color and form. Lucy is my Eden. And no compliment I've ever received matches the sense of accomplishment I feel when Becky, Lucy's generous mother, hands Lucy to me and Lucy reaches out and smiles. Winning Lucy's and my children's and other grandchildren's trust and friendship is the best thing I've ever done. It feels as if it has moral weight. I'm betting it does. I feel as if it has something to do with the why and wherefore of what we're all doing here. I'm betting it does.

One reason why it's so wonderful to be trusted and loved by a baby is that unlike adult relationships, with all those ulterior motives and hidden agendas, I know that Lucy is exactly what she appears to be. Her spontaneous gift of love, trust, and affection is not an intellectually calculated means to an end.

The same guilelessness reemerges at the end of some lives, too. Lucy turned five months old at about the same time that my mother turned ninety-four. Their situations were strangely similar.

Mom lives in Switzerland near my sister Debbie. When I call Mom, she knows who I am and still remembers to ask after Genie. Other than that, Mom has little conversation left these days and must be prompted by whoever is in the room with her to remember the simplest things—it's snowing outside, we had scrambled eggs for lunch, this morning we drove down to Lake Geneva to walk on the quay.

I've told her all about Lucy dozens of times. She's always surprised and re-congratulates me—again—on having had this, my third grandchild. These days I even have to explain to Mom again and again who her grandchild John, Lucy's dad, is. And she seems also to have forgotten Amanda and Ben, my two older grandchildren, who live in Finland with my daughter Jessica and my son-in-law Dani. I ask questions. "What did you do today, Mother?" "What is the weather like?" Mom repeats what I say, and I hear my sister or Mom's other caregivers prompting her. Then Mom relays that information to me, and I pretend I didn't just hear someone else tell her the answer.

Suffering from forgetfulness brought on by several small strokes, my once-vibrant and brilliant mother is no longer able to do much more than my baby granddaughter Lucy can do. Lucy and Mom are passing like ships in the night. Lucy looks into my eyes earnestly as we "converse," me jabbering in French and Italian that she doesn't understand, Lucy wanting to be like the people around her and able to communicate. "I'm a person too!" she seems to be saying with those burbling chirpy little sounds.

As my mother fades away and her great-granddaughter comes into her own, they may never meet. Lucy is a bit young for transatlantic travel, and Mom is too old. But they have met in another way: They are both at about the same place when it comes to being able to speak and remember. Mom is slowly falling asleep. Lucy is waking up.

The best moment in any conversation with my mother is the surprise and joy in her voice at the beginning of our calls when she exclaims, "Oh it's Frank!" She sounds so pleased and, just like my granddaughter, Mom is at a stage of her life when guile, pretense, and calculation are impossible.

In Lucy's case guile has never been there, and she will have to "grow up" in order to learn how to lie. Mom can, at this stage of life, only be herself. She used to be very good at projecting happiness when encountering people she was inwardly cringing at meeting. Her newfound guilelessness means that she is sometimes rude to one or more of the ladies who help my sister take care of her. If Mom is annoyed these days, to think it is to say it! But it also means that when I hear that note of delight and recognition in her voice—the only unprompted part of our phone conversations—the joy is authentic. Mom's joy when she hears my voice strips away the gnawing feeling I carry with me that I've been less than a good son.

Both Lucy and Mom take pleasure in the beginnings and the remains of their ability to communicate to the people most beloved to them. As Mom grows older, the gaps in her conversations grow longer. What remains is a fierce love, even for a son who caused her so much heartache over the years. As Lucy "talks" to me, what I hear is not a series of inarticulate noises, but her desire to enter into an endless conversation, as soon as she learns the words. Mom's great gift to me is that first "It's Frank!" Lucy's great gift is the intensity of the smile that she gives me every time our eyes meet and the tenderness in her voice as she sometimes coos when she sees me. She's too young to fake gladness. Mom is too old and lost in an ocean of diminishing capacity to fake joy.

The calls with my mother are sacred to me because I know that each conversation could be our last. When I tell her she's been a good mother at the end of each call, it contradicts a lifetime of my complaining about my mother and even my incorporating her into some of my books both fiction and nonfiction (including this one) in a less than flattering way. It cuts to the essential relationship that formed when I was in her arms, just as Lucy is in my arms now. It depends on nonverbal communication and a mysterious communion that was what it was before being defined.

Our connection now transcends our differences over religion. The pleasure of our friendship is visceral and bypasses our ideas about each other too. It even bypasses facts: the son who got Genie pregnant when he was seventeen and she was eighteen, the son who has written books presenting his parents in a way that has outraged some of their followers, the son who moved far away (in every sense) and abandoned the evangelical/fundamentalist faith of his youth, to which his missionary parents devoted their lives.

Our connection also softens my unhappy memories of a mother who was too busy with what she believed was God's "call" on her life to care for her children properly. This is the mother who forgot to send me to school until I was almost eleven and who filled our house with strangers she was "ministering" to and, in so doing, turned our home into a public space that was both interesting and traumatizing. And since Mom also folded stories about her children into her talks and books—without our permission—to illustrate points about her spiritual subjects, I grew up with no personal secret safe, all trust stolen. Home never felt safe, let alone private.

All that disappears when Mom and I both say, "I love you." Mom's sincerity springs from the fact that everything else, including her memories of my failings and perhaps of her own, has been stripped away along with those dying brain cells, and she's back to the raw emotion of holding her child. My sincerity is based on the fact that when I contemplate Mom's death, no matter what our differences, fights, and arguments have been, the looming darkness of not hearing her voice strips away all petty complaints.

The sobering thought of losing my mother and the reality that it will happen any day now wipes out everything but the most basic emotion, which turns out not to be blame, or even facts, but simply "I love you Mom, you've been a good mother." And I mean it. She was the best mother she could be, given who she was and her own missionary child background.

My self-awareness seems to have a meaning that is not reflected in Dennett's material universe. That universe is silent, yet I speak. It does not care, but I do. It merely is, but I contemplate it. The universe says nothing to me, yet my mother says "I love you" and means it.

CHAPTER 6

Hitchens Poisons Hitchens

It is now high time to explain that the real reason why man is offended at Christianity is because it is too high, because its goal is not man's goal, because it would make of a man something so extraordinary that he is unable to get it into his head.

Fear and Trembling, Søren Kierkegaard

To rephrase Kierkegaard's apt quote, it is (also) now high time to attempt to explain the black sheep of the New Atheist family, the sexually obsessed, sibling-rival, left-wing radical turned right-wing Jihadist, and one of the least pleasant commentators on the current scene, Christopher Hitchens, author of the bestseller *God Is Not Great*. As best as I can figure him, Christopher Hitchens hates God for two reasons. First, because (judging on the basis of what he's written and is quoted as having said) he likes sex and thinks religious people don't. Second, because (judging on that same basis), he loathes his younger brother Peter Hitchens, also a well-known writer and a rival political commentator, with whom Christopher Hitchens has had a long and bitter feud over theology and politics. Peter Hitchens is a practicing and devout Anglican and a convert from the far, far loony Trotskyite British left that both he and Christopher Hitchens once embraced.

The fact is, I "get" Christopher Hitchens's obsessions and his bizarre rationales for his aggressive atheism and anti-clericalism. I get his split with his religious brother Peter Hitchens too. I understand this chemistry all too well, because my leaving the evangelical/fundamentalist fold was—for a time—a break with my siblings too, one that infuriated my parents' right-wing fundamentalist followers. I get the sex bit too. Sex is all over my novels; in fact it's all over this chapter. So I *get* Hitchens.

God Is Not Great is an entertaining book. On the other hand it's so skewed that, unlike Daniel Dennett's serious and beautiful *Breaking the Spell*, Hitchens's *God Is Not Great* adds little to the discussion of religion besides a kind of furiously demented anti-God entertainment, an odd mix of philosophizing combined with working out the author's very particular psychological problems. The book is entertaining in the same way that professional wrestling and airplane crashes are entertaining. One feels sorry for Hitchens's suffering but sort of glad it happened because his anguished hate of the "other" is riveting.

Hitchens describes how he converted to religion in order to marry. He joined the Greek Orthodox Church to please the family of his first wife. Then he divorced and abandoned that faith. But apparently Orthodoxy meant something more to him than mere convenience, because he writes about how wonderful it felt to shout out "Christ is risen!" at the Easter services, and how he was swept up in that experience. Hitchens also says, "There are days when I miss my old convictions as if they were an amputated limb." Maybe he's talking about those Easter services, or perhaps he's talking about his old Trotskyite certainties.

As Hitchens summarizes his book's argument, it comes to this: "The first [problem] is that religion and churches are manufactured. . . . The second is that ethics and morality are quite independent of faith. The third is that religion is—because it claims a special divine exemption for its practices and beliefs—not just amoral but immoral." What, according to Hitchens, are religion's sins? Religion is "violent, irrational, intolerant, allied to racism and tribalism and bigotry, invested in ignorance and hostile to free inquiry, contemptuous of women and . . . children: organized religion ought to have a great deal on its conscience." Hitchens *also* got sick of expressing gratitude. "Why if god [he uses the lowercase 'g' to make a point] was the creator of all things, were we supposed to 'praise' him so incessantly for doing what came to him naturally? This seemed servile, apart from anything else."

Why thank God when "Religion," Hitchens writes, "spoke its last intelligible or noble or inspiring words a long time ago." And what should Hitchens's readers make of religious people who have been seduced by those "inspiring words" and then been mistaken for heroes? Consider Dietrich Bonhoeffer, the Lutheran pastor hanged by the Nazis for his refusal to collude with them. Well, it turns out that Bonhoeffer's religious heroism was actually a type of humanism, if properly understood.

A couple of pages after Bonhoeffer is dealt with, Hitchens pens a line that could serve as Hitchens's epitaph: "The person who is certain, and claims divine warrant for his certainty, belongs now to the infancy of our species." In which case, what about Hitchens's certainties, or, more to the point, what about Martin Luther King Jr.? He seemed to be in possession of a "divine warrant" or thought he was.

"Anybody," writes Hitchens, "who uses the King legacy to justify the role of religion in public life must accept all the corollaries. . . . Even a glance at the whole record will show, first, that person for person, American free thinkers and agnostics and atheists come out best. The chance that someone's secular [thinking] or freethinking . . . would cause him or her to denounce the whole injustice was extremely high. The chance that someone's religious beliefs would cause him or her to take a stand against slavery and racism was statistically quite small." So Martin Luther King Jr. really must have been some sort of secularist too, because it's just so abnormal for anyone to be *both* religious *and* good.

When it comes to the sins of atheism, Hitchens turns to George Orwell for reassurance that somehow, no matter what it looks like, atheism is not true to itself when being bad but, rather is *authentically atheist* only when it's good. The rest of the time it may *appear* that atheism fails from time to time, but that's not so. "George Orwell . . . whose novels gave us [a] picture of what life in a totalitarian state might truly feel like, was in no doubt about [the fact that] '*a totalitarian state is in its effect a theocracy*.'" (emphasis in the original)

In other words, to Hitchens, Stalin and Hitler and Mao and Pol Pot and their ilk were more to be understood as bad popes than as bad atheists. Evil atheists are not *real* atheists. Real atheists are *by definition* free thinkers who do wonderful things, much like Dawkins's *real scientists*, who are, also by definition, all atheists, or wish they had been, or would have been if only they could have had a chat with Dawkins.

In case we miss the point—about all bad atheists actually being religious people, or at least acting like religious people—Hitchens says that *even if* totalitarian secularism *was* bad, religion *is still* to blame because of the answer to this loaded question: "Given its own record of succumbing to, and promulgating, dictatorship on earth and absolute control in the life to come, how did religion confront the secular totalitarians of our time?" The answer? Consider "the case of the churches [surrendering] to German National Socialism." As for those dependably evil popes, "Despite sharing two important principles with Hitler's movement—those of anti-Semitism and anti-Communism—the Vatican could see [that Nazism] represented a challenge to itself as well." So even if *sometimes* the Vatican (or a local priest or nun or layperson) resisted the Nazis, it was not for any humanitarian reason but simply to maintain the Church's power. The rest of the time popes colluded, and anyway, from Hitchens's point of view, Nazism was *just another religion* carried on under a secular name.

He may call himself an atheist but Christopher, like his brother Peter, is also a perennial convert. In Christopher Hitchens's case, though, conversion was not to an ancient religion (except briefly to curry favor with his in-laws) but, early in life, to the political religious cult of extreme Marxism and then, late in mid life, to neoconservatism and jingoistic American exceptionalism. He made this last conversion to the far right after 9/11, when, after a career as a left-wing anti-imperialist, Christopher became a leading advocate and supporter of George W. Bush's war in Iraq.

This angered his old friends on the left. So Christopher threw them a sop, his Johnny-come-lately jump onto the New Atheist bandwagon. His peace offering was *God Is Not Great*. He got to kill two birds with one stone: attempted reconciliation with the (often) atheist American left, and another way to stick it to his brother Peter.

Hitchens's shot at lefty redemption didn't work. With a "friend" like Hitchens, smart lefties feel they need no enemies. What to do with a man who in a May 2008 *Slate* article on Michelle Obama (in the wake of *L'Affaire* Reverend Wright), alleged that her view of America was the same as that of Stokely Carmichael and Louis Farrakhan?!

Here is how Alexander Cockburn, Hitchens's former, pre–Iraq War colleague at the lefty *Nation* magazine (from which Hitchens dramatically departed in 2005 after he became a shill for Bush on Iraq), has described how people on the left feel about Hitchens:

> What a truly disgusting sack of shit Hitchens is. A guy who called Sid Blumenthal one of his best friends and then tried to have him thrown into prison for perjury; a guy who waited till his friend Edward Said was on his death bed before attacking him in the *Atlantic Monthly*; a guy who knows perfectly well the role Israel plays in US policy but who does not scruple to flail Cindy Sheehan [a mother who turned peace activist after her soldier son was killed in Iraq] as a LaRouchie and anti-Semite because, maybe, she dared mention the word Israel. She lost a son? Hitchens (who

[given Hitchens's support for Bush's war] should perhaps be careful on the topic of sending children off to die) says that's of scant account, and no reason why we should take her seriously. Then he brays about the horrors let loose in Iraq if the troops come home, with no mention of how the invasion he worked for has already unleashed them.

Besides having converted to the war-solves-everything far, far jingoistic neoconservative right, Hitchens seems to have some weird hang-ups, including ones about Israel, maybe related to his basic God phobia and/or his late-in-life claim that he is a Jew via his mother's side of the family—whatever. According to Cockburn, "In 1999 Edward Jay Epstein publicly recalled a dinner in the Royalton Hotel in New York where Epstein said Hitchens had doubted the Holocaust was quite what it's cracked up to be."

Here's a guy that may or may not be a closet Holocaust denier but who publicly proclaimed that he'd refuse to care for his brother's children, should his brother Peter die. As quoted in the *Guardian* in 2005, Christopher said, "The real difference between Peter and myself is the belief in the supernatural. I'm a materialist and he attributes his presence here to a divine plan. I can't stand anyone who believes in God, who invokes the divinity or who is a person of faith."

James Macintyre, who has known both Hitchens brothers for years, dissected their ugly relationship in the June, 11, 2007, issue of *The Independent*: "Christopher revealed that after he discovered his mother died in mysterious circumstances—apparently a suicide pact with a boyfriend in Athens—he found a note his mother had addressed only to 'Christopher.' He has since been quoted as saying, 'If you were the mother of Christopher and Peter, who would be your secret favorite?'"

Although it's hard to imagine a less appealing way of expressing sibling rivalry than citing one's mother's suicide note, apparently the two brothers have had a recent reconciliation. But lest anyone accuse him of being generous, Christopher clarified this "reconciliation" in a 2006 interview in the *Guardian*: "There is no longer any official froideur," he says of their relationship. "But there's no official— what's the word?—*chaleur*, either."

In *God Is Not Great*, Hitchens seems to be impugning his brother's faith without naming him:

> Our [New Atheist] belief is not a belief. Our principles are not a faith. We do not rely solely upon science and reason, because these are necessary rather than sufficient factors, but we distrust anything that contradicts science or outrages reason. We may differ on many things, but what we respect is free inquiry, openmindedness, and the pursuit of ideas for their own sake. We do not hold our convictions dogmatically. . . . We are not immune to the lure of wonder and mystery and awe: we have music and art and literature, and find that the serious ethical dilemmas are better handled by Shakespeare and Tolstoy and Schiller and Dostoyevsky and George Eliot than in the mythical morality tales of the holy books. Literature, not scripture, sustains the mind and—since there is no other metaphor—also the soul. There is no need for us to gather every day, or every seven days, or on any high or auspicious day. . . . ceremonies are abhorrent to us . . .

This would come as news to the faculties at Harvard, Cambridge, or Princeton, given the secular academic community's jealously guarded rituals on graduation day when they do indeed gather to recognize their quasi-religious hierarchies. And the professors of literature at those same schools would be surprised to learn that Hitchens has impressed Shakespeare, Tolstoy, Schiller, Dostoyevsky, and George Eliot into the service of his atheist cause. None of their writings (or lives) are remotely decipherable outside of the religious/ biblical literary tradition (and social context) that permeates the work of every writer he named. Hitchens's misappropriation of their names reminds me of the Mormons' arrogant practice of baptizing dead non-Mormons into their church.

The *Washington Post* reviewer of Hitchens's book pegged Hitchens's ignorance about religion. In his May 6, 2008, review, Stephen Prothero (chair of Boston University's Religion Department) wrote,

> What Hitchens gets wrong is religion itself. . . . [he] assumes a child-ish definition of religion and then criticizes religious people for believing such foolery. But it is Hitchens who is the naïf. . . . Read-ers with any sense of irony—and here I do not exclude believers—will be surprised to see how little inquiring Hitchens has done and how limited and literal is his own ill-prepared reduction of religion. . . . I have never encountered a book whose author is so fundamentally unacquainted with its subject. In the end, this maddeningly dogmatic book does little more than illustrate one of Hitchens's pet themes—the ability of dogma to put reason to sleep.

The question: Why is Hitchens so "maddeningly dogmatic"? The answer, again: sex.

What I *don't* get is why Hitchens believes that the freedom to have sex is tied to freedom *from* religion. Who in his circle (or, for that matter, who anywhere) is *not* having sex these days because of the anything the Pope says? What does Hitchens think all those Muslim sheiks are doing to their twelve-year-old brides in Riyadh? And given the high statistical rates of adultery and divorce in North American evangelical/fundamentalist circles, and (according to stud-ies) the higher-than-average numbers of church-going porn addicts in the Bible belt, who today does Hitchens think is suffering dan-gerous sexual repression because of a belief in God?

Hitchens's preoccupation with sex is woven throughout his book and articles. As he pushes into old age, Hitchens's writing tends to circle back to sex, the wanting and the getting of sex in a schoolboy wanker-style. When asked by an interviewer from the *Village Voice* (March 18, 2008) to speculate on why New York's (then governor)

Elliott Spitzer risked his career by going to whores, Hitchen's answer unintentionally revealed his own bottom line (no pun) concerning men given to acting the part of the alpha male. The interviewer asked,

> So what in the wide world was Eliot Spitzer thinking? "Oh, that's easy," Christopher Hitchens said from his Washington apartment . . . "You wouldn't be doing any of this if one of the objectives was not to increase the amount of pussy that was available to you. That is *what you do*. . . . You don't do it to be, ah, the most approval-rated governor, for fuck's sake." During the 1992 presidential primary season, Hitchens pointed out, the day that Clinton won the endorsement was the very day he hit on Paula Jones. "He said, 'Wait—I could be the next president. . . . Now, where's the next cutie? Because I need that *now*, much more than I did 10 minutes ago,'" Hitchens speculated. And likewise with JFK: "With Kennedy, it's really all over the guy for everyone to see," Hitchens said. "From dawn till dusk, from soup to nuts, from everything he does to the last day he dies: 'I do this to get laid.' What's the point of all this if I don't get an orgasm now? What's the point of being an alpha male? Anyone who doesn't get this," [Hitchens] concluded, "doesn't know."

Besides obsessing over his brother Peter, why does Hitchens bother writing? Take a wild guess. Here's Hitchens's answer as offered in his article on "Why Women Aren't Funny" in *Vanity Fair* of January 2007. "The chief task in life that a man has to perform is that of impressing the opposite sex." Hitchens explains that his method to get into bed with women is to make them laugh "with their mouths wide open." That, he claims, is his best shot. He concludes, "If I am correct about this, which I am, then the explanation for the superior funniness of men is much the same as for the inferior funniness of women." In other words, men are funny in order to impress humorless women into having sex with them.

According to Hitchens, women are humorless because they make babies, and he notes that that's why "episiotomy jokes" fall flat with women and advises would be seducers to avoid dead child jokes too.

In another *Vanity Fair* piece, this time on the history of the blow job, "American As Apple Pie," July 2006, Hitchens bemoans the state of his teeth as one reason why it's been such a slog for him to seduce women at least until he discovered ways of making those humorless baby machines laugh—and found a decent American dentist.

> As one who was stretched on the grim rack of British "National Health" practice, with its gray-and-yellow fangs, its steely-wire braces . . . I can remember barely daring to smile when I first set foot in the New World. Whereas when any sweet American girl smiled at me, I was at once bewitched and slain by the warm, moist cave of her mouth, lined with faultless white teeth and immaculate pink gums and organized around a tenderly coiled yet innocent tongue. The illusion of the tonsilized clitoris will probably never die (and gay men like to keep their tonsils for a reason that I would not dream of mentioning), but while the G-spot and other fantasies have dissipated, the iconic U.S. Prime blowjob is still on a throne.

Welcome to the brave new world of the New Atheist aesthetic. In the first chapter of *God Is Not Great*, Hitchens grouses about his brief encounter with religion, back in his schoolboy days. "Why," he laments, "was the subject of sex considered so toxic?" A few pages later he lays out his basic quarrel with religion. It too is all about sex, though he pads his God-hates-sex bit with another reason (emphasis added):

> There still remain four irreducible objections to religious faith: that it wholly misrepresents the origins of man and the cosmos, that because of this original error it manages to combine the maximum

of servility with the maximum of solipsism, *that it is both the result and the cause of dangerous sexual repression*. . . . I do not think it is arrogant of me to claim that I had already discovered these four objections before my boyish voice had broken.

Hitchens describes the problem of Islam as producing "mobs of sexually repressed young men." He is particularly interested by a Roman Catholic cardinal saying, "I've never seen a little dog using a condom during sexual intercourse with another dog." A few pages later we read, "And there may be someone who can explain the sexual and other cruelties of the religious without any reference to the obsession with celibacy, but that someone will not be me. . . ." And then, "Christianity is too repressed to offer sex in paradise . . . but it has been lavish in its promise of sadistic and everlasting punishment for sexual backsliders." And a little later, "We have no way to quantify the damage done by telling tens of millions of children that masturbation will make them blind."

Hitchens gets to the nub of his grudge against God when he lashes out against what he calls "the three great monotheisms." Hitchens says that the concept of God is a "totalitarian belief." He ends his book with this statement on the all-important last page (emphasis added):

> *Above all*, we are in need of a renewed Enlightenment. . . . The pursuit of unfettered scientific inquiry, and the availability of new findings to masses of people by electronic means, will revolutionize our concepts of research and development. *Very importantly, the divorce between the sexual life and fear, and the sexual life and disease, and the sexual life and tyranny, can now at last be attempted, on the sole condition that we banish all religions from the discourse.*

Hitchens is also fascinated by the temporary marriages offered by religious leaders in Iran and then tells us that

The relationship between physical health and mental health is well understood to have a strong connection to the sexual function, or dysfunction. Can it be a coincidence, then, that all religions claim the right to litigate in matters of sex? To survey the history of sexual dread and proscription, as codified by religion, is to be met with a very disturbing . . . extreme repression. Almost every sexual impulse has been made the occasion for prohibition, guilt, and shame . . . oral sex, anal sex, non-missionary-position sex. . . . Clearly, the human species is designed to experiment with sex.

All Hitchens needs to do to take us that final step into the realm of *Doctor Strangelove* is to add a few comments to his capacious sex writing about maintaining his precious bodily fluids. I can almost hear a plaintive Peter Sellers as Captain Lionel Mandrake begging Hitchens, reincarnated as the deranged base commander General Jack D. Ripper, to put down his machine gun and to

"Just please, do be a good chap and turn on the radio Sir!"

"No Mandrake! The relationship between physical health and mental health is well understood to have a *strong connection to the sexual function!*"

Hitchens is an odd chap but not original. British intellectuals have been worrying about sex for quite some time. The Bloomsbury Group did the Viagra shuffle before, and did it better. The group grew from student friendships at Cambridge in the early twentieth century and included E. M. Forster (author), John Maynard Keynes (economist), Virginia Woolf (author), Vanessa Bell (artist), Duncan Grant (artist), and Clive Bell (art critic), to name a few very accomplished people. They practiced—and wrote about—the free sexuality Hitchens advocates as a grand new idea decades before he was born. They were braver too; penicillin had yet to be discovered.

Hitchens's take on sex is also a mere retread of Bertrand Russell's lifetime anti-God/pro-sex crusade. Russell also fits the stereotypical image of a British sexually disappointed intellectual brooding over other people's genitalia. In *Marriage and Morals* (1929), Russell suggested "trial marriages" that he called "companionate marriage." And even though Russell was a supporter of women's rights, he denounced feminists' "puritanical attitude" toward pornography. He proclaims, "Pioneers of women's rights . . . were for the most part very rigid moralists, whose hope was to impose upon men the moral fetters which hitherto had only been endured by women."

Russell also used a sarcastic tone when addressing anything he thought smacked of "traditional attitudes" about sex. In *Marriage and Morals* he sums up what he regards as the British and American prudish attitude toward sex (circa 1929): "A boy should be taught that in no circumstances is conversation on sexual subjects permissible, not even in marriage. This increases the likelihood that when he marries he will give his wife a disgust of sex and thus preserve her from the risk of adultery." And foreshadowing Dawkins in his suspicion of those Yanks, Russell laments, "Sex relations as a dignified, rational, wholehearted activity in which the complete personality co-operates, do not often, I think, occur in America outside marriage. To this extent the moralists have been successful."

My evangelical/fundamentalist missionary mother's life overlapped Russell's generation, but apparently Russell (and Hitchens) never met people like Edith Schaeffer. If they'd met Mom, perhaps they would have converted! Mom was *always* talking about sex and what a "gift from God" sexual pleasure was. The idea that Mom needed liberating by the likes of Hitchens is ludicrous. Other evangelical women could have taught Hitchens and Russell a thing or two as well. Take Marabel Morgan.

Morgan wrote her multimillion-selling evangelical/fundamentalist anti-feminist sex manual *The Total Woman* in the early 1970s. She advocated—among other aphrodisiacs—that evangelical/fundamentalist housewives wrap themselves in Saran Wrap and/or smear themselves with whipped cream and do it on the kitchen floor.

This seemed to go a step or two beyond barefoot and pregnant in the kitchen. One wag who reviewed the book called it *The Totaled Woman*, given that Morgan's Jesus-loving, oral-sex-giving, born-again, Saran-Wrapped, stay-at-home-mom/concubines would be worn to exhaustion, if they put out with the frequency and energy Morgan recommended.

But Morgan was *nothing* compared to my mom! By the time I was seven, I knew that sex was good. When I was eleven or so, Mom told me how her father (a nineteenth-century missionary to China no less) had given her a book on sexual pleasure so she could get the "right ideas" about enjoying sex and "how to achieve simultaneous orgasms." I mean, did Hitchens ever worry about someday achieving *simultaneous orgasm* when he was *eleven*?

When I was twelve Mom, in her never-ending sharing of red-hot sex information, told me about how Dad took her to a cabaret in Paris while they were on one of their many trips to conduct Bible studies. At the time, I was home from my British boarding school, and Mom regaled me (and, it turns out my sisters, given that in later life we compared notes) with this story while I was back in Switzerland during the holidays. I was at school with a bunch of Hitchens's contemporaries, some of whom didn't know that boys and girls are different "down there." The contrast between their prudish English lack of knowledge and my overabundance of sex information was something of a shocker. Hadn't *all* their mothers obsessively been telling them the "facts of life" again and again and *again*?

But just to make it clear that there were peculiarities to the mixture of sex and evangelicalism, I should say that Mom did not let the trip to the cabaret be in vain; she turned the episode into a bedtime story sex lesson that got in a jab at Dad at the same time. Mom told me about her chagrin when she and Dad met a "non-Christian" American couple in that Paris nightclub:

"We were unable to share the Lord," Mom said with a sigh.

"Why?" I asked.

"You see, dear, they had a floor show."

"What's that?"

"A form of very worldly entertainment, where girls dance in an inappropriate way."

"How do you mean?" I asked.

"Men go there to be aroused. You see, dear, it was your father's idea. He *insisted!* There were women there taking off almost all their clothes."

"What did they take off?"

"Everything dear, except for the merest covering over their most private places."

"Why did you go?"

"Your father was already in a Very Bad Mood. What choice did I have? Your father said he wanted to see the 'real Paris.' The night club was French of course. But the Lord had a *real* rebuke waiting for *him!* As soon as we sat down at the table—and by the way we both ordered ginger ale not anything alcoholic—another couple sat down at the little round table next to ours. And at first when they spoke to us, your father pretended he couldn't understand English. The man persisted, so your father had to say something, and he just pretended we were tourists. Of course I was longing to share the gospel, but how could I? They were a New York Jewish couple. And clearly they had a deep spiritual need; I mean they were in *that place*, weren't they?"

The way Mom explained it, the first part of her sin was to "give in to Fran's weakness" by allowing herself to be "dragged to that place." The second part was having to deny the Lord, not by commission but by omission.

You see, if Mom had told the couple from New York that she and Dad were Christians, let alone missionaries, it would have been a terrible witness and would have hurt Jesus's reputation. You can't lead non-Christians, let alone New York Jews, to the Lord while some woman is making the tassels on her breasts whirl over your husband's head. How can you quote John 3:16 in *that* situation? So

Mom lamented that Dad's sin led to a failed contact with a couple who "will now never hear the gospel."

Of course, this logic may give aid and comfort to the anti-clericals. I mean, what was I supposed to conclude? Sin and *then* repent and witness anyway? Or don't sin and the lost "Jews" you never meet don't ever get the chance to be saved? If my dad had not sinned and dragged Mom to that den of iniquity, she never would have met the lost Jews in the first place. If you *did* witness to those people, while they and you were watching an almost-naked woman dance, did that make almost naked dancing okay? How could it *not* be okay if the Lord used it to bring you into contact with those hard-to-reach New York Jews who would not otherwise hear the gospel?

But back to Hitchens: What no one knows, including (I suspect) Hitchens, is whether Hitchens is serious, or just a Brit former-lefty version of Ann Coulter, cashing in on the American market and dedicated to entertaining (and making a great living off) those of the godless middlebrow of the American left who will still tolerate him, instead of entertaining (and making a good living off) the God-fearing even-lower-Neanderthal-brow Americans of the right who mistake Coulter for a serious (or even decent) person.

Whereas Dennett, Harris, and company write sober books and articles, Hitchens uses his writings (in such august intellectual outlets as *Vanity Fair* magazine) for less lofty purposes. He writes to explain how he hits on women (by telling them dirty jokes); to explain his wandering around in Lebanon and getting in fist fights with Arabs (in press reports early in 2009, he was quoted as saying that some toughs who roughed him up on a Beirut street were fascist thugs attacking him because he was defending democracy by defacing political posters outside a bar); and to defend (in essay form) President Bush's misbegotten Iraq war. Along the way, he penned what he calls a "mildly pro-life" article against abortion one day and, on another day, reminisced about accompanying one of his girlfriends to an abortion clinic to help her dump his baby. And he worked all of this in when he was not writing his book on the Clintons, whom he accused of murder.

Sex and brother Peter aside, Hitchens's views strike me as a version of the no-elephant pebble story. A man says that carrying a particular magic pebble in his pocket keeps elephants out of the room. He *always* carries the pebble, and there *never* are any elephants in any rooms he walks into! Hitchens treats religion as his pet "pebble": People are bad, and religion is always lurking about, so therefore, religion is *making* people bad.

But *does* religion make people worse than they would be without religion? Twenty-first-century Britain is more *atheistic* than ever, yet crime has gone up. Iran became a theocracy and more *religious* than ever, and crime went up there as well (not to mention state-sponsored terror). What do the atheist Britons and religious Iranians have in common? They're human. Whatever they say they believe, they evolved from the same tribe of marauding murdering monkeys we all descended from.

Hitchens's ideas remind me of the "intelligent design" theologian William Paley and his nineteenth-century theories. (Natural theology looked to nature as displaying the beneficence of God. In the scheme of William Paley, who was archdeacon of Carlisle, the seemingly perfect adaptation of creatures to "their station" in life was "due to divine design.") Paley posited the divine design of nature because it *looks* designed. Hitchens seems to buy this theory as it applies to religion. He sees evil all around him. He sees religion all around him. So religion must have *designed* the evil.

Hitchens goes further: This is no mere design, it's a conspiracy! It appears that Hitchens believes that religion, like Ernst Blofeld and all those other great old James Bond villains and organizations, is leading a worldwide plot to destroy humanity. Perhaps the pope is now working for SMERSH or even the dreaded SPECTRE! At the end of Chapter 1 of *God Is Not Great* Hitchens seems to channel not just Paley but also Ian Fleming when Hitchens writes, "People of faith are in their different ways planning your and my destruction, and the destruction of all the hardwon human attainments."

Whatever the merits of his arguments, to put it mildly, Hitchens ideas don't seem to have worked out too well for him personally. If Hitchens being Hitchens is an example of those "hardwon human attainments," the rest of us would do well to avoid them.

CHAPTER 7

The Only Thing Evangelicals Will Never Forgive Is Not Hating the "Other"

Man is spirit. But what is spirit? Spirit is the self. But what is the self?

The Sickness Unto Death, Søren Kierkegaard

Rick Warren is the celebrity founder of an evangelical/fundamentalist "megachurch." He's also the author of *The Purpose Driven Life*, which has sold 30 million copies. Warren is the icon of success that every ambitious evangelical/fundamentalist pastor strives to become, in much the same way that a wedding singer grinding out tunes in some godforsaken Holiday Inn lounge would rather be Bono.

Warren's book is divided into sections: Purpose 1: You Were Planned for God's Pleasure. Purpose 2: You Were Formed for God's Family. Purpose 3: You Were Created to Become Like Christ. Purpose 4: You Were Shaped for Serving God. Purpose 5: You Were

Made for a Mission. "It's not about you," Warren writes. But his church is very much about *him*. He's the star in a cult of personality that fits the celebrity-worshipping temper of our times.

Ask yourself: What will happen to his church when Warren dies, leaves, or is thrown out? Will it remain as successful? Are people there for each other and their community? Are they there for Jesus? Or are they there for Rick Warren?

Fulfillment, satisfaction, and meaning can be found only in "understanding and doing what God placed you on Earth to do," writes Warren. But Warren's message turns out to be less about God than it is about trying to convince his readers to become American-style evangelicals. In other words, to find purpose they have to join the North American individualistic cult of one-stop born-again "salvation" to which Warren belongs. Warren's Christianity (the leftover residue of the simplistic frontier Protestantism we call "evangelicalism" that broke most connections theological, aesthetic, and liturgical to the historic Christian churches of both the East and West) is not to be confused with what Christians through most of the 2,000-year history of their religion would have recognized as even remotely familiar.

According to traditional Christianity, a person was not "saved" or "lost" in a one-stop magical affirmation of "correct" doctrine, but, rather, the *process* of salvation was lived out in a community. Salvation was a path toward God, not a you're-in-or-out event, as in "At two thirty last Wednesday I accepted Jesus." Just as Hillary Clinton said about child rearing, the process of redemption took a village. Pastors were part of that "village" tradition and were inducted into existing communities of faith. They were not self-made and reinventing the faith according to whim. The heart of worship was sacramental continuity and an unbroken connection to generations that came before.

Bishops and priests came and went, but the Church remained. What the Church provided was a set of tools—liturgical sacramental exercises, things to *do* to *train* one to receive God's love by learning to love others as oneself.

Some members of the Church—East and West—did some very, very nasty things. They oppressed women, killed heretics, started wars, buggered choir boys, persecuted Jews, molested pilgrims, and aided and abetted the institution of slavery. But they usually did get one thing right: Spirituality wasn't a matter of celebrity leaders who sprang up then faded away. Some terrible celebrity Christian leaders existed, such as the fifteenth century's nasty, odd, and painting-burning Savonarola of Florence. But celebrities were the exception to an otherwise virtually anonymous pastorate.

Communities built cathedrals over generations. Usually no one who worked on laying the building's foundation was around when it was completed. The name of the cathedral was that of the town where it stood (for instance, Chartres Cathedral) or that of a biblical figure (Notre-Dame for instance). A few egomaniacal popes (or bishops) aside, churches were not about their leaders but about the people who worshipped in them. There were religious orders in the Roman Catholic Church that bore the names of their founders, such as the Franciscans, but when those orders survived their founders, it was because they were folded into a hierarchical orderly structure. There were egomaniacal "saints" who drew attention to their "holiness" by public displays of self-mortification (the so-called Stylites, or "Pillar-Saints," ascetics in the Byzantine Empire who stood on pillars preaching, exposed to the elements, while followers gathered around), but they performed their antics outside of churches. Such individualistic displays didn't penetrate the liturgical practices led by largely anonymous priests.

The North American evangelical/fundamentalist brand of Christianity is the religious version of the American civil religion: consumerist individualism. Today's "Stylites" are more often found in private jets, but they still have followers who conflate holiness with success American style—in other words, as measured by money, possessions, numbers, and (above all) celebrity status. The consumer picks a pastor based on where the action seems to be: "Wow, you ought to hear *our* pastor!" Such "churches" are often founded by a man or woman who started them the way other men and women start a restaurant or a movie company. In Warren's case, he is pastor of a church called Saddleback, but it's more properly known as "Rick Warren's church," just as the Crystal Cathedral came to be known as "Robert Schuller's church," and the Billy Graham Evangelistic Association has its founder's name in the same way as the Ford Motor Company bears the name of its founder.

Warren isn't the first hero-author to capture the imagination of the consumers of American religion. Before Warren there were many other celebrity leaders, including authors C.S. Lewis, Billy Graham, and my father, to name a few of countless stars. As a child I was a C. S. Lewis fan, a member of his far-flung fan base, his "church" of evangelical/fundamentalist fans. I enjoyed his creative riffs on the Bible; they were better than the Bible stories being riffed on. For one thing, Lewis was more compassionate than the severe biblical writers. I liked Lewis's stories that humanized God, books such as *The Great Divorce* about Heaven, salvation, and second chances, where Lewis put forward the comforting "heretical" (to evangelical/fundamentalists) idea you can be saved *after* death. According to my parents, Lewis's ideas about salvation weren't biblical. "We all have to accept Jesus *before* we die. The Bible is *very clear*! Lewis has some *fuzzy* ideas," Mom would say.

My parents tolerated Lewis anyway. Mom read and reread C. S. Lewis's Narnia stories to me. We evangelical/fundamentalists had so few contemporary celebrities to admire. We needed stars to follow but were frustrated by the dearth of a tradition to belong to. With apologies to Gertrude Stein, there was no there there. Having no saints, we made up our own. Our "tradition" was all about correct theology—*our* correct theology, that is. Our "saints" were personalities that gave us a high-profile sense of identity. We embraced what amounted to self-appointed popes and bishops the same way Americans need their presidents to become "kings," even though officially we have no royalty. We weren't about to quibble over a couple of heresies expressed by our one and only bestselling, "sainted" author of the moment—and bestselling into the hated, yet envied, "secular world" that we so feared but also longed to have recognize us as legitimate.

Never mind that Lewis had had several weird sexual relationships, including one with a married woman, or that he was a drunk. How many evangelicals got to teach at Oxford or give lectures on the BBC? Lewis played for *our* team!

Only he didn't. Lewis was no American-style evangelical/fundamentalist but a high-church (in other words formal, liturgically inclined, and old-fashioned) Anglican with a strong bias in favor of the pre-Reformation Orthodox liturgy and Roman mass. He also had Hitchenesque appetites—lots of smoking and drinking that would have gotten him instantly dismissed from any American evangelical/fundamentalist institution. For instance, Wheaton College made faculty sign pledges to never, but *never*, smoke, drink, dance, or play cards, and it would never have allowed Lewis to work there. This makes the fact that The Marion E. Wade Center at Wheaton College sells itself as a "a tribute to the importance of the literary, historical, and Christian heritage" of C. S. Lewis, G. K. Chesterton, and other assorted authors rather ironic. None of these smoking, drinking, and distinctly non-evangelical authors could ever have taught there.

Lewis was apt to work characters from Greek mythology, even Father Christmas, weird Christ figures, and English nationalistic sensibility (he described Heaven as a nicer version of England in his book *The Last Battle*), not to mention Norse myths, into his "evangelical/fundamentalist" books. Never mind! We'll take what we can get when it comes to stand-ins for bishops, tradition, actual writers and an identity. Otherwise whom can we identify *with* in order to identify *ourselves* now that we have cut our link to the historic churches?

Which brings up an interesting point: The curious parasitic habit of evangelicals borrowing intellectual (or artistic) respectability from Christians who never were and never would have been American-style evangelicals—for instance, from Owen Barfield, G. K. Chesterton, C. S. Lewis, George MacDonald, Dorothy L. Sayers, J. R. R. Tolkien, and Charles Williams. These authors (all of whom are studied at Wheaton and some of whose papers are enshrined there) would have shot themselves rather than be condemned to attend, let alone teach at, Wheaton College or any other evangelical/fundamentalist backwater institution like it.

Because in the Protestant world the word *Christian* can mean anything, Protestants need to discover and then hang on to some sort of distinctiveness. One person might be a "C. S. Lewis–type Christian," another might describe herself as a "Francis Schaeffer–type," and so forth. And given Americans' love of material success, there are plenty of people who look at Rick Warren's 50,000-member church and say, "Hey, now *that's* what I call a church! I'm a Rick Warren–type Christian!"

Today the American evangelical/fundamentalist consumer of religion is even more prone to the truism that nothing succeeds like success. Talk about unregulated banks and hedge funds, the biggest unregulated American market is big-time religion (and it's tax-free!). Its success isn't measured in spiritual gain that changes anything for the better. As big-time as religion is in the United States compared to highly secular Europe, nevertheless America's teen sex statistics, abortion rates, spread of STDs, divorce statistics, and rates of child rape are higher than those in non-church-going Europe. So the "success" of Warren's type of born-again entrepreneurship is a failure when measured against actual results in terms of what used to be called the fruits of the Spirit.

Evangelical/fundamentalist leaders don't see it that way. Their faith entertains. It makes money. It nurtures a celebrity culture of its own, with its own TV stations, radio stations, book publishers, author tours, rock concerts, schools, home school programs and colleges. What's not to love? It is no coincidence that other entrepreneurs who aren't believers have gotten in on the act. Media mogul Rupert Murdoch now owns the largest "Christian" publishing company, having bought it out and then folded it into his stable of publishing giants, one of which publishes—that's right—Rick Warren.

One can't picture any scenario in which Warren would be thrown off the evangelical/fundamentalist team, other than if he started to officiate at gay weddings. He answers to no one, let alone to a tradition of liturgical practice, or, God forbid, a bishop, that might diminish the go-it-alone individualism (otherwise known as "God's leading") of market capitalism with a Jesus twist that works so well for Warren. Warren makes past evangelical/fundamentalist superstars such as Lewis, Falwell, Schuller, or my dad seem insignificant. Warren's is star power on an Oprah level. Warren gave the invocation at a president's inauguration. Warren's church is huge. He's the author of the all-time bestselling book ever published in the history of American publishing. God *is* blessing! Right?

Maybe not. A Rick Warren, a C. S. Lewis, and a Francis Schaeffer are the essence of evangelical/fundamentalist success, but they also represent the Achilles heel of American evangelicalism. Personality cults with no accountability and no tradition and no structure to fall back on when the "Dear Leader" dies, or is found to have "fallen"—whatever—are no better than the men and women they're built on. The "something bigger" you thought you joined just turns out to just be some smooth-talking guy named Rick, or maybe Franklin Graham.

Only in the strange—dare I say obscene—world of big-time American consumer religion could the following story be possible, combining as it does the ego, commercialism, betrayal, nepotism, and personality cult aspects of American "Christianity." According to newspaper reports ("A Family at Cross-Purposes: Billy Graham's Sons Argue Over a Final Resting Place," *Washington Post*, December 13, 2006), a family feud erupted in Billy Graham's family over where he and his wife, Ruth, were to be buried. Was it to be in Charlotte, North Carolina, at the Billy Graham "museum" erected in the vicinity of the Billy Graham Evangelistic Association headquarters? Or should their remains go to a small private site near their home in Montreat?

Franklin Graham, the 56-year-old "heir" to Billy's ministry, insisted that the burial spot be at the $28–$30 million, 40,000-square-foot museum. It creates a "farm setting" to look like the place where Billy grew up outside of Charlotte. Other family members—including Ruth Graham—wanted to have a quieter final resting place.

The Washington Post called the family "debate" a struggle worthy of the Old Testament, pitting brother against brother, son against mother. After Ruth's death, Billy was trapped in the middle pondering what to do with her remains. The *Post* said Ruth had signed a *notarized document with six witnesses*, saying she wanted to be buried near her home. After her death her wishes were ignored, and Billy was talked into doing what Franklin wanted.

Ruth (whom I knew and liked and who was close to my mother) was laid to "rest," against her wishes, in what amounts to an amusement park for the greater glory of—what? Consultants had worked with the Walt Disney Company to create a large "barn" and "silo" as a reminder of Billy Graham's early childhood on a dairy farm near Charlotte. Today, visitors wishing to visit Ruth's tomb pass through a 40-foot-tall glass entry cut in the shape of a cross and are greeted by a mechanical talking cow. From there, they walk on paths of straw through rooms of exhibits. At the end, a stone walkway shaped like a cross takes them to a garden where Ruth lies (as will Billy Graham when he dies). The *Post* also reported that tourists have more than one chance to get their names on a mailing list and later, therefore, to be solicited for funds.

The evangelical/fundamentalist religion is no different in its core "values" from the celebrity-worshipping, entertainment-oriented society it claims to be a prophetic witness to. In this vein it's no coincidence that Billy Graham's alma mater, the aforementioned Wheaton College, *also* has a "museum" attached to its campus in which Disneyland-like experiences are offered. This attraction is described on the school's website as a "journey through the Museum [that] takes you on a Walk Through The Gospel, with a stirring three-dimensional presentation of the Christian message." But that is only after you have experienced an "encounter [with] one of the loveliest and most fascinating presentations of the basic Christian message in The Cross of The Millennium. From here, you'll enter a major section of the Museum which highlights the Life and Ministry of Billy Graham."

Since it turns out that Franklin Graham has cornered the market on his parent's remains for his amusement/fund-raising/empire-maintaining park, perhaps Wheaton can cut a deal for at least a lock of hair, toenail, or some other Billy relic, to be placed in a suitable jewel-encrusted reliquary, or, given today's fashions, incorporated into a giant cross-shaped roller coaster ride.

Star power is seductive. For instance, and to put this on my turf, evangelicals aspiring to be writers want to become "the next C. S. Lewis," just as lesser pastors want to become "the next Warren." But being a writer means that your loyalty must be to your reader and to the truth, or, as I put it when pressed, a writer's loyalty must be to the page.

The problem is that evangelical/fundamentalist faith revolves around two directives: Be successful *and* evangelize. That leads to bad choices. For instance, if you are trying to get people "saved" through your writing instead of writing the best and truest books you can write, you are nothing more than a propagandist. Combine this with commercial interests, and not only are you just a propagandist, you are a gutless wonder who doesn't want to offend your market. Translation: no F-word in the dialogue please, because the Christian Booksellers Association bookstores won't stock your book. Oh, and no expressions of doubt either, or embarrassing questions about God, let alone the truth about evangelical leaders. So if you're writing a story about, say, a Marine brigade in combat, you'll have to lie when it comes to dialogue. And if you are writing a memoir, please leave out anything about the flaws of the believers you've known (or your saintly parents) and skip the truth about yourself too, if it's embarrassing. And if you are burying your mother, well, too bad about her wishes, what *use* is a quiet grave in an out-of-the-way place? Why rest in peace when you can help build the mailing list?

Pastors aren't pastors in the evangelical/fundamentalist culture any more than evangelical/fundamentalist "writers" are writers, or intellectuals are actual intellectuals. (How can an intellectual *already* have made up his or her mind about what the truth is?) Rather, "pastors" are the inventors of their own product line sold as religion, offering themselves as just another consumer choice to a culture that picks ministers the way they pick sweaters. Picture how this consumer/market approach would work out for the United States Marine Corps.

If the USMC caved to the consumer culture the way the evangelicals have, each drill instructor would be individually picked by each recruit, some choosing DIs based on looks, others on charm, yet others because this or that DI wore a cool uniform or was "nicer than those other guys." The process might be fun, but the idea that the Marines are identifiable because each Marine knows that all other Marines share the same experience of boot camp, values, and discipline would be lost. The word *Marine* would lose its meaning if all recruits went to boot camps that suited them personally. The Marine Corps would become just another part of the entertainment industry/consumer culture, which is exactly what the evangelical/fundamentalist churches are today, with a therapeutic twist that adds feeling good to the product list.

Empire builders are empire builders, and entertainers are entertainers, regardless of what they call themselves. The Billy Graham Evangelistic Association and the Walt Disney Company are a perfect match. Mea culpa! I only understood the reality of the symbiotic relationship between the consumer/entertainment culture and our star religious-empire builders after I quit being one myself. Judging by the many emails I'm getting from pastors who have read my Calvin Becker Trilogy of novels (which are humorous stories about a preacher's family, seen from the inside), it seems that many a preacher is in the position of Groucho Marx. Groucho said he'd never want to belong to a club that would let someone like him join. The doubt and self-loathing expressed to me by so many pastors is amazing. Of course, they all beg me never to tell anyone what they are telling me.

If I have heard this once, I have heard it (or rather read it in emails) literally hundreds of times. "I can't say this in public, but . . ." has been the start of so many emails from many evangelical and Roman Catholic and (to be truthful) several Orthodox leaders too, as well as ordinary folks living what amount to intellectual/spiritual double lives. Perhaps it's because they are being presented with bad alternatives that they believe they must choose between.

> Frank: After leaving the strait jacket of evangelicalism, I can breathe. . . . I was out of step as an evangelical pastor [with] my quotes of Bob Dylan, celebration of sexuality when the [biblical] passage called for it and a demand for truth though it was only when I was out from the oppression of the movement that I real-ized how much compromise had been interwoven into my life as pastor and leader.
>
> *Cordially, D.*

I can't prove this, but I think that any person who remains a "professional Christian" in the evangelical/fundamentalist world for a lifetime, especially any pastor, risks becoming an atheists and/or a liar. Such individuals put on an act of certainty. Sooner or later they become flakes faking it, or quit. Worse yet, some just stop ask-ing questions. The very fact that a preacher can fool others when he or she has so many doubts makes the self-appointed mediator of faith the deepest cynic of all if, that is, he or she doesn't embrace paradox.

If you have to be correct all the time, while knowing that you are wrong most of the time, you become an actor. Been there, done that. If you think that to "be a Christian" means you have to iden-tify with a club you loathe, you'll have to choose to redefine your faith or lose it—even if it costs you a paycheck and your "good" life.

Making my final break with my evangelical/fundamentalist past was like turning on some sort of creative tap. As my dad's sidekick I'd been a miniature flash-in-the-pan Rick Warren in the making, with a growing following. Back in the 1970s and early 1980s, I was used to huge audiences turning out to hear me speak in places such as the annual Southern Baptist pastors convention; the annual meeting of the National Religious Broadcasters; Dr. Kennedy's church in Coral Gables, Florida; Jerry Falwell's church and college in Lynchburg, Virginia; and on several nationwide seminar tours where Dad and I packed auditoriums. My evangelical "books" sold by the pallet load, whereas my secular books (since) have sold as individual copies. But as an artist and writer, I also knew that even if I could have kept putting up with the "theology"—which I couldn't—let alone tolerated the insane hate-filled, gun-toting, moron-making right-wing politics, the evangelical/fundamentalist subculture is death to artistic creativity. That is because art depends on at least attempted honesty and unconditional questioning.

Since there is no there, there—no tradition—all that governs the evangelical/fundamentalist empire-builders is the self-appointed Church Lady Brigade. You always have moralizing busybodies sniffing around your butt to see if you're pure enough. Good for dogs, maybe; bad for writers. When I left the evangelical/fundamentalist world, I found that I was no longer looking over my shoulder wondering what people—in other words, the Church Ladies—would think.

You see, a Rick Warren looks powerful, but he makes a bad trade, sort of like Prince Charles. You get the life and the palace, but *being Prince Charles* is all you'll ever do. You *are* your job. You are all wrapper and no candy. It's a gilded cage and you are STUCK! It's the worst type-casting imaginable.

Warren can't do more than act the part of Rick Warren *being* Rick Warren. He also has to be "into" whatever the Church Ladies are into at the moment. And woe betide Warren if he expresses any truths about his doubts and failings or, worse yet, casually mentions that he'd rather be, say, a secular Jew free to do or say what he wants without a gaggle of low-IQ evangelicals parsing his every move.

The freedom I found in my local Orthodox Church was surprising. And no, I'm not making a pitch, because there are plenty of Orthodox who leave the Orthodox Church and are liberated by doing that. And as we've seen with the Father Xs of this world, the Orthodox too have their share of Church Ladies ready to form their own little right-wing posses and butt-sniffing Inquisitions.

That said, the Orthodox come from the Byzantine culture, and when it gets down to what I really care about in addition to my faith and my family—art and writing—the Byzantine tradition opened a door to creative freedom for me. The Byzantine/Orthodox emphasis on mystery rather than theology, its long history of encouraging art since the time of the late Roman Empire, and its support for the secular arts inclusive of nudity and sex in art freed me to write what I wanted. Check out the nude reclining "Sleeping Eros" on a silver box in the Metropolitan Museum of Art Byzantine collection (and much more) if you doubt my generalization about the easygoing sexuality in Byzantine art.

Moreover, the Byzantines treasured pagan Roman and Greek art from the pre-Christian era. Unlike today's more militant Muslims or prudish evangelicals (or the "Orthodox" who know nothing about their own Byzantine tradition and are thus thoroughly protestantized), the Byzantines didn't have a problem with the human body. For instance, in the fifth-century Byzantine mosaic of Jesus's baptism found in the baptistery in Ravenna, Italy, Jesus is nude, his penis visible. Even though the so-called Arian Baptistery was erected (in 565), after the condemnation of the Arian cult, the structure was converted into a Catholic oratory named Santa Maria. Greek monks added a monastery during the period of the Orthodox Exarchate of Ravenna. And no one—not the Greeks, the Roman Catholics, or the Byzantines—was affronted by Christ's nudity.

In fact, through most of Byzantine history and Roman Catholic history as well, when, from time-to-time, some monk or other person of an anti-sexual strict bent (following the gloomy restrictive thread of faith that co-mingles with the more enlightened thread running throughout church history) would rage against "pagan art," he was largely ignored. And when, in a pre-Protestant anti-image, Islamic-style purge, certain Byzantine leaders (sometime between 726 and 730) tried to do away with the use of icons in worship, the whole Church rose up and rebelled and eventually (by the end of the eighth century) restored images to worship.

The Byzantines also preserved Roman and Greek philosophy, including that of Plato and Aristotle, which the Byzantines (and some Muslims) kept alive when much of Western Europe was mostly an illiterate cow town. The Western European Renaissance was possible only because the Medici family (and a few others) imported Byzantine scholars, Byzantine libraries, and the Roman and Greek learning and art that the Byzantines had preserved, which then spread from Florence to the rest of Western Europe. And the Byzantines' love of learning for its own sake not only informs the present-day temper of the Orthodox Church but also happened to inspire the people—such as the Florentines who produced the humanist art and culture (and everything else that proceeded from it)—that make my life (and maybe yours) seem worth living.

Most liberating of all, for me, was discovering that the people in my local church community were religious and yet didn't interpret every relationship, whether that with a stranger sitting next to them on an airplane or that with a writer who happened to go to church with them as an opportunity to evangelize, let alone judge. In other words, I can write the most truthful books I can write and also go to church, and the two activities aren't mutually exclusive.

Thus it's no coincidence that I started to write novels only after I left the evangelical/fundamentalist world. It's also no coincidence that C. S. Lewis ruined what could have been a decent literary career by slavishly working Christian propaganda into his "novels," especially once he began to cater to the evangelical/fundamentalist subculture after he became a star. Perhaps this is one reason why Tolkien's *Lord of the Rings* trilogy will stand the test of time better than anything Lewis wrote.

Tolkien—a friend of C. S. Lewis—was also a practicing Christian, and his books have a spiritual tone that seems to have sprung from his beliefs. But Tolkien refused to become a mere theological repackager masquerading as a writer of fantasy literature. He let his imagination rip. The only place I sense that Tolkien censored himself is in the area of sex. I still don't know how or when elves do it!

The perception these days is that being religious, especially Christian, and being a real artist are incompatible. Some of the best writers of the last century who were devout Christians, such as Walker Percy, John Updike, and Flannery O'Conner, are presented in university courses by secular professors so used to the idea that all writing by Christians is propaganda, that when they teach the writing of some of the best contemporary writers who were devout non-evangelical Christians they don't even mention (and in some cases don't seem to know) that many modern celebrated writers were (or are) believers.

So far has the evangelical/fundamentalist rot gone in culture trashing that the fact that people such as O'Conner, Updike, and Percy were good contemporary writers seems to exclude them from being identified *as* Christians. And the evangelical/fundamentalist community wouldn't recognize their writing as writing by Christians, either because it contains too much truth about reality or because it is not Jesus propaganda. In a way in the United States, actual writers (or those working seriously in any of the other arts) who are also Christians are men and women without a home.

Warren, like C. S. Lewis before him, and like many an evangelical/fundamentalist leader or "writer" today, knows that he must park his conscience at the door of his golden cage, or his empire will melt away under the intolerable weight of the gossip of the Church Ladies. Warren got a whiff of this when he was foolish enough to go on *Larry King Live*, in the spring of 2009, and mention that maybe he wasn't as firmly against gay marriage as he was said to have been in the wake of the battle over gay marriage in California during the 2008 election season. As the *Washington Times* reported on April 11, 2009, "I was extremely troubled," said Al Mohler, president of the Southern Baptist Theological Seminary in Louisville, Kentucky. "Absolutely baffling," huffed Wendy Wright, president of the far-right Concerned Women of America organization. Warren learned, if he didn't already know, that the only thing evangelicals will never forgive is any letting up on hating the "other."

That's what my friend Richard Cizik, former vice president of the National Association of Evangelicals, learned. He was being interviewed by Terry Gross on *Fresh Air* in 2009 and mentioned that *maybe* he wasn't against gay civil unions. He didn't even mention gay marriage. He was fired within days. Rich told me that he was never even asked by the board what he'd meant by his remarks and was never given a chance to respond.

Cizik had almost been forced out several years before when James Dobson, of "Focus on the Family" fame, wrote to the NAE board demanding Cizik's dismissal for saying that he thought global warming was real. Cizik got away with that apostasy against the Republican Party, which had long since come to be a stand-in for the "true church" for power-hungry evangelical/fundamentalist leaders such as Dobson. But when Cizik didn't hate gays enough, game over!

Maybe escaping the culture of hate of the "other" was one reason why, as soon as I left the evangelical fold, I began to write fiction and stopped editing my less than attractive feelings and failings out of my nonfiction. When you are no longer defined by what you are *not*, you can begin to be *for* something—say, trying to write a real book and let the chips fall where they may. This may not seem like a very big deal to someone raised in a secular home, but believe me, for me it was.

There was one exception to this newfound freedom. Soon after my joining the Orthodox Church in 1990, and displaying all the embarrassing enthusiasm of a new convert, I did quite a bit of speaking and writing that had a lot more to do with my former fundamentalist attitudes than with anything remotely Orthodox. In that sense I was a mirror image of the Father Xs of this world. But I got over my knee-jerk reactionary illness (at least somewhat), along with getting over my right-wing politics. And by the early 1990s I was well on my way out of the grip not just of fundamentalist "faith" but also of the fundamentalist *emotions* that lead to the right-wing politics of fear and exclusion.

This is a continuing process, and I'm not there yet, nor can I tell you where "there" is. As someone raised on the idea that my loyalty wasn't to the truth but to "our faith," writing the simple truth (as I understand it) still feels revolutionary. With my first novels it was such a relief to be writing whatever I wanted to write, where the point was to let the story's needs, rather than the needs of "Christian" propaganda, let alone the rules of the Church Ladies (or even Orthodox propaganda), dictate the direction of my work. Looking back now, it strikes me as passing strange that to live as a successful evangelical/fundamentalist activist (or even as an Orthodox activist) demanded a sophisticated degree of habitual lying, if not by commission than by omission. One always had to feign a degree of certainty about the Big Questions that no sane person ever feels.

As I said before, when salvation is understood as a journey, there is no pressure to make snap decisions and "get right with God." And because everyone is on the same path—even atheists—those at different stages on that path are not judged as "lost." In that sense what many Fathers of the Church said is understandable and boils down to this: The Church can only say how some people may find the path of salvation, but never who is lost. That means one can try to live as a Christian *and* be free of the guilt-induced need to proselytize. But even more important, one is freed from the illusion of certainty. Since no one is out because of wrong intellectual ideas, no one—including oneself—is ever completely in because the journey never ends. So you can answer "I don't know" to many a question without feeling you are letting yourself, others, or God down.

I understand the impulse to convert others because *I* kept converting! So I understood what another recovering evangelical/fundamentalist meant when she wrote to me this in an email, "To be honest, I miss the sense of belonging, purpose and vision my life had then [as a former evangelical]. I miss the hope I had and the drive to save souls because at least then I believed in something and it gave me reason to get up in the morning. Now I'm rudderless."

That's the longing Warren tapped into when he wrote his book. Converting is habit-forming. Even in my post-evangelical/fundamentalist reincarnation I've been looking for that quick fix, that one agent or editor who is my shining knight, a one-stop road to literary recognition, or (back in the day) that one donor who would underwrite my zealous evangelical/fundamentalist outreach efforts or (more recently) my political fixation on President Obama. You can take the evangelical/fundamentalist out of the evangelical/fundamentalist world, but the harder habit to break—speaking for myself— is the evangelical/fundamentalist addiction to silver-bullet, instant, born-again sorts of "solutions."

When I convert to whatever the next silver bullet is, I'm *sincere.* Later there comes a stage when I'm less sincere. That's because I've started to depend on my newfound belief for a sense of purpose, and for a while, I don't want to rock the boat by asking questions. At that stage I hold on to my new "faith" a bit longer than I'd do otherwise with no psychological vested interest. Jesus will save me! Being a movie director will save me! The Orthodox Church will save me! Being a Republican will save me! Obama will save me! Being a progressive *Huffington Post* blogger will save me!

I'm too afraid to abandon what seemed so true and was such a comfort as each new "church" heaves into sight and I do the American consumer shuffle and reinvent myself—again. I love to belong to a tribe! Why doesn't *everyone* believe in Jesus? Hollywood is great! Obama is so smart! Why don't all young men join the Marines like my son did?! Isn't this a wonderful church!

Atheists do the same thing when they put their trust in authors such as Harris or Dennett to *explain* it all, or invest their faith in Reason, science, politics, or sexual liberation—whatever. But at least atheists aren't claiming that people who disagree with them are going to suffer eternal damnation.

Then I start asking questions. This slick outfit seems to run like a big business. Is this the entertainment industry or spirituality? Can Obama walk on water? My cooling off to my new faith goes like this: I discover that lots of born-again people are just too dumb for words. That there will always be the next "Rick Warren" with all the "answers." That Hollywood sucks! That even in the Greek Orthodox community there are a few very nasty wingnuts lurking. That those "tolerant" left-wing supporters of Obama are just as intolerant as my old right-wing friends and just as into their own closed-minded orthodoxies. That I've joined another this-will-solve-everything cult—*again*. Most of all, I discover that my real problem never was about belonging to the "right" group but about *what is wrong with me*.

CHAPTER 8

Spaceship Jesus Will Come Back and Whisk Us Away

But what is this unknown something with which the Reason collides when inspired by its paradoxical passion, with the result of unsettling even man's knowledge of himself? It is the Unknown. It is not a human being, in so far as we know what man is; nor is it any other known thing. So let us call this unknown something: the God. It is nothing more than a name we assign to it.

Philosophical Fragments, Søren Kierkegaard

Jerry Jenkins and Tim LaHaye's *Left Behind* series of sixteen novels (so far!) represents everything that is most deranged about religion. If I had to choose companions to take my chances with in a lifeboat, and the choice boiled down to picking Tim LaHaye, Jerry Jenkins, or Christopher Hitchens, I'd pick Hitchens in a heartbeat. At least he wouldn't try to sink our boat so that Jesus would come back sooner. He might even bring along a case of wine.

The *Left Behind* novels have sold tens of millions of copies while spawning an "End Times" cult, or rather egging it on. Such products as *Left Behind* wall paper, screen savers, children's books, and video games have become part of the ubiquitous American background noise. Less innocuous symptoms include people stocking up on assault rifles and ammunition, adopting "Christ-centered" home school curricula, fearing higher education, embracing rumor as fact, and learning to love hatred for the "other," as exemplified by a revived anti-immigrant racism, the murder of doctors who do abortions, and even a killing in the Holocaust Museum.

No, I am *not* blaming Jenkins and LaHaye's product line for murder or racism or any other evil intent or result. What I *am* saying is that feeding the paranoid delusions of people on the fringe of the fringe contributes to a dangerous climate that may provoke violence in a few individuals. And convincing folks that Armageddon is on the way, and all we can do is wait, pray, and protect our families from the chaos that will be the "prelude" to the "Return of Christ," is perhaps not the best recipe for political, economic, or personal stability, let alone social cohesion. It may also not be the best philosophy on which to build American foreign policy! The momentum toward what amounts to a whole subculture seceding from the union (in order to await "The End") is irrevocably prying loose a chunk of the American population from both sanity and their fellow citizens.

A time-out for disclosure is in order. I knew Jerry Jenkins quite well many years ago, and we worked on a baseball book project together, with me trying—and failing—to get his book made into a movie. I liked Jerry and he was kind and decent. I also have known Tim LaHaye for years, and some thirty years ago we shared the platform at several fundamentalist events. Both men always treated me well. This may come across as maudlin BS to some people, but I mean it when I say that if I weren't convinced that their hugely "successful" work is about as innocuous as tossing gasoline and lighted matches into a nursery school, I'd never say a word about them. I'm betting that they mean well. It seems to me that they also have no idea what they have helped unleash. You can be very decent *and* very blind.

That said . . . the evangelical/fundamentalists—and hence, from the early 1980s until the election of President Obama in 2008, the Religious Right as it informed U.S. policy through the then dominant Republican Party—are in the grip of an apocalyptic Rapture cult centered on revenge and vindication. This End Times death wish is built on a literalist interpretation of the Book of Revelation. Too bad.

This weird book was the last to be included in the New Testament. It was included as canonical only relatively late in the process after a heated dispute. The historic Churches East and West remain so suspicious of Revelation that to this day it has never been included as part of the cyclical public readings of scripture in Orthodox services. The book of Revelation is read in Roman and Anglican Churches only during Advent. But both Rome and the East were highly suspicious of the book. The West included it in the lectionary late and sparingly. In other words, the book of the Bible that the historical Church found most problematic is the one that American evangelicals latched on to like flies on you know what.

Given that Revelation is now being hyped as the literal—even desired—roadmap to Armageddon, it's worth pausing to note that it's nothing more than a bizarre pastoral letter that was addressed to seven specific churches in Asia at the end of the first century by someone (maybe John or maybe not) who appears to have been far from well when he wrote it. In any case, the letter was not intended for use outside of its liturgical context, not to mention that it reads like Jesus on acid.

The evangelical/fundamentalist literalistic "interpretation" of Revelation is symptomatic of a larger problem: make-it-up-as-you-go-along biblical interpretation suited to hyping whatever the evangelical/fundamentalist flavor of the moment is, in a desperate effort to keep religion relevant. But taken out of the context of being part of a worship cycle, the Bible became something like an extremely sharp butcher knife in the hands of children running around a garden. There's nothing wrong with the knife per se, but context is everything. Enter semiliterate American evangelical/fundamentalist rubes armed with multiple "kitchen knives" and imbued with a frontier "no bishops or kings!" suspicion of any tradition, scholarship, or hierarchy that might moderate their wild-eyed personal "interpretations" of scripture and their burning desire to make a buck.

The *Left Behind* series is really just recycled evangelical/fundamentalist profit taking from scraps of "prophecy" left over from an earlier commercial effort to mine the vein of fearsome End Times gold. A book called *The Late Great Planet Earth* was the 1970s incarnation of this nonsense. It was written by Hal Lindsey, a "writer" who dropped by my parents' ministry of L'Abri several times.

Lindsey's *The Late Great Planet Earth* interpreted Revelation for a generation of paranoid evangelicals who were terrified of the Soviet Union and communism and were convinced that the existence of the modern State of Israel was the sign that Jesus was on the way in our lifetimes, as Lindsey claimed. According to Lindsey, Revelation was "speaking" about the Soviet Union and imminent nuclear attacks between the Soviet Union and the United States. When Mikhail Gorbachev became president of the U.S.S.R., *Planet Earth* groupies claimed Gorbachev was the Antichrist, citing the references in Revelation to the "mark of the beast" as proof because Gorbachev had a birthmark on his forehead!

After everything predicted in the book came to nothing, Lindsey rewrote and "updated" his "interpretations" in many sequels, in what must have been some sort of record for practicing George Orwell's idea of "doublethink" via editorial revision of ever-changing "facts." Trying to follow the prophecy party line eventually got confusing, even for the Lindsey followers, and Lindsey faded into well-deserved obscurity.

This would be amusing, if not for the lives touched by this crazy nonsense. For instance, a good friend of mine was dragged—at age five—to Alaska, where his parents huddled in an "End Times" commune, a place chosen to be out of the way of major cities so that when the bombs fell, his family (and some fellow "pilgrims") could await the Lord's return in safety. My friend's life was almost destroyed by suffering through years of a cruel and bizarre lifestyle in which his family was reduced to eating their goats and bear meat hunted (with the many guns kept by the members of this particular cult) on the "mission's" garbage dump. Of course, school was not a big concern since Jesus was on the way! Discipline was harsh so that everyone could be found "pure of heart" at the Lord's imminent return. After five or six years of this, my friend's miserably duped parents dragged themselves back to a neighborhood near ours where it happened that Genie and I got to know their utterly dislocated and severely damaged children, one of whom grew to become a close friend of ours.

According to Jenkins and LaHaye, who have taken over the Hal Lindsey franchise of apocalypse-for-fun-and-profit and expanded it into a vast industry, the "chosen" will soon be airlifted to safety. The focus on the "signs" leading up to this hoped-for aeronautical excursion is understandably no longer the defunct U.S.S.R. but the ripped-from-the-headlines gift that keeps on giving: the Middle East.

The key to understanding the popularity of this series (and the whole host of other End Times "ministries" from the ever weirder Jack-the-Rapture-is-coming!-Van-Impe to the smoother but no less bizarre pages of *Christianity Today* magazine) isn't some new or sudden interest in prophecy, but the deepening inferiority complex suffered by the evangelical/fundamentalist community.

The words *left behind* are ironically what the books *are* about, but not in the way their authors intended. The evangelical/fundamentalists, from their crudest egocentric celebrities to their "intellectuals" touring college campuses trying to make evangelicalism respectable, have been left behind by modernity. They won't change their literalistic anti-science, anti-education, anti-everything super-stitions, so now they nurse a deep grievance against "the world." This has led to a profound fear of the "other."

Jenkins and LaHaye provide the ultimate revenge fantasy for the culturally left behind against the "elite." The *Left Behind* franchise holds out hope for the self-disenfranchised that *at last* soon every-one will *know* "we" were right and "they" were wrong. They'll *know* because Spaceship Jesus will come back and whisk us away, leaving everyone else to ponder just how very lost they are because they refused to say the words, "I accept Jesus as my personal sav-ior" and join *our* side while there was still time! Even better: *Jesus will kill all those smart-ass Democrat-voting, overeducated fags who have been mocking us*!

Nietzsche talked about "everyday being oneself" and not belong-ing to "the herd," but we *want* to belong. We *have* to belong! We want to find *the* purpose, be it Jesus, or the study of the biological/evolutionary origins of religion, or blogging on left-wing sites and reading all those responses from people *just like us*. We can't change that desire to belong to the winning side. But some evangelical/fundamentalists not only wish to be proved right; they also want revenge.

The bestselling status of the *Left Behind* novels proves that, not unlike Islamist terrorists who behead their enemies, many evangel-ical/fundamentalist readers relish the prospect of God doing lots of messy killing for them as they watch in comfort from on high. They want revenge on all people not like them—forever.

Knowingly or unknowingly, Jenkins and LaHaye cashed in on years of evangelical/fundamentalists' imagined victimhood. I say *imagined*, because the born-agains had one of their very own, George W. Bush, in the White House for eight long, ruinous years and also dominated American politics for the better part of thirty years before that. Nevertheless, their sense of being a victimized mi-nority is still very real—and very marketable. Whether they were winning politically or not, they nurtured a mythology of persecution by the "other." Evangelical/fundamentalists believed that even though they were winning, somehow they had actually lost.

Most of that sense of lost battles is related to the so-called culture wars issues in which evangelical/fundamentalists did not fare so well, from the legalization of abortion to gay rights. But rather than admitting that they were often losing the arguments, or had come across as so mean (or plain dumb) that few outsiders wanted to be like them, they blamed everyone else, from the courts to organizations such as Planned Parenthood, the ACLU, the *New York Times*, and the "left-wing media." Just about any scapegoat would do to deny or disguise the simple fact that fewer Americans wanted to follow the evangelical/fundamentalist Church Ladies into their gloomy cave (and/or the never-never land of the Rapture) and park their brains there.

I used to be part of the self-pitying, whining, evangelical/fundamentalist chorus. I remember going on the *Today Show* with host Jane Pauley back in the late 1970s (or early 1980s). I debated with the head of the American Library Association about my claim that our evangelical/fundamentalist books weren't getting a fair shake from the "cultural elites." We Schaeffers were selling millions of books, but the *New York Times* never reviewed them. I made the point that we were being ignored by the "media elite," which was somewhat ironic, given that I had been invited to appear on *Today* to make that claim.

I dropped out of the evangelical/fundamentalist subculture soon after that *Today* appearance (years later I was back on *Today* in my secular writer incarnation, being interviewed about a book of mine on the military/civilian divide, but I decided not to mention that I'd been on the show about thirty years before in what seemed like either another lifetime or an out-of-body experience).

Others carried on where I left off, pushing the victimhood mythology to the next generation of evangelical/fundamentalists, and they have cultivated a following among the terminally aggrieved based on ceaselessly warning them about "the world." For instance

"An Evangelical Manifesto," a document put together by yet another self-appointed evangelical/fundamentalist "leadership group" (in 2008), was widely circulated in evangelical/fundamentalists circles. It put forward the idea of the evangelical/fundamentalist battle with the dangerous forces of secularism, claiming that "Nothing is more illiberal than to invite people into the public square but insist that they be stripped of the faith that makes them who they are. . . . If this hardens into something like the European animosity toward religion in public life the result would be disastrous for the American republic. . . . [The] striking intolerance shown by the new atheists is a warning sign."

The evangelical/fundamentalist authors of this document were claiming that fundamentalists were being *stripped* of their political power. Worse, we'd soon find that America would be just like—heavens!—*France!* They made this case *during* the Bush presidency!

A host of evangelical/fundamentalist Cassandras tour college campuses reinforcing their followers' perennial chip-on-the-shoulder attitude by telling fearful evangelical/fundamentalist students to hold fast against the secular onslaught. They tell their student listeners (and those students' even more worried parents) to not let "those people"—professors, members of the Democratic Party, moderates, progressives, and such ordinary American men and women as Jews, gays, and members of the educated "elite"—*strip* them of their faith. Hundreds of books by many evangelical/fundamentalist authors could be consolidated into one called *How to Get Through College with Your Fundamentalist Faith Intact So You Won't Wind Up Becoming One of Them.*

Sometimes right-wing paranoia takes an ugly twist. A website maintained by James Von Brunn, an avowed racist and anti-Semite well known to the netherworld of white supremacy—and the assassin who killed a security guard at the Holocaust Museum in June of 2009—said that Brunn tried to carry out a "citizen's arrest" in 1981 on the Federal Reserve Board of Governors, whom he accused of "treason." When he was arrested outside the room where the board was meeting, he was carrying a sawed-off shotgun, a revolver, and a knife. Police said he planned to take members of the Fed hostage.

"Mainstream" (in other words, slightly less nutty and less violent) religious-right Republicans have been saying the same thing as Brunn about the Fed for years, particularly the so-called "dominionists" who believe it's their job to reestablish God's dominion on earth. They preach Old Testament–style vengeance and loony gold-standard "economics" from many "respectable" pulpits. They also hate America (as it is), want a revolution in the name of God, and espouse "pro-life" beliefs, anti-gay hate, racism, and far-right Republican politics. They take the Republican anti-government propaganda to the next step and say that even paying taxes is "unconstitutional." I know them well.

I knew the founders of the dominionist movement—people like the late Reverend Rousas John Rushdoony, the father of "Christian Reconstructionism" and the modern evangelical/fundamentalist home school movement. Rushdoony (whom I met and talked with several times) believed that interracial marriage, which he referred to as "unequal yoking," should be made illegal. He also opposed integration, referred to Southern slavery as "benevolent," and said that "some people are by nature slaves." Rushdoony was also a Holocaust denier. And yet his home school materials are a mainstay of the right-wing evangelical home school movement to this day. In Rushdoony's 1973 book, *The Institutes of Biblical Law*, he says that fundamentalist Christians must "take control of governments and impose strict biblical law" on America and then the world. That would mean the death penalty for "practicing homosexuals."

Many evangelical leaders deny holding Reconstructionist beliefs, but Beverly and Tim LaHaye (of Concerned Women for America and the co-author of the novels we're talking about in this chapter), Donald Wildmon (of the American Family Association), and the late D. James Kennedy (of Coral Ridge Ministries and a friend of mine before I left the movement) served alongside Rushdoony on the secretive

Coalition for Revival, a group formed in 1981 to "reclaim America for Christ." I went to some of the early meetings.

The New Atheists have played into the evangelical/fundamentalist's hands. Each side fans the flames of victimhood. "An atheist can never be president!" says one side. "A Christian never gets a fair shake in the *New York Times*!" claims the other. Each side is led by opportunists claiming to speak for a beleaguered minority.

Indeed, Dawkins needs the evangelicals and they need him. As the authors of *An Evangelical Manifesto* wrote, "striking intolerance shown by the new atheists is a warning sign." Conversely, how would Dawkins's followers use their Scarlet A pins to open their conversations if America weren't full of evangelical/fundamentalists? The fundamentalists in both camps *need* to *claim* they are hated. The leaders push their followers to fear each other to maintain their identity—and lecture fees.

But getting back to the Apocalypse—since all the good God-fearing folks are going to be forced to be *Europeans* anyway, why not end it all now? Jenkins and LaHaye's "I told you so" to all those "elites" who aren't like "us" comes packaged as ultra-violence. The promotional copy for one of the books in the *Left Behind* series—*Shadowed*—promises plenty of killing: "After God intervenes with a miracle of global proportions, the tide is turned on international atheism!" Those Europeans the evangelical/fundamentalist leaders warned all "Real Americans" about are about to get theirs!

If you want to know what it means to turn the tide on "international atheism," here's an example from *Glorious Appearing*, in which Jesus slaughters unbelievers.

The riders not thrown leaped from their horses and tried to control them with the reins, but even as they struggled, their own flesh dissolved, their eyes melted, and their tongues disintegrated. . . . [T]he soldiers stood briefly as skeletons in now-baggy uniforms, then dropped in heaps of bones as the blinded horses continued to fume and rant and rave. Seconds later the same plague afflicted the horses, their flesh and eyes and tongues melting away, leaving grotesque skeletons standing, before they too rattled to the pavement.

Many evangelical/fundamentalist's can't get enough of this garbage. They've been sucking it up since the early 1970s, and now, in the *Left Behind* books, the message has gone viral. The video game *Left Behind: Eternal Forces* was developed by a publicly traded company, Left Behind Games. The player controls a "Tribulation Forces" team and is invited to "use the power of prayer to strengthen your troops in combat and wield modern military weaponry throughout the game world." The game blesses religious violence. It's the Americanized version of some Islamic sheik drumming hate of the infidel into young minds in some dusty Pakistani madrassa. It's legal evangelical Jihad training, a fantasy foreshadowing of the all-too-real killings of abortion doctors and others hated as "anti-Christ."

The expanding *Left Behind* entertainment empire also feeds the dangerous delusions of Christian Zionists, who are convinced that the world is heading to a final Battle of Armageddon and *who see this as a good thing*! Christian Zionists, led by many "respectable" mega-pastors—including Reverend John Hagee—believe that war in the Middle East is God's will. In his book *Jerusalem Countdown: A Warning to the World*, Hagee maintains that Russia and the Arabs will invade Israel and then will be destroyed by God. This will cause the Antichrist—the head of the European Union—to stir up a confrontation over Israel between China and the West.

Perhaps, in the era of Obama, Hagee will do a fast rewrite and say that President Obama is the Antichrist, because the same folks who are into Christian Zionism are also into the far, far loony right of the Republican Party represented by oddities like Sarah Palin. These are the same people who insist that President Obama is a "secret Muslim," "not an American," and/or "a communist," "more European than American," or whichever one of those contradictory things is worse—not like *us* anyway, that's for sure.

Christian Zionists support any violent action by the State of Israel against Arabs and Palestinians because the increasingly brutal State of Israel is, in the fevered evangelical/fundamentalist mind, the nation presently standing in for Jesus as avenger on evildoers everywhere, by which they mean Arabs and others not like us. Christian Zionists are yet another reason why I and countless other Christians, including many of the more moderate evangelicals, mainline Protestants, Roman Catholics, and Orthodox are hesitant to be labeled "Christian." Who wants to be confused with some of the most dangerous and stupid people in the world: nuclear-armed, paranoid evangelical/fundamentalist Bible thumpers rooting for Armageddon and worrying in paranoid "official" documents about being forced to become like "the Europeans"? (Just a thought: does that make high-speed rail service a tool of the Devil?)

Perhaps I'm not alone when I say that it would be tempting to walk away from trying to follow Jesus, if for no other reason than to avoid the constant hassle of having to explain what I'm *not*. Fortunately, I have role models who are far from today's right-wing evangelical/fundamentalists.

It seems to me that a lot of us *non*-evangelical, *non*-fundamentalist followers of Jesus find ourselves where Marc Chagall found himself vis-à-vis his faith in God and the public perception of what that faith means. Chagall is proof that not all people who identify with Christianity and Judaism (or religion in general) are of the Hagee, LaHaye, Rushdoony, and Jenkins ilk.

Chagall was an ambassador for a Judaism of peace and redemption, not a pusher of the eternal war of ethnic-religion-based Christian and/or Jewish Zionism, let alone a purveyor of fear of the "other" say, Europeans, Arabs, or gays. Chagall extends an olive branch to humanity and envisions an inclusive Judaism, not the clenched fist of race-based Zionist otherness and exclusion that the far-right hardliners in the modern State of Israel have become.

Chagall painted faith subjects infused with the Jewish and Christian symbolism that had been part of his formative years in prerevolutionary Russia. Chagall was one of the twentieth century's great painters, but he paid a price for being out of step with the critics of his day, most of whom were preoccupied with "brave" mid-twentieth-century angst and nihilism. Chagall refused to remove biblical themes from his visual vocabulary long after all such "sentiment" (indeed, any figurative representation at all) was supposed to have been rejected by thinking artists. Chagall—much like Pierre Bonnard, Georges Rouault, and several other outcasts from the inner circle of early to mid-twentieth-century critical acclaim—has since transcended his critics.

Standing outside the Metropolitan Opera House at Lincoln Center at night and looking through the glass front of the building at Chagall's huge paintings *The Triumph of Music* and *The Sources of Music*, the viewer is transported into a mind within which a loving humane vision of the God of Judaism and Christianity finds a home. Chagall didn't paint theological or political "statements" but cut to the heart of the redemptive message of all faiths.

Chagall didn't claim he had *the* truth but saw himself as a servant of beauty and a practitioner of grace-filled thanksgiving. His art was a doorway to reconciliation among three bloody and often inhumane faith traditions: Judaism, Christianity, and Secularism.

Chagall gave us a spiritual way of seeing that is the opposite of paranoid victimology and evangelical/fundamentalist and/or Zionist rage. Where Jenkins and LaHaye offer a blood-soaked, angry God as video game "entertainment," Chagall gave us brides and angels floating in an eternal sky of hope and love, where tragedy is a prelude to joy. In Chagall's mercy-drenched vision all are saved; Jew, "pagan," and gentile alike are redeemed. Only hatred and exclusion have no place in his paradise.

In a 1979 interview Chagall said, "I went back to the great universal book, the Bible. Since my childhood, it has filled me with vision about the fate of the world and inspired me in my work. In moments of doubt, its highly poetic grandeur and wisdom comforted me. For me it is like second nature. . . . Since in my inner life the spirit and world of the Bible occupy a large place, I have tried to express it. It is essential to show the elements of the world that are not visible and not just to reproduce nature in all its aspects."

As Jonathan Wilson writes in his book *Marc Chagall*,

> Chagall's relationship to the figure of Jesus Christ is ultimately mysterious . . . unclassifiable, and contradictory. It is the Jesus of a Jewish child who grew up in an environment of churches and Russian Orthodox icons; of a Jewish painter both attuned to and rebelling against a two-thousand-year tradition of Christian iconography in art; of a Jew in love with the stories of the Hebrew Bible and yet well-versed in the parables of the New Testament, drawn to the poetry of that book and excited by its gaunt philosophy.

I happen to empathize with Chagall. As a person of faith—both chosen and inherited—where do I fit as a writer? Where did Chagall "fit"? Where do love and mystery and mercy fit in the literalist-minded armed camp of atheist against believer, when the whole debate is tinged with a deadly fear of the other?

How can one *be* a Christian when those such as Rushdoony, Jenkins, and LaHaye describe themselves as such? How can one be an atheist when a T-shirt vendor such as Dawkins has foisted himself on thoughtful and humane non-believers? Chagall shows the way for all of us, whatever we believe. His life and art demonstrate that it is possible to buck the trend of cynicism and to believe in each other more than in the rightness of our particular ideas.

PART II

Patience With Each Other, Patience With God

CHAPTER 9

So Naked Before a Just and Angry God

They like to give it this turn: the human race has outgrown Christianity.

Journals, Søren Kierkegaard

In the second part of this book I'll shift from essay-laced-with-memoir, to memoir-and-memory with a touch of essay. Beliefs and lives are shaped by good (or bad) examples set by others. So I'll be looking at some of the lives that have touched mine. I'll also be approaching the answers offered here having learned one thing: *I am my only insurmountable problem.*

There are no silver bullets, born-again, political, atheist, or religious, to slay what ails me. The solution is not a one-time born-again experience or correct ideas, but an incremental chipping away at those things I, and those closest to me, like least about me.

That said, I can't explain why I said, "Thank you, Jesus," as I did the other night when I happened to open the front door to fetch firewood and saw a new crescent moon perfectly lined up in a small triangle with Venus and Mars. All three were shimmering through a fogbank in the cold December sky. Of course, they weren't really "lined up." All that was happening was an optical illusion from my earthbound perspective.

I don't have the capacity or time to learn everything about the workings of the solar system. I don't understand the universe beyond it, how all this got here, what I'm doing here, or whether my life has a meaning in some transcendent sense. I have no final explanation for why picking up that load of firewood and knowing that I could not only heat my home but also care for my little granddaughter, asleep up on the middle floor, was so deeply satisfying.

My reaction to that extraterrestrial vision was not to try and answer all of the questions related to the planets, firewood, my knee-jerk thank you to Jesus, or the workings of the universe; it was to fetch Genie so we could exclaim, "Isn't that amazing?" Those words didn't come close to expressing what I was feeling. Nor were they scientific explanations of why the rather rare alignment of those planets and our moon was occurring that night.

Nevertheless, "Isn't that amazing?" was just as valid an expression of one aspect of what I experienced as any words ever spoken about planets, gravity, and dark matter would have been, and it was just as accurate and precise as talking about how light was entering my eyes and how my brain was "seeing" that light, filling in the gaps and presenting a "picture" to me that I recognized as planets and a moon.

The reason why all these ways of thinking about the moon and the planets—scientific, aesthetic, and spiritual—are equally valid is that all words—lyrical, spiritual, or scientific—are metaphors. That's why Warren is so wrong. That's why Dawkins is so wrong. There is not *one approach* to purpose, let alone to truth. There are many. Descriptions of those approaches are only approximations of the illusive reality that Einstein described as "something that our mind cannot grasp and this beauty and sublimity reaches us only indirectly and as a feeble reflection."

We can't live in each other's brains, let alone in the heads of the people on some church council a thousand years ago who wrote whatever creed we're repeating, or in the minds of the Bible's authors, or, for that matter, in the minds of scientists like such as Einstein. When they used the word *God* or *universe* or *truth*, what were they actually picturing? We'll never know what their perception was for the same reason that the Supreme Court justices rarely agree unanimously on the original intent of the authors of the Constitution.

When it comes to trying to sort out the competing threads in Christianity, the idea of "right belief" goes back to the gospel-writing period but was maximized by the scholastics who were part of the thread of nit-picking, rules-orientated, literalistic fundamentalist Christianity. The idea of correct theology as a rationalistic proposition needed for salvation was rooted primarily in the Aristotelian Roman Catholic Scholastic movement—in other words, those theologians who longed for academic certainty about the most nonacademic of subjects: God. They harked back to pre-Christian philosophy to look for some method through which to view religion in a more "scientific" way. They discovered their "method" in Aristotle's systematic approach to philosophy.

Thomas Aquinas was the leading scholastic. He believed that truth is known through reason, or what he called "natural revelation," and through faith, which he called "supernatural revelation." Aquinas viewed theology as a science. (Scholasticism was dominant in the medieval Christian universities from the eleventh century to the fifteenth century.) But how can we discover spiritual truth by parsing terms? This way lies the madness that drove Aquinas to pen such gems as these: "As regards the individual nature, woman is defective and misbegotten, for the active power of the male seed tends to the production of a perfect likeness in the masculine sex; while the production of a woman comes from defect in the active power." Or this: "If forgers and malefactors are put to death by the secular power, there is much more reason for excommunicating and even putting to death one convicted of heresy."

Aquinas's rationalism was just a foretaste of the theology of the Calvinist Protestants. Jonathan Edwards was the epitome of this

Reformed "logic." Edwards was the leading evangelical/fundamentalist evangelist in the eighteenth century's Great Awakening. Here's a bit of a sermon he preached called "Sinners in the Hands of an Angry God" (delivered in Enfield, Massachusetts, in 1741).

> There is nothing that keeps wicked men, at any one moment, out of hell, but the mere pleasure of God. By "the mere pleasure of God," I mean his sovereign pleasure, his arbitrary will, restrained by no obligation, hindered by no manner of difficulty. . . . The bow of God's wrath is bent, and the arrow made ready on the string, and Justice bends the arrow at your heart, and strains the bow, and it is nothing but the mere pleasure of God, and that of an angry God, without any promise or obligation at all, that keeps the arrow one moment from being made drunk with your blood. . . . If you cry to God to pity you, He will be so far from pitying you in your doleful case, or showing you the least regard or favor, that instead of that he'll only tread you under foot.

If Chagall is at one end of the religious spectrum, Edwards is at the other. On the other hand, the struggle between the merciful side and the harsh side of religion—the two threads—was also evident even in Edwards's personality. His essay "Nature of the True Virtue," seems to be by a different person than the man who preached "Sinners in the Hands of an Angry God." (In "Nature of the True Virtue," Edwards says that true virtue is based on benevolence and love).

Whatever Edwards's personal struggles between the light and dark sides of the Protestant religion, he has come to symbolize the ugly side of Christianity. Fortunately, the view of some of the earliest Fathers of the historic Church could not be further from Aquinas's and Edward's rougher statements. Those Fathers would "get" Chagall and would have been shocked by Aquinas and Edwards.

In the context of our necessarily subjective perception, an atheist telling religious people that they the atheists have the facts and that the rest of us are deluded is a sign of hubris. It's just as arrogantly insane as an otherwise genial fellow like Rick Warren telling atheists that the Creator wants to keep them alive for *eternity* in order to burn them, just because the atheists believed the "wrong" words or didn't pray the so-called sinner's prayer. Warren wouldn't put it that way, but however one dances around it, that is the heart of the demented evangelical/fundamentalist message.

The cure for hubris (Protestant or otherwise) is, I think, to experience God through failure, beauty, tragedy, community, and love. Sometimes our learning curve away from self is forced on us, if not by God then by God's angels say, by Mr. and Mrs. Parke.

Certain experiences changed my life. Being sent to Great Walstead School (a boarding school for boys in Lindfield, Sussex, England) just before I turned eleven was one such experience. Mr. Parke was the headmaster, and Mrs. Parke was both a teacher and his eagle-eyed helpmeet. She (like her husband) gave "her" boys opportunities that I came to fully appreciate only years later.

The school turned my "island" (as I think of my weird childhood) into a peninsula. It almost made me feel normal. Eventually, when Genie showed up (more in the role of a terrific-looking archangel than a mere angel!) my peninsula gradually drifted into a continent of shared human experience. But without GW, I'd never have believed that it was possible for me to function at all in the wide world outside my parents' inward-looking mission.

Great Walstead School sat at the end of a long, oak-lined driveway. The grounds covered 294 acres of fields, woods, ponds, a small river, playing fields, and lawns nestled in a gently hilly landscape midway between London and Brighton. GW was "a short train journey from Victoria Station," according to the school brochure that Mom read aloud to me several times. (Why my parents sent me there is another story I've told elsewhere.)

When Mom and I arrived by taxi from the Hayward's Heath station, we passed the school's small farm. Next to the farm—it consisted of two tumble-down cow barns—sat Walstead House, the Elizabethan half-timbered cottage that the older boys lived in and that at first I mistook for the main building, until the taxi drove around the corner and the view of a large Victorian manor house appeared.

Mom and I took a quick tour, along with several other new boys and their parents, while following one of the Sixth Form (senior) boys. The two other new boys on our tour were much younger than I, the ages you were supposed to be when you started school. Our guide seemed scarily old. Boys came to GW at age six and then, between thirteen and fourteen, went on to a public school, which is what they called the private boys or girls boarding high schools in England. (After GW I was sent to one, but hated it and at age fifteen ran away, also another story.)

Our thirteen-year-old guide had the beginnings of whiskers, was a head taller than I, and never looked at me or the other two little boys in our party. He addressed his somewhat formal remarks to Mom and the other parents as though he were reading from a travel brochure.

"The main house has fifteen-to twenty-foot ceilings. Notice the wide staircase descending to the entrance hall. Boys are *not allowed* to use the main stairs! Here's the common room, library, the headmaster's study."

Behind the main house was a series of decaying huts linked by rickety, half-covered passages.

"We built these ourselves," the boy said. "Great Walstead is a DIY sort of place."

"DIY?" asked Mom.

"That's short for do it yourself," said the boy.

He said that the huts had been bought from a nearby Royal Air Force base at the end of World War II. These served as our classrooms, "as cold in winter as they are jolly hot in summer. In winter the huts are heated by portable kerosene stoves, and the bloody windows have to be opened."

Mom gave him a look the boy didn't seem to notice. She hadn't liked that he had said, "bloody." It wasn't taking the Lord's name in vain, but it didn't sound right to her.

"The huts are almost impossible to sweep no matter how hard the boys assigned to sweeping duty work. The good news is that most of the huts are propped on blocks and have loose floorboards. We pry one up and sweep everything through the hole!"

The other parents laughed. Mom didn't.

I was afraid of Mr. and Mrs. Parke—at first. I was not a great student. I spent all three years at the school desperately trying to catch up after a failed "home schooling" effort by my parents. The fact that I was also dyslexic—something no one knew about at the time—was no help.

GW was simple to the point of being Spartan. Our staff ranged from eccentric and doddering old men and women, who seemed to have just always been there lurking in the narrow passages, to several youthful and inexperienced teachers. But somehow the school was more than the sum of its parts. As Mr. Parke explained to me many years later, "My idea about which teachers I'd employ or keep on as masters was that they should be interesting. That's a lot more important than all this 'teacher-training' nonsense. Teachers needed to be able to hold the boys' attention."

Bubble held our attention all right! Bubble—also known as Mr. Albon was a teacher who would have been fired anywhere else. He had been at the school since around 1920 when it was founded. He was short and had colorless strands of hair plastered above a pale, bitter face that was dwarfed by his red-veined, bulbous nose. He was slope-shouldered, wore filthy gray trousers (victim to years of tea spills) that made his lap look like some sort of milky Jackson Pollock, a blue fraying-at-the-elbows cardigan he never changed, a wool burgundy tie, and a "white" shirt that had many years ago turned into a stained yellowing excrescence below a collar so grimy that it looked as if it were made of gray material, a bit like fungus.

Having Bubble for a master was something like having Gollum for a teacher. Only Bubble didn't disgust us by gnawing raw fish. Rather, he revolted and riveted us by snorting huge quantities of filthy, face-staining snuff, he never bathed, and he smelled oddly of pepper and was clearly drunk at times, although he did know a lot about music and made science interesting. No one liked Bubble, but we loved being taught by him. Who else would send a boy to detention for saying he believed in the Genesis story? Who else would sit reading the scores of Wagner operas, while silently mouthing the music, as if listening to a performance that only he could hear, when he was supposed to be leading a chapel service? What other teacher would help us remember the periodic tables by setting them to filthy limericks?

The first term I was at GW, Bubble wouldn't direct that year's end-of-term production, now that it was settled that it had to be Gilbert and Sullivan and that no rewriting of the lyrics would be allowed. So Bubble was angry because Mr. Parke had just banned him from directing yet another Wagner-derived opera.

I didn't know why at the time, but more than forty years later I found out that this ban was imposed because Bubble was a former wartime "German-lover" and fascist-sympathizer, so having to sit through Wagner-more-bloody-Wagner got the parents reminiscing over Bubble's best-forgotten wartime sympathies. Most of the parents hated Wagner anyway. They favored English operettas followed by cucumber sandwiches and afternoon tea. Besides, Bubble had once set bits of the *Ring* to "questionable limericks." The headmaster before Mr. Parke had made a point of never attending Bubble's rehearsals so that later he could truthfully tell irate parents that "I had no idea of what was in the play!"

Anyway, one afternoon there was plenty of smirking going on. We knew Bubble was sloshed—again. Ross and Weeks had found him on the drive sitting in a puddle actually holding a bottle! Wonderful! Splendid! Topping! Ripping! They pulled him out and fetched Matron (the school nurse) because his condition seemed to fall into a medical category. A bit later Bubble wasn't propped against the rhododendrons next to the driveway any longer, so we assumed that he'd been bundled back into the squalid room he lived in next to the barn.

Bubble (I later learned) was a former Anglo-Catholic, but by the time I got to GW he'd lost his faith and become our resident atheist. The interesting thing was that Mr. Parke kept Bubble on after Bubble lost his faith, even though their views differed sharply and GW was an evangelical school in that casual, breezy, laid-back and tolerant way of doing religion that the English are especially good at. This was a powerful object lesson to me about how attractive faith is when it's tolerant. We also had several declared agnostics on the staff and one other strident atheist, my favorite teacher Mr. Mellor, who also was a fine jazz pianist. Mr. Parke's forbearance was a long way from L'Abri's style where, if workers didn't toe the theological line, my parents asked them to leave.

Bubble's hatred of God made even the most pagan among us feign a deep love of religion just to goad him into some outrageous statement—"You Christians are a bloody nuisance and should be shot! I agree with Stalin!"—that would then be gleefully repeated. And what could the other teachers do about little boys shouting, "I agree with Stalin! Christians must be shot!" when they could truthfully answer rebukes with "But I was just repeating what Mr. Albon said, sir."

During the opening stages of World War II, Bubble had volunteered for the local Home Guard regiment, probably as a way to repair his reputation. Using his flair for making explosives, he had trained local volunteers to defend Britain with homemade weapons that, in a last ditch effort if all else failed, might stop the Germans. Bubble kept up his interest in anything that went bang! And he would march us out to the old tennis court to play Home Guard as a "science project" and have us make *and throw* flaming Molotov cocktails concocted in the empty scotch, rum, and gin bottles he always seemed to have handy. Our bombs sent mushrooms of fire and billowing smoke high into the air as Matron stood on the sidelines imploring, "Mind out!" and "Don't blow yourselves to bits!"

Building bombs, to say nothing of setting them off and surviving, is a confidence builder! But no one built confidence like Mrs. Parke.

The first time I saw Mrs. Parke was about an hour after Mom left me at the school. Mrs. Parke walked into the school's front hall. (I'd been hiding in some rhododendron bushes for over an hour trying to pull myself together.) Mrs. Parke was wearing a white apron over a gray, knee-length skirt and briskly drying her hands on a dishtowel. Maybe it was the disconcertingly steady way she met my eyes, but diminutive or not, she exuded a no-nonsense cast iron will, and I felt a twinge of fear. Mrs. Parke must have been working in the kitchen with "cook" on a parents' tea, which was about to be served to the hoard of mothers and fathers dropping off their boys. She briefly looked me up and down, taking me in the way a chef might dispassionately gauge the freshness of a crate of fish of dubious provenance. "Go see Matron, and put your things away," she said in an all-business voice and bustled away.

I wanted to ask whom or what Matron was, and where he, she, or it might be found, and how to get there. But I didn't dare.

About five minutes later Mrs. Parke bustled back through the hall. This time she was helping a very little boy drag a full-sized steamer trunk through the front door, on which several cricket bats were piled, along with an air rifle and a gleaming new hatchet. She noticed I hadn't budged and barked, "Spink Two, will you *please* collect this new boy and *do something* about him! You've been assigned to be Schaeffer's shadow, haven't you?"

I was surprised that Mrs. Parke knew my name. A tall thin lad wearing wire-rimmed glasses ran in from another room. He came to a full stop in front of Mrs. Parke and put his hands by his sides before he answered her.

"Yes, Mrs. Parke."

"For *goodness's sake*, Spink Two, will you *do* some *shadowing*! Why are you just standing there? Do something *useful*!"

I was swept into a whirlwind of unpacking, finding the place in the "boot room" to put my boots, where the dormitory was that I'd been assigned to, how to get from the classrooms back to the main school through a labyrinth of halls, as my shadow mumbled a dizzying explanation of each new mystery. Everyone else seemed to be speaking in a private code designed to exclude a newcomer. The boys, the staff, the parents dropping off their sons all seemed to have been born and raised in the school and moved effortlessly through what looked to me to like a series of complex ritual dances that I'd never get the hang of.

The strangeness of boarding school, how far from home I was, and how lonely I felt after Mom abandoned me in the rhododendron thicket was driven home by the smell of Peg's cleaning. On my first day at GW, I didn't know that the smell catching in my throat and making me want to gag was Peg's cleaning smell. Later I discovered that the stench of tar and ammonia—as if the stink of urine in some French train station bathroom had been mixed with hot tar used to patch potholes—came from the pale brown, oozy liquid Peg poured out of a big industrial-sized container into her galvanized bucket.

Peg was fierce. She was also drab-looking as the brown-gray water and bits of hair and grime slopping around in the pail into which she dipped her mildewed mops. Woe betide the boy who was rude to Peg or to Fred, our cockney cleaning staff of two—our "domestics." They of the deeply sallow, yellowy-gray chain-smoker complexions, and the small, stunted, years-of-bad-lower-class-English-wartime-and-postwar-diet bodies, lived together in a room deep in the bowels of the oldest and most decrepit part of the school, somewhere off past the kitchen. Were they fifty, sixty, eighty? Were Peg and Fred brother and sister? Married? No one knew, or, if they did, they weren't saying.

Fred followed Peg ten steps behind, even on their weekly walk down the school drive to go to Lindfield and catch the bus to Brighton and their "day out at the seaside." It was the only day Peg didn't wear her ill-fitting maid's uniform with a Victorian white cap and snap-on starched cuffs.

There was more than a little irony in the fact that Peg and Fred were our cleaning staff, because they were the dirtiest people in the school. Fred never took off his filthy brown mechanic's overalls. And Peg and Fred moved around the school in a haze of evil-smelling smoke, their own personal rancid atmosphere created by the filter-less cigarettes clenched in their thin, liver-colored lips. Their "fags" always seemed to be just about to burn down to a revolting saliva-soaked line and go out. Peg's eyes were set in a permanent smoke-induced squint through which she glared angrily at the world.

Peg and Fred were objects of curiosity but not mockery, in spite of Peg's rapid-fire cockney speech, made almost unintelligible by a cleft palette that transformed her head into a sounding board wherein words seemed to squirt from her nose, echoing as if they'd been shouted down a long empty water pipe. Stare at her for too long—for instance, when she was blowing gushing columns of smoke from blackened nostrils that gaped on either side of her enormous beaky nose—or smile in a way she mistook for a smile *about* her rather than *to* her, and there would follow the shrill scream "I'll tell Mr. Parkes of you!" and sometimes a wild slap. And that boy's smile would evaporate. Because if there was one thing our headmaster Mr. Parke—why Peg added the "s" at the end of his name I never learned—would *not* tolerate, it was rude-ness to or bulling of people who were "less advantaged than you lucky boys."

A few months into my first term at the school, Mrs. Parke stopped me in the narrow, musty-smelling back hall that led down to our dining area. "Schaeffer!" she called, after she popped her head out of the staff sitting room door while I'd been walking past.

"Yes, Mrs. Parke," I said, nervously wondering what I'd done now, and also wondering how on earth she knew I was passing.

"Why haven't you tried out for *Pinafore* yet?"

"I can't do that sort of thing, Mrs. Parke."

"And jolly well *why not*?"

"I can't learn words," I blurted.

"Reading and spelling have *nothing* to do with opera, Schaeffer. How do you know you're no good at *opera*?"

"But, Mrs. Parke, I'm no good at anything."

"A play isn't 'learning,' it's *acting*. All you have to do is *pretend*."

"But—"

"Can you remember music?"

"What do you mean?"

"I mean if I hum this, Da, Da, Ta, *Tah*, what is it?"

"Beethoven's Fifth, I think."

"*Brilliant*! You *see*!? You *can* remember anything as well as anyone else once it's set to music, so you jolly well come to the rehearsal today."

"But—"

"I shall read the words out loud to you, and then we'll sing them *together*! It will be rather jolly!"

"Yes, Mrs. Parke."

It always *was* "Yes, Mrs. Parke." So a few weeks later I found myself in the school play and rehearsing madly in our dining room/theater and finding out that I could do things I'd never thought possible. Mrs. Parke was thumping away on the tuneless old upright piano with one hand and directing with the other. Mrs. Macdonald was up on a ladder with all the boys who didn't have a part in the play clustered around her. They were painting the scenery: a vast seascape backdrop nailed to the wall of the dining room.

It wasn't all plays. During my second term at GW, Nichol and I ganged up on Higgins.

We called him "Higginbottom," and it drove him mad. Higgins was about my age and had something wrong with him. He flew into sudden and uncontrollable rages over the most petty provocations. The rest of the time he kept to himself. He had no friends.

Higgins was short and stocky and moved like a clumsy bear cub. He had a rather dark complexion, ruddy as if he had spent most of his days outdoors. Higgins would glance up from under a shock of thick, wiry hair falling over deep-set, dark, and brooding eyes just a bit too close together, giving his face a pinched look. When he was upset, his cheeks suddenly flushed crimson, as if Higgins had had a splash of vermilion paint dashed onto his face. Tease him a bit more, and he would put his head down and charge in such a blind, incoherent, roaring fury that his aggression was totally ineffectual, reducing Nichol and me to fits of laughter—and Higgins to tears.

One night Nichol and I were asleep in our dorm, which happened, that term, to be way up near the water tank in the top of the school, almost in the attic. Mr. Parke woke us up. He told us to follow him.

The other four or five boys in the dorm room watched us put on our dressing gowns and follow the Head. I didn't bother with my slippers. Mr. Parke had already stalked out and I didn't dare delay following him. The others seemed to shrink back into their pillows and stare through eyes wide with curiosity, and not a little morbid pleasure, at someone else's dramatic and highly unusual misfortune.

Mr. Parke was young for a headmaster, handsome, tall, and thin, his thick, wiry salt-and-pepper hair divided by an uneven part into a shaggy mop that bounced as he walked. He had dark eyes that— from the point of view of a terrified little boy—seemed piercing. Mr. Parke was wearing a dark green plaid tie, a white shirt, rumpled gray flannel trousers, and a shabby tweed jacket. His golden Labrador retriever Bret pressed against his legs as Mr. Parke walked and always left hair on his trousers.

What on earth could merit this abrupt hauling away in the middle of the night? From time to time during summer term, the Head was known to roust us all out for rollicking midnight swims, but whoever heard of two boys being summoned at this hour? It was winter term. The pool was frozen. And no one could have mistaken

Mr. Parke's equally frozen "Schaeffer, Nichol, come to my study—
at once" as an invitation to anything pleasant.

We walked in near darkness, finding our way by the occasional
glow from some single low-wattage bulb far down a hallway. We
followed Mr. Parke down three flights of narrow, rickety back stairs,
out to a landing, then down the wide, grand staircase to the main
hall. That was a shock. What could this breach of protocol mean?
Expelled? A firing squad?

Striding on legs twice as long as ours, Mr. Parke was far ahead
of us. We began to run after him and then remembered the "no running indoors" rule. No point compounding the trouble we were in.
We slowed to a panicked fast trot.

We found ourselves in the Head's study staring at the usual clut-
ter and trying to avoid Mr. Parke's eyes while we stood at attention
in front of his big Victorian mahogany desk. It was piled high with
papers, open books, letters, and assorted lost and found items: a
cricket bat or two, several air rifles, pens and watches, and two
swords Mr. Parke had recently confiscated from a boy who had
wanted to carry naval cutlasses to class.

"Do you know why you two are here?" Mr. Parke asked.

"No, sir," we replied.

"It came to my attention that you've been bullying Higgins. He
didn't sneak on you. You know I have my sources?"

"Yes, sir."

Indeed we did know. There was no point trying to deny anything—ever. We believed Parke when he said Higgins hadn't told on
us. No one ever sneaked, and also we knew that Mr. Parke knew
everything!

Adam and Eve were never so naked before a just and angry God
as Nichol and I were before Mr. Parke. We stood there praying for
the floor to swallow us. He'd used the word *bullying*. We knew that
we stood accused of the worst crime. We were dead men.

"My sources tell me you two have been winding him up. Is this
true?"

"Yes, sir," we whispered.

"Very well," Parke said quietly. He looked down at a book, opened it, and began to read.

Mr. Parke didn't look up. Nichol and I shifted uneasily. Then, almost as an afterthought: "Stand outside the study door while I decide your fate."

We stepped into the darkened hall. The only illumination came from Mr. Parke's desk lamp. It cast a long square of dim light through the open door and across the black and white marble floor. The rest of the hall was a black void, something that went nicely with the feeling in the pit of my stomach.

We stood silently facing the wall next to the study door—it was always open—shivering in our pajamas and dressing gowns, which provided inadequate protection from the frigid air. The floor felt like ice below my bare feet. The stale, sour mayonnaise smell of the ubiquitous "salad cream" (all-purpose and awful salad dressing) wafted out of the open door of the staff dining room nearby. The hall clock chimed. We didn't speak but exchanged frozen, despairing glances as the doom-laden minutes dragged past. The half hours came and went as the bell on the school clock struck 10:30, then 11:00, then midnight, then 1:00, then 1:30. Legs were numb. Heartbeats slowed. Then he spoke.

"You may come in now."

Blood pumping, heart pounding, we were sure that after so long a wait we'd each get six of the best, trousers—or in this case, pajamas—down.

"Well?" asked Parke, looking up from his book, "How did you enjoy that?"

"Not very much, sir," we mumbled.

Mr. Parke closed his book with a snap and sat back in his chair. He sighed then nodded slowly before he spoke.

"Now you know how Higgins spends his days. You see, you chaps are happy boys. When you get up in the morning, it isn't with a sense of dread. You're expecting a pleasant day. When Higgins gets up, he's expecting unpleasantness. He knows that chaps like you think it's funny to wind him up, to take advantage of the fact that he loses self-control. Well, for him that is a sort of hell. Would you make fun of him if he were a cripple, Schaeffer?"

"No, sir."

His words hit home. No one at the school had ever so much as mentioned my polio and my thin atrophied left leg. This had been a great relief to me, and the shame of my hypocrisy welled up.

"And you, Nichol? Would you fight a boy smaller than yourself, some little chap in First Form?"

"No, sir," Nichol said, and his face flushed. He was powerfully built and tall for his age, a great athlete and one of our best cricket bowlers. The idea of being labeled a big chap who picked on the little chaps was intolerable.

"Well, here's the thing, lads, now you know how Higgins feels not knowing what will happen to him. You've been waiting for several hours not knowing. Not much fun, eh?"

"No, sir."

"What do you think I should do to you chaps?"

"Give us a whacking?" Nichol suggested in a shaky voice.

I cast an involuntary glance in the direction of the school safe. Yes, there it was, the dreaded gym shoe surrounded by dust balls and nestled under the old safe. Mr. Parke almost never actually used it, but the idea of that shoe-of-death hovered in all our brains, the final guarantee of order among 183 boys. Any teacher could get our attention by casually saying, "Would you like to explain this to Mr. Parke?" There was ultimate justice waiting for anyone who pushed his luck.

We expected the fateful, "Fetch the gym shoe." But Mr. Parke was saying something else. "You certainly deserve it, but no, I think that wait was enough."

Heartfelt stunned relief: "Thank you, sir!"

Mr. Parke held out a biscuit tin. We each took one of the slightly stale cookies with trembling fingers. We ate them in silence, solemnly.

Then, brightly smiling, his usual friendly self: "I have a job for you two! From now on I want you to provide Higgins with just as many pleasant surprises as you've given him nasty ones. Mercy, gentlemen! Mercy! Take him along. Change his life! I'm holding you two personally accountable. You are to become his secret guardian angels. And he mustn't know. I don't want to find him alone in the library again. I want to see him coming back from the woods with the whole gang, muddy, happy, and bedraggled as you lot!"

"Yes, sir."

"Words are dreadful weapons, aren't they?"

"Yes, sir."

"Never bully anyone again."

"We won't, sir."

Mr. Parke smiled. He held out his hand. We shook. A handshake was a sacred bond between gentlemen, between men like our Head, men we wanted to be like someday, and be liked by. Higgins's life was about to change for the better.

The wisdom and mercy of our headmaster was what I followed, not a theory. He did not try to convert me to a better way. He *was* the better way. His teaching me didn't depend on my believing what he believed. It depended on his setting an example for me to follow— an example that cost him a night's sleep. Mr. Parke spoke no grand words. He traveled with two scared little boys a few steps down a path to greater kindness, to empathy, to learning to walk in another's shoes. *That* is the purpose driven life.

CHAPTER 10

There Is More in Man Than the Mere Breath of His Body

But he who in self-love shrinks from the touch of love can neither understand it nor summon the courage to venture it, since it means his downfall. Such is then the passion of love; self-love is indeed submerged but not annihilated; it is taken captive.

Philosophical Fragments, Søren Kierkegaard

We Schaeffers believed *in* The Book! We believed in the Bible more than we believed in God. And our interpretation of the Bible wasn't as benign as Chagall's. My parents were kind and compassionate people, but according to their literal interpretation of our official theology, we Schaeffers were part of that mean-spirited vengeful Reformed thread within the Christian tradition that takes every last word of the Bible as a directive from God. Or, even more than that, I think we believed—though we never said—that somehow God lived *in* the Bible and was thus constrained and described

by it. We believed that the Bible explained God's character through
revelation.

Luckily for us Schaeffer children and for all who came in contact
with my parents, Mom and Dad were much better people than their
theology; in fact, they were nicer than the "God of the Bible" they
paid lip service to. Had they lived consistently according to the
Bible's harsher teachings (harsh when they're taken literally, or as
revelation, that is), they would have become monsters serving a god
about whom some very disturbing and highly unlikely stories had
been written.

As regards our official Reformed theology, we *knew* God was
angry with humankind and always had been. He was so angry that
he wrestled with the decision whether to kill all of us in a flood or
to save just one family—Noah's—so that later God could sacrifice
his only son to save everyone descended from the one family he
didn't kill or send them to Hell for eternity.

God did this because Adam and Eve, not to mention Noah's
great, great grandchildren—that's you and me—wouldn't live up to
God's pre-creation expectations. We were a big disappointment to
God, and the "just penalty" was to torture us for eternity. So say
the holders to the demented thread found in both Roman Catholic
and Protestant theology, a form of voyeuristic sadism also found in
other religions, and, I'm sorry to say, in some persons within the
past and present Orthodox Church too. This retributive sadism is
based on a dreary fear of the Lord, not fear in the sense of respect
for but literally "fear of" as in scared of, and this provides more
ammunition for the atheists than they could ever dream up.

When I was two, my parents were kicked out of Champéry, a
small village high up in the Swiss Alps located in the Roman
Catholic canton (state) of Valais. They were expelled because they
"led a local man to Christ." In other words, Mom and Dad convinced him to trust our angry Calvinist Protestant getting-ready-to-
burn-you Jesus as his "savior" rather than to trust his angry Roman

Catholic will-send-unbaptized-babies-to-baby-Hell-bleeding-on-a-cross-forever Jesus.

The local bishop pulled strings with the cantonal authorities and had our family's residency permits revoked. In 1954 we moved across the valley to another little village, called Huémoz, located in the Protestant—and therefore more accommodating to American evangelical/fundamentalist missionaries—canton of Vaud. The Swiss Protestants there were the "wrong sort" Dad said, "theological liberals," but at least they let us stay. That's where my parents started their ministry of L'Abri Fellowship.

Mom and Dad assumed that folding their children into the ministry, volunteering us to share our chalet with strangers who had come to seek the Lord, was fine with us. It wasn't. We Schaeffer children grew up feeling guilty if we didn't use every opportunity to talk about Jesus to the strangers who were invading our house.

I don't think our experience was unique. After she read my memoir, Billy Graham's daughter Ruth wrote to me and said that she had enjoyed the book. She mentioned her childhood memory of visiting our family along with her dad when she and I were both nine. But the line that stuck with me was when Ruth described herself (and the other Graham children) as "sacrificial lambs." I understood her just as she'd understood my book in a special "inside" way.

Children of ministers, and especially those of high-powered celebrity religious leaders, are members of a small and rather strange little club. Faith is complicated enough even if it isn't the family business. Loving God *while* you are selling Him is close to impossible. God is no longer your friend but a job. You are always left feeling guilty, because there is no way to tell when you've done enough witnessing to the "lost." And of course your parents' "call" to serve God trumps their family obligations. The whole family is a "witness" and therefore a showcase for God. And showcases are by nature false. Lifetimes are spent not mentioning (and even covering up) your family's faults as a matter of "duty to God" in the same way that the

military will try to cover up friendly fire deaths as an extension of
some sort of face-saving idea that conflates patriotism with keeping
the military's reputation unblemished. The result is that when it comes
to families involved in "full time ministry," inevitably you live a lie.
And even the lies are lied about because instead of being admitted
they are dressed up like some sort of state secret needed to protect
God via protecting His very fallen—and sometimes downright mad
and/or corrupt representatives—here on earth. After that anything
and everything can be justified, say from burying one's mother in a
place she's begged not to be buried "for the good of the Lord's work,"
to the sort of double standard we maintained in my family wherein
we covered up my father's abuse of my mother, or in my case the several years I spent profiting off "God's work" after I'd stopped believing in right wing Christianity because I liked those right wing
speaking fees and book royalties.

You have no honest conversations either. You are in the same fix
that Dawkins's atheist missionaries will find themselves in: always
waiting to have that meaningful (and manipulative) talk with the
apostates in order to convert them. Like the wearers of Dawkins's
disingenuous A pin, what we Schaeffers were after was not what we
pretended. Conversations had to be *steered* to the desired result.

In other words, our faith made us into well-intentioned two-faced
liars. We weren't really interested in what anyone was saying, just in
what "door" their conversation might "open" through which we
could enter to convert them. If they were already converted, then we
steered the conversation to whatever subject we needed to get to in
order to convince them to adopt a theology closer to ours than to that
of whatever other evangelical/fundamentalist group they were asso-
ciated with. We did this to other believers because we just *knew* that
our brand of Christianity was best. Anyway, if you can't get other believers to join your church or group, how do you "grow"? It wasn't
good enough to believe in Jesus; you had to do it *our* way.

The only reason why I still place my hope in God is that I had
the good fortune to abandon a position of leadership in the evan-

gelical/fundamentalist world when I was still young enough to make a new life. Genie and I lost about two-thirds of our income, which no amount of my secular writing (even though I've been moderately successful, including a stint on *Oprah*) or my movie-directing career in Hollywood (albeit on low-budget movies) ever replaced. I gained something, though: the ability to look in a mirror without cringing. I started to treat Genie and my children better too. Unhappy men serving a weird, angry God make bad husbands, especially if "serving God" provides an excuse for covering up (and thus never dealing with) one's faults in the name of protecting one's ministry. And conversations became conversations rather than evangelistic ploys, as I discovered that other people— even though they might not be like me and might have ideas opposite to mine—sometimes actually have something to say, when you're not just waiting to pounce and deliver a "spiritual" coup de grâce.

Evangelical/fundamentalists who stick with the program are forced to try to reconcile the irreconcilable. They either go nuts— that would be those theologians spending lifetimes writing things like "An Evangelical Manifesto," talking to themselves and to the like-minded about how their impossible (and paranoid) ideas are actually relevant—or they secretly quit believing but don't say so. Given that faith is also their paycheck, and given that nothing terrifies a "professional Christian" like the prospect of having to get a real job, they just keep going through the motions, not only wasting their lives but perhaps also losing their souls if, that is, you buy into their own boilerplate claim that sincere faith is needed in order to be saved.

How does one have faith in God after surviving an evangelical/ fundamentalist background? One place to start discovering faith after the craziness is to try and unpack the misbegotten "foundation" of what amounts to the evangelical madness.

Evangelical/fundamentalists have bought into an idea that my mother used to phrase as a dire warning: "If you pick and choose between verses in the Bible, the whole thing will unravel! If it's not *all true*, none of it is!" Because picking and choosing is what thinking *is*, thinking becomes a threat. Who knows where asking questions might lead? And that is why all so-called evangelical/fundamentalist intellectual activity has such a hollow ring to it. It begins with its "answer" and then twists itself into knots trying to justify the conclusion.

It's as if you were reading a novel and the printer had bound the book wrong and put the last chapter first. All pretense of open inquiry is just that: a pretense. There are no evangelical/fundamentalist intellectuals by definition, because no matter how they dress their work up or spend lifetimes hanging around universities or think tanks, feverishly working to garner a little secular respect, it's all playacting. The "last chapter"—God exists, and Jesus saves and I'll go to Heaven—is already written. Of course, fundamentalist atheists face the same problem. Is there anything that could change their minds?

What the evangelical/fundamentalists won't admit is that all fundamentalists *do* pick and choose, by necessity. So even their claim of consistent belief in the Bible is two-faced. If they didn't pick and choose by omission if not by commission, they'd all be in jail—literally. Seen any adulterers stoned to death in a church? Somewhat less dramatically, but just as tellingly, if you are an evangelical/fundamentalist churchgoer, have you recently heard that Bible verse in Genesis about how "the sons of God saw the daughters of men that they *were* fair; and they took them wives" preached on? What about Sunday school lessons on the following story from Genesis? "There were giants in the earth in those days; and also after that, when the sons of God came in unto the daughters of men, and they bore children to them, the same *became* mighty men which *were* of old, men of renown"? Or have you heard pro-lifers using the example of God killing King David's innocent baby—conceived during David's affair—as an example of God's unconditional love for innocent babies? And why isn't *this* verse on bumper stickers? "If a damsel *that is* a virgin be betrothed unto an husband, and a man find her in the city, and lie with her: Then ye shall bring them both out unto the gate of that city, and ye shall stone them with stones that they may die."

Having elevated the Bible (or at least the nicer bits that they like) to the status of a magic book in which God is trapped and kept somewhat like a tame pet, evangelical/fundamentalists can't admit that the Bible has flaws and is just plain crazy in places. Like a child idealizing an all-too-human father, their world comes crashing down if they admit the truth. Of course, it crashes only because their basic premise was wrong. The point never was to worship a book but to experience God's love.

Why Bible idolatry is a particularly evangelical/fundamentalist blind spot is that, unlike the earlier Christianity (in the more enlightened thread anyway), evangelical/fundamentalist Protestants have forgotten and/or banished the idea that an oral tradition coexisted with the Bible within the life of the Church. They also have forgotten that some of the earliest Christians wrote that God is not to be defined or hedged in by theology, even by descriptions about Him in the Bible.

As I noted before, Evagrius Ponticus summed up this view, exhorting us, "Do not define the Deity: for it is only of things which are made or are composite that there can be definitions." In fact, a whole anti-theology following this train of thought came to be called apophatic theology, or the theology of not knowing, or negative theology. It speaks only about what may *not* be said about God. And this way of perceiving God is found not just in Christianity but in other religions too.

This theology takes a mystical approach related to individual experiences of the Divine beyond ordinary perception. It teaches that the Divine is ineffable, something that can be recognized only when it is felt, then remembered. And therefore all descriptions of this sense will be false, because by definition the experience of God eludes description.

Apophatic descriptions of God acknowledge (1) that neither the existence of God nor nonexistence, as we understand these words in the material world, applies to God, (2) that God is divinely simple and that one should never claim God is "one" or "three" or any "type" of being, (3) that we can't say that God is "wise," because that implies knowledge of what wisdom is on a divine scale, and (4) that to say that God is "good" also limits God to what that word means in the context of human behavior.

Some of the earliest Church Fathers believed that portions of scripture pointed to this apophatic approach. God is said to reveal Himself in a "still small voice." Paul speaks of an "unknown God." Tertullian said, "That which is infinite is known only to itself." St. Cyril of Jerusalem says, "For we may not explain what God is but candidly confess that we have not exact knowledge concerning Him." Clement of Alexandria, Gregory of Nyssa, John Chrysostom, and Basil the Great all spoke of God in apophatic terms. And of course the Hindu scriptures also reflect an apophatic view, as do some traditions within Islam.

This might be called the humble thread that runs through many religions parallel to the deadly we-know-it-all thread of theological hubris. And yes, this is very different from the idea of the "revelation of God's character" through an "inspired" scripture, where God, as if writing a memoir dictated to scribes, "reveals" Himself. The apophatic thread has existed in Christian and Jewish thinking side-by-side with the literal and fundamentalist thread. The point isn't to say which is correct (though I have my druthers!) but to note that even people who want to stick by original or ancient ways of Jewish and/or Christian beliefs have choices.

One reason why the evangelical/fundamentalists are so defensive about the Bible is that they know all too well that the Bible can be used to say anything once you begin using it to try to define the Deity as revealed therein. They know this because of the thousands of splits in their denominations that shatter again and again into ever-smaller fragments. They know this because they have grown up hearing the Bible used to justify as "God's will" things that are wrong, crazy or even evil in the personal context of believers using the Bible to justify their actions. "But the Bible says that we need to put the Lord first, and what could be a greater witness to future generations than this theme park and a visit to Ruth and Billy's grave? Just think how many will be saved . . . " or, "But the Bible says women are to submit to men. That is why Daddy has to hit Mommy sometimes."

Nearly all evangelical groups have split at one time or another because one person decided he or she had a better, truer interpretation of some Bible passage regarding God's revelation of Himself through the Bible. These fights are often incredibly petty. For instance, my parents split from one group over the burning issue of the timing of the return of Christ. Would Jesus snatch away all believers in the Rapture *before* or *after* the "Tribulation?" I can't remember which side they were on, because this happened in my early childhood. But I know the conflict left bitter scars.

Sometimes the differences between evangelical/fundamentalists are less of a joke. Not so very long ago, one set of American preachers used the pro-slavery verses in the Bible to uphold slavery. Another group used the verses on love and compassion to fight slavery. They were reading the same Bible. They all believed that their Bible, including what it said about slavery, was their sole means to understand God. Many had been to the same seminaries. And there is no reason to believe that both sets of preachers weren't intelligent and sincere. In other words, religion embodies the paradox of human existence: Good and evil duke it out in the arena of religion too, just as they do in the rest of life, and the Bible is often nothing but the handy pretext.

Recognizing that paradox is *the way things are* is about more than theological conflicts. Science (grudgingly) embraces paradox too. Take, for example, what seems to be the contradiction between Einstein's proven Theory of General Relativity and Quantum Mechanics. The first theory holds that if you know the initial conditions of a physical system with absolute certainty, then you can know the future outcome of the system you are modeling. Theoretically, then, everything in the universe is as predictable as the speed of light—if you have enough information. The second theory (Quantum Mechanics) says that you can never know the initial conditions exactly and also that you can't know what will happen in the future of any physical system. You can only know, to a greater or lesser extent, the *probability* of something happening because, for instance, some particles can be in two places at once. Quantum Mechanics might be described as the apophatic science of uncertainty.

Although this apophatic paradox is recognized in science, it nevertheless makes physicists nervous in the same way that apophatic theology makes some Christians nervous. "If we can't *know*," they all seem to say, "then how can we KNOW?!" I picture Charlie Brown screaming "*Arrrrg!*" yet again, as Lucy snatches away the football and he falls on his back. Another placekick foiled! Another certainty undone!

There is a lot work going on to try to marry the theories of General Relativity and Quantum Mechanics in some grand unified theory. But for now, either we don't know enough to find one "theory of everything," or such a theory can't ever be found. Maybe randomness and predictability exist side by side in a way our minds can't reconcile without suffering the fate of Homer Simpson when Bart triumphantly exclaimed, "Cool, I broke his brain!"

But if we embrace paradox as *the actual way of life* and embrace the paradox of apophatic theology as *the essence of faith in God*, then hope in God comes into focus. Maybe we can even learn, grow, change our minds, and evolve without worrying about everything unraveling. Maybe the point is that if we can stop relying on our trust in a *system* to hold that "ball" of certainty steady and just stop trying so hard, we will be more likely to succeed in making our peace with paradox.

Embracing paradox—in other words, admitting the truth of our limits—is not good enough for many people, though, especially for pastors, religious leaders, and/or the New Atheists earning a living by selling certainty. They feed a public who crave lifetime warranties. Churches, seminaries, Dawkins's website, and other bastions of fundamentalism will not keep the pay checks coming if you stand up and say, "I could be, and, given the odds, probably am, wrong," let alone "I can only *know* what I *don't* know!"

The public that evangelical/fundamentalist religion and the New Atheists cater to want to believe that there *really are* knives that will never need sharpening! They want that "lifetime warranty," never mind that deep down they know that there is nothing that can hold an edge without sharpening, no matter what the theological or philosophical or scientific equivalent of the "amazing knife set offer" for "just three easy payments of only $19.95" claims. But as Darwin discovered, claims of absolute truth, without a nod to inconsistency, are made to be abandoned.

"There is more in man than the mere breath of his body," Darwin said. Later, he renounced that mystical spiritual idea after he lost his religious faith. He abandoned faith in God after the death of his beloved daughter, and because he had come to distrust a literal interpretation of the Bible. Like many Victorians, he came to distrust the Bible as a book that condoned "the dreaded doctrine of eternal Hell," as he put it.

In *History, Humanity and Evolution* (a collection of essays he edited in 1989), James R. Moore writes,

> The circumstances under which Darwin came at last to reject Christianity were full of pain. . . . Intellectual considerations weighed heavily with him, but his decisive objection was moral. Rewards and penalties took place in the present life, not another. The loss of [his daughter] Annie in 1851 was the point of no return. . . . The perfect child, a vengeful God Christianity broke on the back of a conundrum.

The reason why Darwin believed that his theory of evolution negated Christian belief also had a lot to do with the Anglican so-called

natural theology (that I mentioned in Chapter 6). In *Natural The-*
ology Evidences of the Deity, Collected from the Appearances of
Nature, William Paley wrote, "Does one man in a million know how
oval frames are turned? Ignorance of this kind exalts our opinion
of the unseen and unknown artist's skill, if he be unseen and unknown, but raises no doubt in our minds of the existence and agency
of such an artist." Darwin came up with an alternative explanation even while at first drawing on the same tradition—when he still
had some idea of a design—to explain his new biology of adaptation by natural selection.

Although he lost faith in Christian doctrine per se, Darwin was
nevertheless a theist at the time he wrote *On the Origin of Species*,
evincing a belief in some sort of design visible in creation. Eventually he came to doubt design and purpose altogether and wound up
as an agnostic. Given the choices Darwin was presented with, a literalistic, angry, vengeful, religion on the one hand and a flawed design theory or faith in reason on the other, he made the only sane
choice. But I think there is a better alternative: Take the sum total
of human experience, discount it by a wide margin because we *know*
we'll never know, take the one overarching lesson from reality—
humility—to heart, and move forward together.

I believe Darwin was right: We are animals. I believe Jesus was
right: We are animals *plus*. "Man does not live by bread alone."

Where it seems to me that Darwin was mistaken was in thinking
he had to make a choice between these two ways of seeing what we
humans are and, more importantly, *can become* if we choose to. I
think that, unfortunately, Darwin was looking at Christian teaching only in the past tense and as "history," rather than as a moral
lesson about *moral evolution* that is timeless.

The best way to understand Darwin and Jesus, I believe, is to
look to the example Jesus set in the context of the reality of evolution. Jesus demonstrated by example that selflessness is the door to
redemption. Darwin gave us the tools to understand that existence
is not static, predestined, or fixed. Can we take Darwin's liberating

truth and Jesus's selfless example and *choose* to shape our next step of moral evolution accordingly? I hope so.

If we are to survive as a species, it will take faith in evolution, *and* faith in our ability to change and adapt, *and* a willingness to sacrifice for each other to overcome the destruction we have wrought on our planet and against one another. If religion is to help rather than hinder that process, then it must grasp the apophatic tradition available within itself and reject the false and cruel "certainties" that coexist with it.

The point is not to argue over how we got here but to agree on a better vision of *where* we want to evolve to now, not just physically but also ethically. *That* is a project that we believers, and we agnostics and we atheists, can and should agree on. We don't have to "fit" our ideas about how we perceive things together in order to work together. We can be the same "particle" but exist in two places at once.

St. Maximos's teaching about the Church and the Eucharist expresses the idea of accepting paradox that I'm trying to get at. Maximos lived in the sixth and seventh centuries and was a monk, a theologian, and a scholar. Maximos says that "lovers of God" are granted to see with inner eyes "the Word and God Himself." Maximos might be describing many an African American church service, or the Orthodox liturgy, or even a meeting of young mothers at a breast-feeding group. Maximos teaches that the soul is granted to "see the Word," who leads it to the spiritual understanding that is "immaterial, simple, immutable, divine, free of all form and shape." In other words, authentic spiritual apophatic experience is the exact opposite of intellectually organized theology, and of "fact" and "history." And biblical "revelation"—just as is mother love—isn't about books on the subject but is expressed in those moments of tenderness that transcend description and are seen with inner eyes. (That is one reason that many of the Fathers of the early monastic tradition put forth the idea that true theology is prayer, rather than intellectual ideas.)

Through "the spiritual kiss," Maximos says, the soul comes to the Word of God, because it gathers to itself the words of salvation. The declaration in the Liturgy "One is holy, one is Lord," chanted by all the people, represents the gathering *beyond understanding*.

What are examples of seeing with our inner eyes? To me it's losing myself within an African American congregation where all are singing as one in the Spirit. It's found in the instant recognition between young mothers as they pass each other holding their children, when each mother is so filled with love for her child that both mothers instantly empathize with the other. It's the "Ranger Creed" shouted by young Rangers at their graduation ceremony after the month-long "indoctrination" training as these young warriors prepare to become members of the fabled 75th Ranger Regiment, ready to lay down their lives for our country. In one mighty voice they shout their creed, one line of which is "I will never leave a fallen comrade!"

According to Maximos, the distribution of the sacrament is participation in the divine life, "and in this way men and women also may be called gods by grace." The call by the priest as he summons believers to partake of communion, "With fear of God, faith and love draw near," indicates that salvation is a journey dependent *not* on "right thinking" but on *love*, which is what the fear of the God, who cannot be described, *is*. The Rangers do not say that they will rescue only a fallen comrade who has the right ideas, whose skin is the right color, whom they personally like, or who goes to their church. The promise of faithfulness is unconditional, based only on faith and love.

As the congregants in African American churches clap, sing, or solemnly process, or as new Rangers put on their hard-won tan berets for the first time at their graduation ceremony, or as mothers push a stroller through the park and wave to other mothers, we *are* liturgy. We *are* "faith and love drawing near." We *are* all vowing to "fight on . . . though I be the lone survivor," along with those Rangers. We have love, as Maximos says, and love is God's gift. We see this not with our eyes but *with inner eyes*. It is revealed to us not in a book, but *through our experience*. It is the revelation we have been waiting for and evolving toward. It is the *reason* we are here. It is our destiny. It is our purpose. It is our hope. That's my hope, anyway.

The God of love is in that rolling thunder pouring from a Hammond B-3 electric organ, providing the heart-stopping link that holds together so much luminous black gospel music. The God of love is in the perfume of clouds of incense at the Orthodox midnight Easter service as we shout "Christ is risen!" The God of love is in those first imperishable notes on Miles Davis's album *Kind of Blue*. The God of love is in the tender way Lucy lays her cheek on mine and we cling to each other for dear life as this speck of a spaceship we call Earth hurtles into the vast unknown.

A certain sort of note, musical phrase, facial expression, or whiff of perfume can convey emotion and insight even if that feeling can't be described. Is it any less real or true because it is seen only with our inner eyes?

Why does Suk's *Serenade for Strings* evoke such pangs of loving tragedy? Why did it evoke that feeling in me *before* I read that the music was composed as a tribute to Suk's beloved wife Otilka, who died so young? How did I *know* what the music *meant* before I "knew"? Why did it make me think of Genie and of my love for her? Why did it make me feel mournful even before I read Suk's biography? Why did the sound of those young voices shouting the Ranger Creed bring tears of gratitude to my eyes?

Yes, I know, there are studies on music and emotion, brain waves and responses. For instance, using magnetic resonance technology, researchers at Dartmouth College mapped the area of the brain that processes melodies; it is known as the rostromedial prefrontal cortex. But those studies probe the how, not the why, of the deep satisfaction we have when experiencing emotional empathy in nonverbal or even preverbal communication with a composer through his or her music. The scientists tell us *how* brains work, but not *what we are* when we become one with Mahalia Jackson as she lifts up her gorgeous voice and sings "Every Time I Feel the Spirit."

The smell of incense, the sound of Byzantine chant in Greek—in a language I don't speak—the glitter of an old icon in a darkened church, the voices of a gospel choir, the heartfelt cry of young warriors "speak" to me in nonverbal, nonintellectual ways. At those moments I'm not visiting a black church as a white man, I'm not visiting Fort Benning and the Rangers, nor am I trying to figure out what the Greek chant "means." I am not *doing* anything at all. I am *being* human. And I believe I am experiencing God.

Lucy will not remember my bonding with her in terms of "On Wednesday, May 3, 2009, at 4:23 P.M., my grandfather put a blanket on the kitchen table, and while I lay there, he rubbed my hands and feet and made me smile and I felt dreamy, happy, and secure and Suk was playing in the background." Nonetheless Lucy's memories will be retained in some part of her brain that makes her feel closer to me than to strangers.

The liturgical ritual of bonding with her grandfather will not be lost. Memory is not shaped by a series of born-again moments, let alone correct intellectual beliefs. Rather, it's built on thousands of small, repeated steps in a seamless journey to infinity. If you want to understand the power of repeated actions—the learning curve implied by the *doing* of liturgy, of *doing* and *being*, rather than merely *saying* and *thinking*—then watch (or watch again) the film *Groundhog Day*. It's one of the most powerful statements of what spirituality *is*.

A stranger coming into an unfamiliar church sees only what is happening that day: The old priest shuffles along, maybe a few people straggle in, a sketchy choir feebly sings. The person who grew up in that tradition and that community, repeating the process again and again (à la Bill Murray in *Groundhog Day*), "sees" and "hears" with inner eyes and ears. He or she sees every service he or she attended, his or her grandfather's funeral, the many midnight services, the friends no longer present, the sons and daughters who were blessed by pastor and people before they left for war, and who were mourned when they did not return. That liturgy is not just one particular Sunday service to that person, and it is not happening in one time or place. Rather, it's a lifetime made sacred and remembered as it is lived in the eternal present.

Love doesn't depend on remembering facts. I can still love my mother and be loved by her, even if both of us would fail a written test with questions such as "When was the first time you understood a story you were reading about love?" or "Explain the principal psychological attributes of maternal love." The connections of love can be rekindled too. Sometimes angels visit one last time.

On a bright morning in the fall of 2007, Mrs. Parke walked into Genie's and my sunroom. The Parkes had arrived the evening before for their visit to Genie and me—also their first visit to America.

In her crisp, upper-crust British accent—its tone of authority undiminished—Mrs. Parke pronounced the view of our lawn, the marsh with its dense carpet of shimmering marsh grasses, and the swiftly flowing Merrimack River "magnificent." This wasn't just a polite guest-to-host comment. It was also a "Well done!" offered to one of Mrs. Parke's old boys for succeeding well enough—in spite of many dire predictions—to own a house at all, let alone one with a view.

In October, daylight fades early north of Boston. By the time Mr. and Mrs. Parke got to my house the evening before, it was already dark. The morning dawned clear. The maples outside the kitchen windows were at their peak of autumn color, a vivid, fiery red. The river sparkled. The sky was gold on the horizon, changing to a dark cobalt blue above.

Mrs. Parke was ensconced among the hibiscus, two rosemary bushes, and the bay tree in our sunroom. She was drinking the tea I'd prepared. I was fervently hoping that years of American shortcuts with tea wouldn't betray me. Had I correctly remembered the steps she taught us when I was on kitchen duty? "Warm the pot, pour out the warming water, add the tea, pour in the boiling water, let it steep. *That* is *how* it's done!"

That first morning of her visit, the eighty-year-old Mrs. Parke was perched on the edge of her chair looking like some fierce little bird, bright brown eyes shining, her thick steel gray hair swept back into the tight bun that I remembered so well crowning her diminutive wiry figure. Maybe it was the disconcertingly steady way Mrs. Parke met my glance, but diminutive or not, over forty years later, she still exuded the no-nonsense, cast-iron will that I so clearly remembered. I felt a twinge of the old awe.

Eunice—"Mrs. Parke" to me, no matter how old I've grown or how many times she has told me to call her Eunice—was as pretty as ever. If elves had wives that got older but never faded, Mrs. Parke looked the way I imagine they would look. She also still seemed restless, as if she didn't like to sit in one place too long. And she still didn't hesitate to make slightly judgmental observations: "There really is *no need* to fuss so! One sort of marmalade would have done splendidly!" She had kept her ascetic habits too.

The first morning of the visit when Mrs. Parke took her shower, I noticed that it lasted under two minutes. It seemed to me that she emerged from the bathroom just seconds after I heard the water turn off, dressed and ready for the day. She strode into the kitchen wearing a tweed skirt, a white blouse, and a gray cardigan that could have been the same outfit I last saw, through tears, when I was saying goodbye to her (I was thirteen) at the end of my last day at her school. I apologized for still being in my pajamas. "Nonsense, I used to bathe you!" Mrs. Parke answered.

So she had, while presiding over our Wednesday and Saturday bath-night ritual. She kept order while we—the thirty or so boys assigned to the big middle-floor bathroom—hopped in and out of the four ancient, cast-iron claw-foot tubs that sat in a row on the cracked linoleum. We, the shivering throng, shared the lukewarm two-inch-deep murky water. It was changed only after three of us had bathed, one after the other. Being first to bathe was coveted.

We didn't mind the filth left by others, but we did dread how fast the water went from tepid to cold. Complaints ("It's gone cold, Mrs. Parke!") were swiftly countered. ("Hot water costs money!")

In the spring of 2007 I'd visited the Parkes in England. That's when I reconnected with them. There had been a note or two, and I'd kept track of the Parkes through friends. All along I thought that sooner or later I'd run into them again. Then it hit me: I wasn't going to just "run into them." I booked a flight to London. I didn't tell the Parkes that the only reason I was coming to England was that I wanted to see them and make sure I had a chance to thank them. I said that I'd be "in the area." Might I "drop by"?

They invited me to stay. For three days we took walks accompanied by their rescued greyhound "Lady," made a memorable Sunday visit to their small Anglican church overlooking the East Sussex downs, and spent hours sitting together in their cozy living room in the cottage they'd retired to.

Mrs. Parke told me a tellingly funny story about how, when my father went to Great Walstead to look it over before I was sent there, the only question he asked the Parkes was on their "view of Karl Barth." Barth was a liberal Swiss Protestant Reformed theologian with whom my dad was obsessed. To Dad he represented everything terrible about the "direction of liberalism." (Barth had embraced a non-literal view of the Bible.) So there Dad was, about to drop off a practically illiterate ten-year-old son at a real school at last—a son that he'd managed to somehow not bother with educating because he'd been so busy with the "Lord's work"—and all Dad was interested in was the headmaster's theological correctness and his view of Barth!

"I really couldn't quite believe it," Mrs. Parke said and began to laugh. "He asked nothing about the teachers, just asked that odd question, and I had the distinct feeling that had I said I liked Barth who, by the way, I hadn't the foggiest idea about—he'd have been on the next train to London and we'd never have seen you at the school. At the time I remember thinking that his son had rather more urgent concerns. Given the fact that you could barely write your name, I didn't think it likely that you'd be reading much Barth!"

In the evenings we watched Mrs. Parke's favorite DVDs of Mozart operas. I'd forgotten how much she knew about, and loved, Mozart.

Before I left I invited them to visit us in the States. To my surprise they accepted.

Almost fifty years before I served Mrs. Parke breakfast in my sunroom, as a new boy at GW, my problem was simple: How to act normal in boarding school? It would have to be an act, because normal boys didn't think about being normal. They didn't think about anything. They just were. I just *wasn't*.

Other boys were boys. I was a country of one. They were waiting for the next holiday and making plans about what to do on Saturday afternoon. I was waiting for the return of Christ and making plans about surviving the Last Judgment. They could all read well and knew Latin. I sounded out words and couldn't spell anything.

I didn't know that Mrs. Parke would conspire with God (and opera) to save me. She put me in three operas and, during my last term, gave me the role of the evil Count in *The Marriage of Figaro*. She made me a star! She made me *count!* Because of her vote of confidence, I decided that maybe I could learn to read better, maybe even do math. Who knew, perhaps I could even become like the other chaps.

We sat watching a fabulous production of *Figaro* that had been recorded in Covent Garden at the Royal Opera House the year before "the best ever," Mrs. Parke declared it. Almost half a century after I had unsteadily warbled my lines in the school dining room, while marching around the tiny stage dressed in the costume designed and sewn by Matron and her assistants, Mrs. Parke reached out and took my hand and said, "You were really quite good in that production."

"Thank you for giving me a chance," I said.

She must have known what I really meant, because she gave my hand an extra tight squeeze and answered, "Don't worry, you've done splendidly."

You *can* go home again.

I have no argument, vocabulary, or intellectual system with which to prove that love exists. I don't need an argument. Mrs. Parke saw me with inner eyes, and even decades later she could answer my thoughts. My atheist friends will win every argument with me about how they believe that love is just one more chemical reaction taking place in the brain and how researchers have found that oxytocin is involved in the bonding of male and the female prairie voles. Like humans, voles form bonds with each other that last. End of argument; we, like the voles, are nothing! *Fine!* But why was one boy with a lousy voice, to whom it took twice as long as the other boys to teach anything, given a chance to sing?

If love is "just a chemical," so is whatever motivates the researchers who declared this a fact. Does that invalidate the results of their research? I don't think so. Rather, it puts their science in perspective. Paradoxes should not be resolved but celebrated. Love will still be something real when I am dust and—God willing—Lucy is ninety-four years old, forgetting everything she knew, including that I existed. Even if she doesn't remember me, she will be a different person because I loved her.

I will love the Parkes when they are gone. They may never meet Lucy, but each book I read her aloud is my tribute to them. This book is a tribute to them too, as are the novels by this grown-up boy who could barely read so he was taught to sing instead. And once he did that, he gained the confidence to learn other skills that, years later, led "the worst speller this school has ever seen, my lad" to become a writer. Lucy's children may never know the Parkes' names. But if my great, great grandchildren remember what was passed down to my children by me, and then on to them, they will live in homes where people are given second chances for reasons that can't be explained.

CHAPTER 11

That "Truth Button" Should Humble Everyone

So also with the Paradox in its relation to the Reason, only that the passion in this case has another name; or rather, we must seek to find a name for it.

Philosophical Fragments, Søren Kierkegaard

Our thirty-eighth anniversary was golden. We were in New York City. Genie and I took the M-4 bus to the Cloisters and then ended our day in Central Park watching Shakespeare's *Cymbeline* performed in the open air. The Cloisters is an extension of the Metropolitan Museum of Art. It's perched at the top end of Manhattan, literally at the top of the island (if north is "up" and south is "down"). The Cloisters sits on a high, rocky promontory and overlooks the Hudson River. The museum was built from various bits and pieces of medieval monasteries and churches that were carted back to America from all over Europe, rebuilt, and then filled with art.

Genie and I visited our favorites: the garden with "our" four quince trees surrounded by beautifully kept little plots of herbs;

"our" fifteenth-century boxwood "Standing Virgin and Child" carved by Gerheart von Leiden, and Robert Campin's fifteenth-century *Annunciation* triptych, where Joseph sits at his workbench making mousetraps. These art objects are ours because we've been going to the Cloisters for years. That has been possible because there has been a continuity to our relationship. That continuity was not planned. It isn't reasonable. It's an unreasonable paradoxical mistake.

If being rational is the key to success and to truth, then somehow Genie and I missed the lesson. Our marriage is one of those sorts of "mistakes" that Robert Altman said he depended on to make good movies.

Only a few weeks after Genie got to L'Abri—she was traveling in Europe as a high school graduation gift from her parents in 1969—we were practically living together. Yes, I know, that's strange considering that the context of our fornication was an evangelical/fundamentalist mission, but this *was* "the sixties," and the place was overrun with long-haired backpackers. Besides, in spite of their theology, my parents were not prudes, and on top of that they seemed to have forgotten I existed.

Because all the dorms at L'Abri were full, Genie was staying in a rented room half a mile down the road in the village. When Genie walked to our chalet, if it had been snowing in the night, she sometimes passed the words "*I Love Genie*" stomped out in giant letters on the fresh snow. I made these passionate hillside billboards by moonlight during my walks home, after spending most of the night in Genie's room.

All those talks by Mom about ovaries and the seed and the egg did no good. The only part I'd retained was the part about how good sex is. Mom was right about that. I got Genie pregnant, but not for a while, not until almost a year later.

Early in 1970 I was in New York having my first art show (at the now closed Frisch gallery). Genie attended the opening. Then she called a friend and asked her to sneak into her parent's bedroom back in San Mateo and get her passport and send it to New York.

You see, Genie had gone home at last, after having disobeyed her parents by staying in Europe with me for the better part of a year, instead of going to college. (Her original trip was supposed to last only a few weeks. Genie had stopped at L'Abri by chance when her older sister Pam, who was traveling with her, wanted to visit a friend.) Then Genie had gone home, briefly, and then flown to New York to visit me only ten days later. She decided—after I begged her to never leave me again—that she'd made a mistake going home at all and would stay with me. Ten days later, and against the wishes of her parents, Genie, aided and abetted by my parents, got aboard the *Leonardo Da Vinci* of the Italia Line.

We sailed out of New York harbor after my show's opening and headed back to Europe. My parents accommodated Genie because they liked her. Of course, they also helped her because she'd become born-again. She was now "saved" and no longer like her "heathen" Roman Catholic parents, who, from our evangelical/fundamentalist point of view, weren't "real Christians."

Thus Mom and Dad helped eighteen-year-old Genie disobey her parents, skip college, and break her parents' hearts—all because my parents didn't approve of Catholics, and Genie was now "one of us." So my parents' loyalty to Genie as a "fellow believer" trumped whatever common sense they had, much less courtesy to her parents, who might tempt Genie away from her newfound faith. Best of all—in the juicy details department—my dad (bless him!) used his first royalty check from his first bestselling evangelical book *Escape from Reason* to pay for Genie's ticket!

During the voyage Genie discovered her period was late. So actually I must have gotten her pregnant about a month before in Europe. All mistakes. All bad. All things *I do not want my children or grandchildren to do*—ever! And nuts too, given that my parents' rationale for helping Genie more or less elope with their *seventeen-year-old* (!) son was a theological "reason" that was in direct moral conflict with their theological beliefs about sex before marriage.

And yet, this happy combination of fornication, nutty theology, teenage lust, a stolen passport, and art shows ended up just the way these things are supposed to *not* to end up: with a couple in their fifties, in love and wandering around New York some thirty-nine years later with their third grandchild waiting back at home, and with Genie and me long since reconciled with her sweet and forgiving parents. Go figure.

If my children did what we did to Genie's parents, I'd go ballistic. I think we were wrong. That said, what would I change about our sexual activities, my parents' bizarre complicity, Genie lying to her mother and father, and an unplanned pregnancy at the worse time imaginable?

Nothing!

Any other egg in Genie's ovary and any other sperm carelessly contributed by me would not have become Jessica. The world would be unthinkable without my daughter in it. And the world would be unthinkable without *her* children, Amanda and Benjamin, in it. And the world would be empty and gray without my sons Francis and John. And the world would be poorer if I hadn't known Jessica's husband Dani Stromback, a kind and talented composer, great father, and terrific musician whose inspired piano compositions I am enjoying on his latest CD (*For Sleepless Nights*) at this moment as I write. And then there are Lucy and her mother Becky, who knocks on my office door every morning and carries her baby to me in what amounts to a second sunrise. Change anything—the sex, the lies, the crazy theology, the timing, the betrayal of two sets of parents, the betrayal of one set of parents by another set of parents, *anything*—and my life evaporates.

How can this paradoxical, contradictory, amoral way of looking at life be okay? From the evangelical/fundamentalist point of view, what Genie and I did was sinful. From the rationalistic point of view of modern psychology, science, or just your average high school councilor, what we did was wrong. What advice do you think Planned Parenthood would have given us?

Science? Reason? Planning? Rationality? Moral behavior? Smart behavior? Good choices? No. *Grace, mystery, love,* and (above all) *embracing paradox* are what count. And that paradox, that truth button, that grace, should humble everyone who thinks she or he has correct ideas about the way things *should* be, *must* be, *ought* to be, *have* to be—either "according to the latest scientific studies" *or* according to "what the Bible says." With all due respect to Dawkins, mystery trumps everything. With all due respect to the theologians, every true story begins with the words "In spite of what I thought at the time. . . . "

Why do I love Genie now? Because I do.

Of course, I can come up with "reasons" for our love after having been together for almost forty years. She's beautiful, she makes sex sweet, she's familiar, she's reassuring and kind, generous, forgiving, a force to be reckoned with when stirred to anger, the mother of our children, the grandmother of our grandchildren, my best friend, smart, well read, and humble and we both love the same art. Did I *know* any of that when I had sex with her when we were teens? Of course not. She wasn't that person then, either. I don't know who she was. I don't even know who that young man was who got her pregnant.

And *that* is the way real life is. And *that* is how we "decide" all the important questions in our lives: We never know anything. Life happens. We learn as we experience living and learn from living. My son Francis was headed into a foreign policy career after a stellar performance at the Georgetown School of Foreign Service. He took a temporary job at his old high school. One year slipped into the next. Francis didn't know it at the time, but he'd just stumbled into his beloved vocation as a teacher. He's a great teacher, now in his twelfth year at that school, and can't imagine another life. A chance temporary job led to a wonderful and purpose-filled career.

It's only regarding unimportant stuff, such as buying major appliances, that we can go online and find out the "facts." When it comes to the person we spend our lives with, or having babies, or careers we end up killing ourselves for, or life-altering snap judgments like volunteering for military service, let alone the friends we meet and make and keep, we shoot the rapids, take our chances, and improvise. We learn as we do, not as we think about doing.

And that is how faith in God is too. Sure, we who believe (or try to) have "reasons," mostly made up after the fact, like my reasons for falling in love that I've discovered in hindsight. But the truth is that Genie was there, I was there, and it happened. The truth is also that we either experience God or we don't. And just as in a marriage, once we have experienced God, we either choose to work to maintain that relationship or let it fade. In that sense we can choose to believe, just as on days when I'd rather be sleeping with another woman, I choose to stay married.

What does this prove? Nothing, except that people who tell you that you must choose between rational intellectual systems and faith in God are lying.

Visiting the Cloisters makes a point about the way things *are*, as opposed to all our ideas *about* the way they *should* be. It makes a point about choosing to believe once we have experienced God based on the sort of life we want and the sort of world we want to create for ourselves and others.

Robert Campin's painting is displayed in a room decorated with pieces of furniture and pottery reminiscent of the Flemish rooms in which Campin placed Mary, the angel, and Joseph. Joseph's shop shutters are in the up position in Campin's painting, and if you look closely, you can see the rust marks below the nails from all the many years they've been exposed to the weather on the town square of the oddly Flemish Nazareth. Mary receives word from the angel. The ubiquitous lily stirs in the breeze as the Holy Spirit wafts into the room, while the painting's patrons kneel outside, anticipating their eternal reward for having had the good sense to pay Campin for this fine triple-panel devotional work.

The Hudson flows far below the museum's ramparts and shimmers as seen through the leaded windows set in the thick stone walls.

Across the wide river there is nothing visible but trees. The view is unspoiled, almost as the Native Americans would have seen it before the Dutch (and then the British) colonists killed them. There is no hint that you are in a huge city.

Nelson Rockefeller bought the land visible from the Cloisters on the opposite bank. Thus visitors can lose themselves in another time and place, with no reminders of the modern world. The only fly in the ointment is one Roman Catholic convent that would not sell to Rockefeller. (Rockefeller wanted to have it pulled down.) The Catholics held out, so the pristine view is very slightly adulterated by the sight of this one neo-Victorian building about a mile away.

Faith in God, hope of an afterlife, belief in a balancing of the books of justice—the scent of Heaven is thick and sweet in the Cloisters, exuded from the spirit of monasticism and prayer and of the contemplative art on display. The monks who walked on these bits and pieces of transplanted stone, past these columns, and under these arches would be pleased. Their spirit, disjointed and reassembled in the Cloisters as it may be, lives.

Score one for the Middle Ages!

Science may have proved the monks' fondest beliefs about the cosmos to be wrong, but the monks win aesthetically, hands down. Children behave well in the Cloisters. People talk quietly. The Met's handpicked scholars who lead tours of incredible quality, especially when hosting school groups, can't avoid giving a lesson about Christianity and Judaism in order to explain the art. They become the long-dead monks' evangelistic accomplices because of the power of the worldview pervading every inch of the space, from Campin's painting to the Unicorn tapestries (the Unicorn represents Christ) to the tombs where each carved object has a symbolic spiritual meaning. Turning the sacred architecture and art into mere artifacts has not stripped them of the ghosts of faith.

A New Atheist who believes in a linear progress of history from lesser to greater enlightenment has a lot of explaining to do in the Cloisters. Why is the "logical" architecture of so many American high schools able to do no more than produce buildings that look and feel like prisons? Why did these monks, with all their "dumb" ideas, make buildings wherein one feels peaceful? Clean water, street lights, and MRIs are wonderful, but not all movement has been in a forward direction. Present most people with the courtyards at the Cloisters, then show them a Bauhaus-derived, mid-twentieth-century "logical" apartment labyrinth in London, New York, or Berlin, and ask them where they feel more comfortable. Standing under the Cloisters' arches is a good place to argue that some things were done better in the religion-steeped past.

That evening in Central Park, Genie and I joined a happy crowd of about three hundred people, including many delighted children, sitting or standing or lying on lawns and rock outcroppings or propped against tree trunks. We were watching that outstanding performance of *Cymbeline* that we had stumbled on. The actors had to shout their lines to be heard by the widely scattered throng, but they managed to give subtle performances nonetheless, reflecting the depth of talent available in New York and the skill of Stephen Burdman, the New York Classical Theatre's director and his remarkable talent for staging outdoor productions. For the last half-hour of the play, fireflies twinkled and flitted in the twilight. Children were chasing them on the edges of the crowd. Woody Allen in his most romantic Manhattan-is-Heaven mood could not have portrayed the park as more iconic.

Genie's face lights up with childlike expectation whenever she sees fireflies. To her they are more than luminous little insects; they spark luminous memories of her childhood visits to a beloved grandmother in Arkansas. She also loves Central Park, and she'll walk there on any pretext. Genie loves Shakespeare's comedies too. It was the best anniversary we've ever had.

Genie never looked lovelier than she did watching that play. Of course, she looks different from the eighteen-year-old I first met. I've tired her out, and some wrinkles (and lots of sweet laugh lines) are there to prove it. But Genie is my best friend, and she loves fireflies.

She still chases them in our garden. She is funny too. I'm not saying that Genie has removed death's sting, but Genie has made me less afraid of getting old.

Cliché or not, she's shown me that some things do get better with time—love, for one thing. That's because these days we really know each other. So our love is founded on the many times we've forgiven each other or, to be honest, the few times I've forgiven Genie's rare stumbles and the many, many, many times she's forgiven me.

CHAPTER 12

How Do Spiritual Catalysts Work?

The ethical is the universal, and as such it is again the divine.

Fear and Trembling, Søren Kierkegaard

We all need someone to focus our minds on what matters. For me that someone has been Genie. Call her my catalyst, something like the obelisk in Stanley Kubrick's film *2001: A Space Odyssey*. The apes (that would be me) discover, gingerly approach, and finally touch and gather around the obelisk that has mysteriously appeared in their midst. This foreign object stirs them into a frenzy of curiosity and creativity. It changes their behavior. Outside intervention is the essential missing ingredient for the apes' next evolutionary step, both biological and spiritual. It sparks a new level of consciousness that they could not have arrived at alone. (Okay, I know they then club each other senseless, but I'm editing that out of my metaphor!)

What was the obelisk-like intervention that began life on earth? Let's assume that a meteor strike generated the heat, gases, and molecular changes that set the stage for life. One hypothesis is that life began in another part of the universe and arrived on Earth as, say, a single-celled organism embedded in a frozen meteor. Another, more widely credited idea is that life began about 3.5 billion years ago as the result of a sequence of chemical reactions that took place spontaneously. Whatever.

What equivalent conditions or events might have initiated the process of *ethical evolution* required to take the human race to a better place than kill-or-be-killed? How did we go from rapacious apes to the monks who produced the art, culture, life, and spirituality that pervade the Cloisters, not to mention the Met's wonderful curators? Let's call it legal, religious, and tribal taboos—Ten Commandment–type, Thou-Shall-Not proclamations—that prohibited revenge, rape, and pillage and replaced the selfish interests of the individual with the rule of law for a common good. The New Atheists are correct that all these things *could* have happened without religion. But they didn't. They happened in all cultures through religion.

What if we're actually at the beginning of our evolution as an animal species, and not nearly so advanced as our word *modern* implies? What if, in the sphere of moral evolution, instead of an obelisk to catalyze the next step, it took the person of Jesus to lead the way? What if the process of human development will eventually be measured in millions of years from the time we stood up, walked around, and started to talk and/or kill each other, rather than in the short 100,000 years from our ancestral evolutionary home to the present, let alone our eye-blink 10,000 years of "civilization," made possible by a mere fluke: a break in the earth's normally harsher climate?

What if, in another 100,000 years, the intellectual distance between Einstein and a fruit fly is less than the moral and spiritual gap that has evolved between Einstein and the descendents of today's human race? What if (in the unlikely event that anyone cares or remembers us) both Hitchens's ideas and mine will someday be so far out of whack with what is then known to be true that we'll be lumped together as just two more "Dark Age" ignoramuses floundering in unenlightened obscurity scratching crude marks on a cave wall?

So how do our spiritual catalysts work? The Marine Corps provides a good allegory.

I had the privilege of living on Parris Island when writing my novel *Baby Jack*—about service and sacrifice and the class war that is the great divide between those who volunteer and those who don't. What I observed living on Recruit Training Depot, Parris Island, stunned me in many ways, not least of which was the powerful parallels to spirituality evident in the methods of recruit training. I hadn't been expecting to see what turned out to the best illustration of the *process* of spiritual growth I've ever encountered.

The Marines break recruits down and then build them up again as new creatures. On Parris Island (and at the Marine Corps Recruit Depot in San Diego) drill instructors (DIs) say one thing but mean another. Yelling and "brutal" training produce some of the calmest, most polite and free-spirited men and women I've ever met: United States Marines. The training involves well-disguised love in action. It offers Marines their best chance at staying alive in combat, not to mention a chance to become better human beings. (Yes, I know, not all Marines are great. Once in a while they wind up in clock towers shooting people, and they are trained to kill. But then, not all hedge fund managers turn out so great either. And I've met some really obnoxious vegans too. Hold the emails.)

A DI cajoles and screams his or her recruits into obedience to produce a team that doesn't need to scream to get things done. Above all, the DIs lead from the front—showing, not just saying; doing, not just describing. The Marines achieve the spectacular change that takes place in their recruits through a means that, to secular observers—I use the word *secular* because the Marine Corps is as much a religion as a military force—looks as if the DIs are trying to strip the recruits of their ability to make choices. In fact the opposite is the true. By breaking down the recruit and destroying his or her selfishness—the usual American hyper-individualism and consumerist "me first" mindset—the drill instructor is, in fact, creating a future Marine who will put the good of his or her fellow

Marines first and will thereby be able to make creative decisions that entail sacrifice.

When they are learning drill maneuvers, such as how to carry a rifle on a parade deck and do a port arms, Marine recruits appear to be wasting time. However, these "useless" lessons are actually about survival. This is true even though the ability to march in step and snap a rifle prettily to one's chest is meaningless, in and of itself, in combat. But the discipline, pride of accomplishment, and unit cohesion learned through the art of drill is not meaningless. It's one reason Marines win battles.

By breaking recruits down and rebuilding them as stronger versions of themselves, the DIs liberate their recruits to a life of freedom that comes only with competence combined with a willingness to sacrifice for others. The essence of the liberation experienced in Marine recruit training is the ability to walk in another's shoes, to first lose one's life in order to regain it, to die to self and then to be resurrected as a member of a team with a higher purpose.

To emphasize the most essential lesson of boot camp—teamwork—the recruit is never allowed to refer to himself or herself in the first person. From the moment they step onto the fabled yellow footprints of Parris Island—when recruits arrive they step onto footprints stenciled on the pavement and thus are automatically formed up—until they receive the eagle, globe, and anchor emblem at graduation, recruits must always refer to themselves as "this recruit" never as "I" or "me." Recruits earn the right to become a Marine, and with that high honor they reclaim the right to use the first person again.

The process of moral evolution shaped in all of our "boot camps" is long. It's uneven. The journey is made in fits and starts. The enlightened coexist with the unenlightened. It's a messy and ugly process. Our species' boot camp is on a cosmic timeline absurdly out of sync with our oh-so-short individual lives. And as a species, we are only on Training Day One, as far as I can tell.

When it comes to our individual metaphorical boot camps, the new recruit caught up in the details of "recruit training" is really learning an altogether different lesson from what it *seems* is being taught. What the Marine Corps cares about is that the recruits leave behind the selfish "me" civilian culture. What the Marine Corps wants is Marines who have replaced "me" with "we." What the Marine Corps is doing is using its own form of hyperbole, similar to Jesus's exaggeration when (as recorded in Luke) Jesus said, "If anyone comes to me and does not hate his own father and mother and wife and children and brothers and sisters, yes, and even his own life, he cannot be my disciple."

Jesus required that obedience to the higher call take precedence over human concerns. The Marine Corps demands that the recruit also leave behind father, mother, brother, sister, and all familiar habits and become a new man or woman: a Marine. And in order to do that, the recruit volunteers to give up everything he or she takes for granted as normal and be plunged into an alternative reality wherein he or she learns to relate to the world all over again as part of a community rather than as a solitary individual.

Marines do not need to remember how to do port arms after they learn that the Marine next to them is more important than they are. And by the same token, no one needs the Ten Commandments if she or he actually practices the full meaning of "Love thy neighbor."

The process of growing up as an individual and as a species never stops. The lessons implicit in our "recruit training" led us to question the religion that was part of our earlier "boot camp." If this unprovable idea of mine has a nugget of sense, it suggests that perhaps God leads His children to and through atheism as a stage on their journey. Maybe He does this for the same reason as any parents who want their children to grow up and think for themselves.

I believe that we'll get to a point in our evolution when atheists and religious people move beyond our respective "boot camps" and abandon the habit of taking things so literally. Liberated from that narrow perspective, we will perceive the overarching truth: The sum of our parts adds up to something altogether unexpected, a spiritual

animal whose existence doesn't make sense but—nevertheless—here
we are! There are two ways to see this contradiction. We can regard
it as an urgent problem to be solved or as a paradox to be celebrated. I choose the latter.

I think that atheism and fundamentalist religion as we know
them will last barely a geological eye-blink just a few hundred or a
few thousand years more. Then we will begin to understand that we
are spiritual beings *and* animals; that the universe is impersonal *and*
love preceded it; that we believe *and* we doubt; that a particle may
be in one place *and* in another place at the same time; and that love
is a chemical reaction *and* a revelation. Above all, I hope that we
will someday understand that *apophatic paradox is the blessed, creative, and freeing nature of reality*, not a "problem."

It strikes me that the monastic tradition of silence and inner stillness holds clues to the understanding that paradox must not be resolved. We'll never know the end of this movie. We *are* the movie,
and this movie is being shot in subtle tones, not in stark black and
white or vivid color. And our director is an Bob Altman type. He
uses the mistakes as "truth buttons," and changes plans creatively.
Like Altman, He also works with the actors and will listen to—and
enjoy—their ideas, even change the script to accommodate them allowing for improvisation.

I believe that someday the celebration of the spiritual/material paradox will break down what now seems to be a "Berlin Wall" between
secularism and religion in a way that transcends the boundaries of
the world's monastic communities and science labs and explodes into
the realm of general knowledge, just as the once far-fetched idea of a
round earth revolving around the sun exploded from the theory of
one or two scientists, eventually to become general knowledge. Mean-
while, speaking as a father, I know that my concern for my children
was not what they believed about me, but how they behaved and how
they treated their mother, their siblings, their home, and their schools.
My concern was not whether my children believed the right things
about school but whether they did their homework. My concern was

not whether they believed the correct things about families but whether they were polite to their mother.

Concentrating on belief rather than on character leads some people—be they atheist or religious—to get stuck on the training rules and miss the whole point of "boot camp." They never get their "eagle, globe, and anchor" emblem and graduate. It's as if there were platoons of recruits stuck on Parris Island who had never graduated and who, now as crazy old men, are still marching around yelling cadence, having mistaken the training phase for *being* Marines. Rifle drill and doing a perfect port arms are seen by this lost platoon of fundamentalist recruits as the end point, not a step along the road.

That is *exactly* what all fundamentalism is: people mistaking the steps of training—the rules, myths, and "ditties"—for the goal. And because the mistake is a massive one, all sorts of cruelties and fictions are used to reinforce this false and endless recruit training. The permanent recruit from our "lost platoon" codifies the preliminary stage of shouting and breaking down, makes it permanent, and calls it doctrine. The permanent recruit (as it were) also tries to go into battle using port arms to fight the enemy, not knowing that what happened on the parade deck wasn't to be taken literally, but was a step to build the character needed to fight messy, always improvised, battles.

Three months of boot camp is enough for anyone! If you spend a lifetime there, you'll go crazy and take a lot of people with you. Enter "Christians" stalking the grieving families of soldiers killed in our wars, desecrating the solemnity of their funerals with screams of "God hates fags!" and "God hates America!" Why? Because the young man or woman being laid to rest volunteered to defend our country, and our country has laws defending the rights of gay men and women and permits abortion.

I kept notes when I was on Parris Island writing *Baby Jack*. I had, as they say, carte blanche, because the general in charge had read my son John's and my book *Keeping Faith* and liked it. So I was able to observe the nuances of training night and day, with no escort and no part of training off limits. I was able to learn that even in the midst of boot camp, as training moves into the last weeks, the DIs and recruits begin to turn a corner. That is when the spirit behind the training becomes apparent. That is when the DIs loosen up and start to let the recruits share some personal information the Marine way, of course.

Parris Island:

19:30—SDI (Senior Drill Instructor) time in the 1077 squad bay—SDI Baker passes out letters, some of the recruits have to do push-ups to earn their mail, either because they get so much or because someone has written something on an envelope such as "Go Army!" that SDI Baker considers an insult.

The SDI perches on a locker, and the recruits sit cross-legged around him on the floor, God among his angels. The SDI sits still for a moment, looking at his recruits. No one dares to move so much as a finger. Then he slowly spits his tobacco juice into his ubiquitous Dr Pepper can.

"Who hasn't told his story?" asks Baker.

Hands go up. Baker barks out a name.

A recruit stands.

"This recruit was bouncing around in confusion. His MOS [military specialty] is infantry. And he joined the Marines because of the war."

"Aye, recruit," murmur the other recruits.

Another recruit stands.

"This recruit is from Guatemala and moved to New Jersey with his mom when he was twelve, and this recruit is 0–300 [infantry]— he joined because his friend was killed in Iraq and this recruit went down to the recruiting station the day of his friend's funeral. This recruit hopes to soon become an American citizen."

"Aye, recruit," from all the other recruits.

"This recruit joined to see the world."

"Aye, recruit."

"This recruit joined to show my friends I had bigger balls than they do."

"Aye, recruit!"

"This recruit joined because his dad's a Marine."

"Aye, recruit."

"This recruit joined because he wanted to be proud of something."

"Aye, recruit."

"This recruit joined because he loves America."

"Aye, recruit."

"This recruit wants to get all his bad habits out."

"Aye, recruit."

"This recruit wants to protect his family."

"Aye, recruit."

"This recruit will be the happiest person alive in just one week, because he will be a Marine!"

Thunderous: "AYE, RECRUIT!"

By the last weeks of training, the DIs let the recruits in on the secret: Training was training, but being a good Marine is not the same thing as being a good recruit. The recruits begin to understand that the purpose of training was not to succeed in boot camp but to *become* "the happiest person alive . . . because he will be a Marine" and to *leave* boot camp connected to the larger (and timeless) truth that serving others is a joyful experience.

CHAPTER 13

"Shedding over Every Daily Task the Light of Love"

How does the learner then become a believer or disciple? When the Reason is set aside and he receives the condition. When does he receive the condition? In the Moment. What does this condition condition? The understanding of the Eternal.

Philosophical Fragments, Søren Kierkegaard

Frank: My folks were Catholics converted to Evangelicals, I was saved in the 2nd grade, baptized by immersion at 12, grew up in an evangelical denomination where we didn't smoke or dance. . . . But in recent years, I confess, not much of this makes sense to me any more. I try to keep my doubts to myself. . . . I need things to make sense. I believe in the message of the Bible, but not in its literal interpretation. . . . I really don't have anyone to talk to about this. . . . My husband becomes upset and can't believe what he's hearing. I don't want to give up my faith; I just need it to make sense . . . I would love to know your opinion. Have you ever felt this way?

J.

Dear J: Have I felt this way? Only forever.

Very Best, Frank

I've been so fortunate. So has my son John: wife, baby, home, family, college after wartime service in the Marines. He not only survived but prospered. A young man I'll call Martin was not so fortunate.

When I returned from a trip to England in the summer of 2008, Genie told me that Martin's mother had called to say he had just committed suicide. He was a godson of mine. I'd sponsored Martin at his baptism at our Orthodox church ten years before. (Converts need a sponsor.) He was about twenty years old then. At age thirty-one, Martin stabbed himself in the heart with a kitchen knife while lying alone on his bed.

Martin had walked out of the residential psychiatric center in Minneapolis where he was living, after they lowered the dose of his medication. He was suffering from a severe case of schizophrenia. While in his apartment he killed himself.

Martin was trying to enjoy life and meet a women who could understand his situation and yet love him, studying French, Greek, and theology, and struggling to find the correct combination of medications. When he was in Newburyport visiting his mother, sometimes Martin would come to our door distraught and hearing voices, barely coherent and angry. Most of the time Martin was sweet, kind, gentle, funny, smart, and interested in everything. His illness got the better of him.

I talked to Martin's mother on the phone for a long time after Genie told me what had happened. "He had an accident," I said, grasping for some sort of a summing up of our conversation. "He collided with his illness."

"Yes, an accident," said Martin's mom.

I wish I had called him more often. Martin used to send me sweet postcards. Did I answer them all?

You know you didn't!

I was in England the week before Martin died. I was there to go to my very dear old friend John Bazlinton's funeral. I saw Sandra, John's wife, and their daughter Chloe, my goddaughter. We had not seen each other for about ten years, although we'd often talked on the phone. Still, it was a shock. Sandra, Chloe, and I had all grown older. Chloe had just had her first baby. Jacob was born while Chloe and her husband were living in China.

Chloe leaned over her father's coffin to say goodbye while holding baby Jacob. That's as close as John Bazlinton got to meeting his grandson. The timing of his death was so cruel. John collapsed with an aneurysm. Six weeks later he was dead. Chloe was in China and eight months pregnant unable to travel to say farewell to her dad. Grandfather and grandson missed meeting by mere days.

John Bazlinton was a true friend. He gave me my first art show at his gallery in London when I was twenty. John and Sandra remained close to Genie and me. Sandra is one of the most beautiful human beings I have ever known. Chloe grew up into a lovely, sensitive, and creative woman; just who I would have expected Sandra and John's child to become. Seeing Sandra and Chloe suffer was devastating.

John and Sandra always called Genie and me, no matter how long it had been since we'd seen each other, and no matter how far away Genie and I moved. John and Sandra also happened to convert to the Orthodox Church about ten years before he died. John had wandered as a spiritual refugee for a lifetime that began in a family of nine children, all of whom were (at one time) caught up in a group known as the Closed Brethren, an evangelical/fundamentalist cultic offshoot of an offshoot so weird that they could have no fellowship with anyone outside their small denomination.

The Closed Brethren followed the typical evangelical/fundamentalist pattern of splits, only they wound up more splintered and extreme than most. Their roots were in the Plymouth Brethren denomination that split into the Open Brethren and the Closed, or Exclusive, Brethren. Yet another group that formed, the Taylor/Symington/Hales group, embraced a "separatist" doctrine that became more and more extreme as time passed. And—of course—there was an ultimate split based on one of the leaders allegedly having an affair with a married woman, and a further schism took place.

My aunt Janet—my mother's older sister—joined the U.S. branch of this outfit in the late 1950s. Aunt Janet was ordered to leave her husband and two young sons, because they didn't join the group and she could have no fellowship with them, including even eating in the same room. She moved out, once my aunt was forbidden to sleep in the same house as "unbelievers."

Soon after she left her family and moved into a group home run by the cult, my aunt had a devastating accident. What the leaders of her group did was to send one of my cousins the bloodied postcard she'd been on the way to the post office to mail to him when a car hit her. The pastor of the group enclosed a note with the postcard telling my cousin that his mother's blood showed that God was punishing him for not joining the group and was also punishing his mother for trying to send him the card. The leaders of the group took all the money settled on my aunt by the insurance company. Her children were never allowed to visit during her lifetime. Aunt Janet never saw her family again, except once, over forty years later, when my cousin briefly forced his way past her "protectors" posted at a hospital door by the cult's local chapter leaders as my aunt lay dying in a Massachusetts hospital.

That gap, which all evangelical/fundamentalists say they believe is established between the "saved" and "lost"—now and for eternity—was enforced here in this life by the Closed Brethren. In the midst of the Closed Brethren's ever-shrinking world, followers like my aunt were totally walled off from their families. The few times my mother called her sister (and Aunt Janet answered the phone), Mom said she could hear my aunt breathing into the phone, but because my aunt could have no fellowship with unbelievers, she wouldn't speak, no matter how much Mom implored her to.

It must have been a nightmare of self-revelation for Mom because my aunt Janet was doing nothing more than practicing an exaggerated version of what Mom believed herself. My parents believed that the lost were to be eternally separated from the saved. And my parents always said that here in this life, no one could be complete as a person without accepting Jesus, so the separation began right here on earth. (This concept of a chasm between people is paralleled by the gap that today's excruciatingly self-aware New Atheists and their followers impose when they divide the human race into their version of the "enlightened" and the "deluded.")

To be a worker in L'Abri, you had not only to be saved, but the right kind of saved. Mom and Dad would talk about this or that person being "our kind of person" or "real L'Abri material." My parents just never took their version of exclusion to the ultimate dead end that Aunt Janet's group did.

In a way the Closed Brethren were to the evangelical/fundamentalists what Richard Rorty, Christopher Hitchens, and Peter Singer are to the New Atheist movement: the more extreme (and therefore embarrassing) version of what more mainstream atheists in essence are. In fact, what Janet did to her family was similar in spirit to what my parents and I did to Genie's mother and father when we Schaeffers stole Genie away. We acted not for love's sake alone but also because our family was "saved" and the Walsh clan (Genie's family) was "lost." We were so "correct," so "right with God," that in our eyes this justified practically anything we wanted to do.

My parents based their whole lives on the difference they felt between themselves and the rest of the world, even the Christian world, even the evangelical/fundamentalist world. That's why they had to start all those "conversations" with strangers in order to save them. That's why they always urged their children to "only marry a Christian" and not just any evangelical believer either, but "our kind." Genie being pregnant was a problem, but not the end of the world. The end of the world would have been if I'd married an "unbeliever."

I have, or had, four friends more or less my age, who go way back: John Bazlinton, Francis Ackerman, Steve Hawley, and Frank Gruber. John B. is dead; Francis A. is my oldest friend. We have lots in common. Francis grew up on my mountainside in Switzerland and was also the son of expatriate Americans. Francis also went to British boarding schools and moved back to America as a grownup, just as I did. (He became an assistant attorney general in Maine.) We first met when we were both nine years old. Now Francis has Parkinson's disease, and he has recently been diagnosed with leukemia.

Steve Hawley is a successful neo-realist painter, and we've known each other since 1980. Genie modeled for him for many years. Steve suffered a career-changing accident when someone plowed their car into him when Steve was riding his bike. Steve almost died. He spent several years convalescing, and of course his art career was damaged. It took him years just to get back to where he'd been on the day he was hurled to the ground and lay in a spreading pool of blood.

John Bazlinton is lying in the old rambling graveyard in London where I left him after tossing a little dirt on his simple pine coffin. Frank Gruber (whom I first met in the 1980s) is well, but some members of his family struggle with serious health issues. John Bazlinton died at sixty-five when a vein in his brain betrayed him. Francis A.'s body freezes up, and he has to gobble medication just to hold a fork steady. Steve is still wondering how things could have been if several years of one of his most productive creative periods hadn't been stolen from him by a careless driver.

Of my four best friends, then, one is dead and one is seriously ill. One has a head that is held together by titanium plates. One worries about health problems among his family members. Who are our cosmic parents? Where are they when we need them? Is life just? Francis A. is the kindest, brightest, and most charitable person I know, but apparently that is not good enough. Is the God who—according to evangelical/fundamentalist theology—did all these bad things to all my friends our father? I hope not!

My mother never did get over her sister's betrayal of her family. It must have been shocking for my mother to see the logic of the sort of Christianity my parents believed in lived out to a radical extreme. I think that was one reason why, as the years passed, my parents became more moderate in terms of the way L'Abri was run. By the mid-1960s everyone was welcome. Dad talked more and more about art and culture, and less and less about theology. And all the taboos I grew up with regarding drinking, smoking, dancing and even sex were just not mentioned anymore. I think that my aunt Janet provided a kind of shock therapy to Mom and Dad, a case in point illustrating where the logic of becoming ever purer, ever more "correct," and ever more exclusive in one's theology leads. I think it was the same sort of experience that old leftists had in the Stalin era, when they finally confronted what their ideas had wrought.

The search for our cosmic parents, for God, for truth, for the "right" group to belong to—which is all that religion, politics, cosmology, and evolutionary biology are—reminds me of the stories I've read about adopted children growing up and starting legal battles to get their files opened. They, and we, ask, "Who are my real parents? Where do I belong? Did they dump us, or do they love us? And what's this legacy of suicide, aneurisms, religion-gone-mad, cancer, and Parkinson's they left us mired in?"

A meteor may have been our parent, providing the catalyst for that first molecular change on the path to life. It's a nice story anyway, more comforting than the stories about an angry, exclusivist God creating us in the Garden of Eden in order to torture us with suicide-inducing voices or aneurisms or accidents or Parkinson's or sisters who do to you what you yourself would never have done unto another. Did the meteor love us? There doesn't seem to be much comfort in discovering who our "biological parents"—hot gasses and some lucky molecules, and/or a mean God—might be.

I throw a jacket over my bathrobe and pajamas, shuffle on my broken-down lambskin slippers, and jump into the car with my son John at 5:18 A.M. I take him to the station, a seven-minute car ride away, where he boards the early train to go to work in Boston. Usually Genie plays taxi driver, but this morning she is away visiting her mother in California. Becky is with the baby. It's dark; John leaves in the dark and will come home in the dark at around 7:20 P.M.

During the day I'll work on this book, write emails, do some blogging, and miss Genie. I'll also be helping Becky with Lucy while John is at work. Each time I pick Lucy up or hold her while I walk around the kitchen with her napping in my arms, I'm thinking about John working in Boston, working to support his child, working so Lucy has health insurance, a car seat, money saved for her in case of emergencies, a future. I'm also thinking about what my friend John Bazlinton missed.

The connection between Lucy's biological, cosmic, and human parents and herself is not just a series of facts learned about a meteor and evolution, or a body of myths devised to help us grasp God's creation. It's my son John leaving early every morning so he can provide for her. It's Becky up in the night breast-feeding her baby and sliding into a sleep-deprived dream world where everything becomes obsessing about naps, sleep patterns, the relative merits of breast-feeding and bottle-feeding, and which baby book to read and trust. Whichever she chooses, it will conflict with other baby books by equally impressive experts: To let the baby cry or not? To start solid foods at three months or five? And an infinity of other dilemmas—a microcosm of life revolving around one tiny creature.

It is a shock to realize that my aunt believed it was God's will for her to walk away from two young sons that, by all accounts, she loved. She must have once held them as I hold Lucy. She sacrificed her sons to God the same way Isaac was almost sacrificed by Abraham in the most demented of all Bible stories. God sent an angel to stop the killing. In Aunt Janet's case, the angel never arrived.

There is no theological answer as to "why God allows" suffering, some of the worst of which is caused by God's followers and done in God's name. There is no answer as to why God seems to be such a lousy parent. All the nonsense about how God permits suffering because of our free will—blah, blah, blah—is just scared religious people making excuses for their mean and/or grossly incompetent God.

What is the source of comfort, if any? It's not found by making excuses for God or for Nature. It's found in the reality of living by the light of the gift of love.

For today, it's enough to hold Lucy close and to help Becky so she can take a shower and run errands while John works. When Genie is home, we take turns pitching in to give this grandchild the most affection we can provide. That joy balances the horror of life's woes. It also opens the door to suffering, because love invites loss. There would be no horror at death without the loss that comes from loved ones being wrenched from us. Without love, death loses its sting. What a terrible price to pay for the sweetest gift.

Love raises the stakes of loss to infinity. When Steve's wife Barbara sat next to his bed at Massachusetts General Hospital week after week, she was imprisoned there because of love. When my mother called her sister and said "I love you," only to be greeted by silence, her sister was rejecting the love that my mother had embraced, the love that enabled my mother to transcend the theology of exclusion that her sister practiced in its bitterest form.

When Chloe mourns her father, it is in the context of her love. When she was a very young child, Chloe used to take baths with her beloved daddy. John served them tea, toast, and marmalade in the bath, and father and daughter took their afternoon tea on a special tray that he had made to fit over the tub. Later in life, Chloe learned to draw birds when John took her to bird reserves and shared his expert ornithological knowledge with his little girl. Later still they collected discarded furniture from rubbish tips on the streets of London, and John would rebuild it. Chloe loved her eccentric father and he loved her.

That is all we'll get in the way of the answer to suffering.

Some of the biblical writers are honest on this score. "For who knoweth what *is* good for man in *this* life, all the days of his vain life which he spendeth as a shadow?" writes the author of Ecclesiastes. Atheists say that those of us who "cling to religion" are victims of our needy emotions and that we hide behind words like *mystery* to leave an escape hatch open to immortality. I reject that idea. I don't care whether I live forever or not. Nor do I have an answer for the apparent meanness of God and/or Nature, other than to note that love and loss go hand in hand.

Had Barbara lost Steve, I don't think that she would have wished she had never known him. Sandra misses John but is glad they had so many years together. Chloe is fatherless, but her love remains. Francis A. is facing the unknown, but he has a loving family and loyal friends by his side. My mother loved her sister, and to this day she sometimes weeps when Janet's name is mentioned. So my aunt's extreme error was (in a way) trumped by Mom's love. It was a privilege to know Martin, even if in the end his illness killed him.

There is no good, let alone final answer about suffering and loss. This is a question of embracing the paradox. What I care about is that my life not be stripped of meaning and beauty in the here and now by overeager busybodies bent on converting me to their atheist cult *or* by religious zealots who soft-peddle lies about a God who solves everything. He doesn't. Ask Martin's mother. Ask my mother about her sister Janet.

There must be a better way than navigating between an indifferent universe and a Disney "god" of canned, happy evangelical endings or the angry hate-filled god whom my aunt followed and who "told" her to trash her family in favor of a simplistic purity that no one can or should ever attain. Rigid purity is the ultimate denial of paradox. And that denial is the only blasphemy there is. It's the blasphemy committed against God by all fundamentalists with every false certainty they mouth about Him.

Bertrand Russell longed for some way to sum all this up but avoided the false comfort of false certainty. In his lyrical *A Free Man's Worship*, written in 1903, Russell described the problem of mortality so well:

> But the beauty of Tragedy does but make visible a quality which, in more or less obvious shapes, is present always and everywhere in life. In the spectacle of Death, in the endurance of intolerable pain, and in the irrevocableness of a vanished past, there is a sacredness, an overpowering awe, a feeling of the vastness, the depth, the inexhaustible mystery of existence, in which, as by some strange marriage of pain, the sufferer is bound to the world by bonds of sorrow. . . . Victory, in this struggle with the powers of darkness, is the true baptism into the glorious company of heroes, the true initiation into the overmastering beauty of human existence. From that awful encounter of the soul with the outer world, enunciation, wisdom, and charity are born; and with their birth a new life begins. . . . To abandon the struggle for private happiness, to expel all eagerness of temporary desire, to burn with passion for eternal things—this is emancipation, and this is the free man's worship. . . . United with his fellow-men by the strongest of all ties, the tie of a common doom, the free man finds that a new vision is with him always, shedding over every daily task the light of love.

It seems to me that Russell the atheist best articulates the message of faith in God regarding suffering: "shedding over every daily task the light of love." Amen.

With or without my questions answered, I'm glad that my friend John Bazlinton had a religious funeral where we could shed our tears in the light of love. It is comforting to have a means to lift such devastating moments out of the ordinary. As Russell wrote, "in the endurance of intolerable pain, and in the irrevocableness of a vanished past, there is a sacredness."

John Bazlinton's funeral—held in a lovely Russian Orthodox cathedral in London—was the place where Chloe, Sandra, and his other family members and friends could mourn, where dignity if not logic, was provided by the ancient rituals. I think we all, Orthodox and non-Orthodox alike, found comfort standing on the solid ground of settled custom that afternoon.

When I send my son John off to work on a frigid winter morning, I make the sign of the cross over him three times. I'm glad I have a way of expressing my blessing beyond mere words or a hug. Making that sign of the cross expresses all the longing I have to arm my son against a future I have no way to intervene in. It is also an act of humility, a way to say that I am not all-powerful but share the vulnerable predicament we all find ourselves in. And when I hold Lucy, I'm thinking that—whoever those cosmic parents of ours were, those first molecules, that first squiggle—I'm thankful to be here. I express that gratitude each day when Lucy and I stand before the icons Genie and I keep in our hall and I light a candle. Lucy and I say thank you to God or rather I do, and she stares at the flame.

I am saying thank you in the same way that my son John is thanking me by being a good father to his daughter, by sacrificing for her as I have sacrificed for him and as my parents sacrificed for me. In that continuity—that continuing story about love—we hand on the one real gift we can give and the hope that the cumulative total of our knowledge, someday, as more fully realized beings, may open the family file and that we may find the real answer to the question "Who are we?" For now, my answer is "We are givers of thanks."

Bertrand Russell put it so well in the prologue to his autobiography:

> Three passions, simple but overwhelmingly strong, have governed my life: the longing for love, the search for knowledge, and unbearable pity for the suffering of mankind. These passions, like great winds, have blown me hither and thither, in a wayward course, over a great ocean of anguish, reaching to the very verge

of despair. I have sought love, first, because it brings ecstasy—ecstasy so great that I would often have sacrificed all the rest of life for a few hours of this joy.

I pass the wood-burning stove, and the glow it casts through its Pyrex glass door illuminates the darkened kitchen on this winter day. I'm holding Lucy. Her bare feet are cupped in my hand; my head is bent at an awkward angle that, if witnessed by a Red Cross worker visiting a prison camp, would rate as a "stress position" and torture! But if I move she'll wake up.

For weeks I've spent most days with a stiff neck and cramped shoulders. I've learned to enjoy this "torture" because it's the result of holding Lucy as I walk around that kitchen table (again!) with her feet in my hand, her bottom perched on my forearm and the back of her head cupped in the other hand. I hum along with Beethoven's Sixth. As long as my humming continues, and I don't shift the positions of my arms, she stays asleep.

My communion with my granddaughter is complete. And through her, my communion with my son away at work is complete as well. He would so much rather be where I am.

Does love predate brain chemistry? Does love predate the planet I'm standing on? Does love predate the universe? I think it does. I'll take the tears in exchange for a chance to hold Lucy.

Love hurts. I kept a diary when John went to war.

February 26, 2003
Marine Barracks Ft. Meade

It was snowing hard. I sat at the base visitor center waiting for my boy for an hour. When John strode in we hugged, then walked over to the desk to get my visitor pass.

"I have some news for you," John said. "But I'll wait till later to tell you."

The security officer filling in the information on my visitor pass piped up: "Is it news of a deployment?"

"Maybe," growled John.

We stepped out into the snow.

"It looks like I could be sent to the sandbox in two weeks," said John.

I knew something like this might happen, what with all that is going on with our wars. I'm feeling ill, empty; trying to be cheerful for John's sake.

John's room in the barracks is strewn with all his new gear. I will sleep in the extra bed.

John tries on his new bulletproof vest and a desert cammie jacket. I take pictures with my old film camera. I only have five shots left on the roll. As the camera winds back after the last shot, I think of all the thousands of photographs I've taken of my son. I have to push back thoughts such as: Will these be the last pictures of John I take?

February 27, 2003

I said my goodbyes to John this morning. I woke up in the dark a little before he did and listened to him breathing. Before I went to sleep I kept surreptitiously raising my head to watch him. I didn't want to sleep while I still had the chance to look at my boy.

When John woke up I borrowed his prayer book and sat on the edge of his bed, and we said our prayers. As I made the sign of the cross over his chest, I could not help but think of the bulletproof vest and pray that if he got shot the bullet would hit the thick ceramic plate.

The words of the ancient prayers comforted me. I held his hand as we prayed. At first his grip was tight; I think he was remembering all he had to do that day. But as we prayed his grip relaxed.

"Heavenly King, Comforter, Spirit of Truth, Who art everywhere present and fills all things . . . " I pray for another minute or so and conclude with "Hear me, O Lord. Lord, I have cried unto Thee, hear me."

We were standing in a snowy parking lot opposite the base. I shook his hand, then kissed him goodbye.

"God bless you, John. Come home safe," I said.

"I'll work on it," John answered.

"I love you, John. You are a good son. I'm proud of you."

"I love you too, Dad."

John walked away.

I called after him, "I love you!"

John turned and kissed the air. I got back in the rented car but did not drive away until he was out of sight because I was so hungry for the sight of him and I could not get the tears out of my eyes.

I hold Lucy tighter when I remember her father going to war and all the nights I prayed for John. Love radiates out and infects our beginning, present and future. It is Russell's "ecstasy so great that I would often have sacrificed all the rest of life for a few hours of this joy." Love is not the product of human emotion, but I believe that human emotion is the product of love and that love predates our existence. The parent becomes the child. The child becomes the parent. John went to war while his father—I the protector—stayed home safe and in agony. I will die, but Lucy will hold her child against the cheek that was pressed against mine. Chloe has lost her father. She has not lost his love.

Love abides.

CHAPTER 14

He Never Left a Trace That He'd Been There

Consciousness of being an individual is the primary consciousness in a man, which is his eternal consciousness. But that man is slow to pass judgment who bears in mind, that he is an individual, and that the final and highest responsibility for the judgment rests solely upon him.

Purity of Heart Is to Will One Thing, Søren Kierkegaard

If you want to know what God will perhaps be like—if you ever meet—get to know Mr. Bratchi. I first met Mr. Bratchi when I was five years old. He died when I was forty-seven. Monsieur Bratchi was the village stonemason. He was just "Bratchi" to my family. Before you built anything you called Bratchi, even if it was going to be a carpentry job. Mason or not, he knew everything about building. If you were smart you took his advice, especially if you were a family of American missionaries living in Switzerland and were not much liked by the local villagers because we were foreign, some sort of "religious nutcases."

We were totally dependent on the few villagers who would talk to us in a civil way. Mom would say things like "Bratchi says we shouldn't put the window there, he says it faces the weather and won't last," or "Bratchi says to use *mélèzes* wood for the rail. So it won't rot." "Well, if Bratchi says . . . ," Dad would answer and then instruct Mom or "the girls" (my three big sisters, who spoke French better than my mother) to tell Bratchi that we would be doing whatever he recommended.

When I was five years old Mr. Bratchi came to build us a new fireplace. We lived about half a mile up the road from the village center in a big old chalet, where my parents founded their ministry. Because I spoke French, grew up near the village, and knew everyone, I gained entrance to the villagers' homes and lives, including Bratchi's, in a way that my parents and older sisters never did.

Bratchi was short and wiry. He had a somewhat dour, lined face and a workman's thick, stubby fingernails. I rarely saw him laugh. But this wasn't because he was unfriendly. It was because I saw him mostly at work. He would whistle, tunelessly but happily, but only during the cleanup after work. When he worked it was in silence. Bratchi engaged in his work as if it were a sacred trust and much too weighty a matter for him to make small talk when performing what he called *mon métier* (my profession).

By mid-afternoon Bratchi's fast-growing whiskers began to give him a Homer Simpson five o'clock shadow. But Bratchi had a personality the opposite of Homer's. Bratchi would have found nothing amusing about watching even a cartoon character doing anything badly.

In the village of Huémoz, everyone besides our family lived huddled together in the cluster of chalets that, from the mountainside above, looked like forty or fifty big square brown puzzle pieces jammed together. The peasants' chalets were so close to each other that the old roofs almost touched. Cows, pigs, goats, rabbits, and chickens outnumbered people about ten to one.

Everyone knew everything about everyone—from our village whore's latest outrage (she introduced her skimpily clad, illegitimate daughter into the family business at the village café when her girl was about fourteen) to a local wife-abuser's latest drunken mayhem.

We knew who was born a few months early (if you did the math from the wedding day) and just why the old lady who never spoke had hanged herself when she was eighty-three. (She once told a neighbor that because no one ever visited her, she was afraid of falling and dying in pain alone.)

Village gossip notwithstanding, Bratchi kept his thoughts to himself. As my parents' ministry expanded, I grew up watching him build additions on our chalet and the other L'Abri properties. Because I was "home schooled"—in other words, forgotten by my distracted parents—I could watch Bratchi from morning until evening whenever I wanted to.

Bratchi never asked why I wasn't in school. I was an American, and therefore from another planet, so what business was it of his? If I broke the silence, I felt as if I were talking in church. We'd spend whole days where the only words I heard him speak were "*C'est l'heure de mes dix heures*" ("It's time for my ten o'clock snack") and "*C'est midi*" ("It's noon"), when he went home for lunch.

Bratchi always began work at 6:30, took his bread and cheese break at 10:00, and walked home at noon accompanied by the sound of the clanging village church bell announcing midday. Bratchi came back to work at 1:30, worked until 5:00, and then carefully packed up his tools after cleaning everything meticulously. Next he would clean the spot he'd used to clean the tools, hosing all traces of cement and sand away. He never left a trace that he'd been there, not a splotch of cement, no empty bags— nothing. Local carpenters could confidently leave blond, untreated pine exposed right next to where Bratchi worked. No need to treat or varnish. No need to wait until all the masonry work was complete. He never carelessly splashed cement on naked wood, the way some masons did.

Bratchi was kind to me the way a good old dog is kind: He didn't say much but let me sit next to him. And if Bratchi didn't answer my questions—when I was still young enough not to notice what an intrusion they were—it was because he knew the only real answer to my many versions of "Tell me how to do that" was to watch and then to learn by doing, failing, then trying again.

What Bratchi built stayed built. And anyone he recommended with his highest praise, *"Il travaille comme il faut"* ("He works the way he should"), could be trusted to do a perfect job, be it plumbing or carpentry. Bratchi's philosophy of work—and therefore of life, because what besides work counted?—seemed to be that any building or wall he put up should be able to double as a bunker in time of war. His buildings were to our village what the Alps are to Switzerland and what Switzerland (before plastic Swatch watches, drugs, and graffiti) once was to Europe: unsentimental and defined by non-negotiable solidity.

Our village was a tight-knit community, with the exception of us Schaeffers, of course. There were many grudges, many cliques. Grudges can be bonds of a sort too. However, the village could not have functioned if people had let their differences, even their hatreds, keep them from cooperating. They might not have been on speaking terms, but when, for instance, it was someone's turn to use the tractor to power the band saw and cut firewood, one enemy would hand off the village saw to his neighbor, even if they exchanged no greeting.

Disputes were unavoidable in a village of about two hundred strong-willed, terminally gossipy peasants. There was a small but determined anti-Bratchi group. Mentioning his name to some people provoked a sneer, even a spit of cigar-soaked phlegm. This sneer came only from the village's losers. The villagers who took the best care of their livestock and their families liked Bratchi.

I think the resentment of Bratchi in some quarters arose because he was a bit different from the other villagers, all of whom were farmers. As a mason, he drove a small VW flatbed truck to work. Almost no one else owned a vehicle in those days. And he kept to himself. Maybe Bratchi's success was also resented, especially by the farmers who sold watered milk, or hadn't had their cows properly vaccinated, or could be found in the café from noon until evening drinking white wine. Bratchi's very existence was a rebuke to failure.

One of the few times I ever saw Bratchi flush in anger was when my mother wanted him to hurry a job. He firmly said, "*Non, il faut faire ça comme il faut*" ("No, this has to be done the right way.") A better translation might be "It has to be done the way it *has* to be done." There *was* a right way to do things, an I-have-to-do-it-this-way-because-that-is-the-law-of-the-universe way. The most ignorant or gullible client got the same high quality of work, and at the same fair price, as the most astute. The mortar between bricks was as precise and finished inside the walls as on the visible outside. To Bratchi there wasn't a visible part of a job and an invisible part. It all was his work.

What a client saw, and got, was what God saw, not that Bratchi ever said whether he believed in God. He never argued when, in outrageously incorrect pigeon French, my mother would ask him to invite Jesus into his heart. But later he'd act as if it had never happened, as if he'd seen something untoward, like an inadvertent glimpse of my mother naked, and it would be uncouth to bring up the subject again—ever.

Some villagers just wouldn't speak to Bratchi. It was nothing personal, just business as usual where fitting in was a given. I knew about not fitting in. A few of the village boys sometimes mocked me because of my atrophied leg. They were just anti-anything out of the ordinary. I was an outsider. And they were equally hard on each other.

No special favors were owed anyone. Someone with a polio-stricken leg was just lucky to be alive. Life was hard. Everyone knew that. Runt piglets were dispatched as soon as they were born. So were calves that didn't thrive. A polio leg wasn't something to be celebrated or coddled; it was just another fact like age, like death, like women's waters breaking while they were in a field working just before they gave birth. Life was hard enough without trying to see anything from someone else's point of view. What would be the point of that? There was no feel-good fakery about everyone being a winner.

Even in the 1950s, the higher up the mountainside one lived, the more old-fashioned—some might say backward—everything was, including attitudes toward infirmity. And our village was fairly high up our mountain. Huémoz nestled midway up the steep foothills rising from the Rhône Valley. We lived below dark forests that ended abruptly, about 2,000 vertical feet above us, under the rocky peaks. Little had changed in our village since the 1800s, or for that matter since the 1500s. So even though I was born into the mid-twentieth century and lived just barely thirty miles from the bustling city of Lausanne, in my childhood I lived next to and observed what amounted to medieval peasant life.

Brueghel the Elder's bucolic and slightly sinister paintings of peasants working, sleeping, defecating, and/or frantically making merry could have been drawn from the lives I saw as a child: lives lived as they had been in every farming village in Europe since the Middle Ages, a type of life that was, unbeknownst to me, about to disappear.

Who knew that we were all about to become mindless consumers and forgo all prudence, when it came to living in sustainable harmony with our environment, as the villagers and their ancestors had lived on our mountainside for centuries? But there were a few signs of the changes to come. When I was about eight, the village store owner installed a small freezer and began to sell ice cream. And one or two of the more prosperous villagers had recently acquired secondhand Jeeps. They were battered, olive green American army Jeeps that had made their way onto the local market.

In the summertime, those Jeeps were used to ferry the huge fifty-liter milk cans back from the high alpine communal pastures. It would never have occurred to the farmers to use their Jeeps for anything as frivolous as a shopping trip. Why go anywhere besides the village store? Aside from replacement parts for the more complicated farmer's tools, such as the village's communally owned band saw, no one bought anything anyway. Women made their own clothes. Everything was locally grown, except for sugar, pepper, and flour. Even our salt came from the local mine in Bex, which had been there at the base of our mountain since Roman times.

Everything had its place and season. If it was spring, the cows were led to the high pastures a full day's walk away, just above the tree line, to graze on the wide flower-strewn meadows below the looming peaks. It was a big event when the cows were led to the high pasture. The dawn's quiet gave way to the sweetly sonorous cow bells, and I'd leap from my bed and race down to the road to watch the huge brown and white cows trudge past and to see which farm boy was assigned the job of living with the cows all summer in the farmer's *haut pâturage* (high pasture) barn.

If it was winter, pigs were killed and turned into tangy smoked sausages, while their recently spilled blood froze in bright puddles on the narrow dirt roads next to the farms. Things didn't need much explaining. Things were what they were and what they always had been.

No one needed the so-called facts of life explained. Work let you live. Sex led to pregnancy for rabbits, pigs, dogs, cats, cows, village girls, your mother, your sister—whomever. If the cows ate the wild onions that grew on the side of the road near the cemetery, their milk tasted oniony for a few days, and you knew just where the farmer had let them wander. Wine made you drunk. Pine was for building. Beech was for burning.

When a family raked hay in the hot summer sun (and how else could hay get made other than as a family activity?) the fact that the matrons of the family worked stripped down to their huge lacy white bras was no more sexually provocative than the men working in their undershirts. Farm women were the farmer's partners first and their wives and daughters second. Families were teams.

Families did whatever it took to cultivate a small plot of vegetables, raise ten cows or so, milk them, slaughter the pig, and keep chickens. And together they cut hay, turned it with pitchforks and rakes, loaded it on the cart, tossed it into the hayloft, and then fed it through the winter months to the cows, which patiently chomped on the dried grass and field flowers forked down into their warm, fusty-smelling stalls. The stalls were mucked out once a day and the steaming manure added to the pile that would, in the spring, be spread on the fields to nourish the grass that turned into hay that turned into milk, meat, and manure. The cycle always started over, as it had for your father and grandfather and mother and grandmother since time immemorial.

There was no room for luxury or sentiment, let alone bathing suits or T-shirts to wear while turning the hay, any more than there was time for a "personal relationship with Jesus." He belonged in the village church where you went at Christmas and Easter, or if someone died, was baptized, or married. Who wanted to get dressed up every Sunday anyway? There was your good outfit and your work clothes. Good clothes were a nuisance. They required heating tubs of water and bathing. The men wore smelly, dark wool trousers held up by wide suspenders, nail-studded boots, and collarless old shirts. The women wore heavy stockings, knee-length shapeless skirts, and long-sleeved cotton blouses. When it was cold, the men wore vests and the women put on a shawl or lumpy homemade cardigan.

As she worked, the peasant wife never looked up, let alone gazed at the peaks, let alone ever said how beautiful they were. All she would have seen if she had looked up was the fact that the early snow was already dusting the spiky teeth of Les Dents du Midi, an unwelcome reminder that the short summer was already waning, that more work lay ahead, that the rain the week before had set the haying back several days, that her husband still needed to pile up a lot more wood for the stove by the back door. Anyway, she was in a reverie of the kind that comes to those who do the same job well again and again, until thoughts disappear and only the rhythm of the work exists.

When I watched Bratchi I'd be lost in a reverie too, mesmerized by shovel strokes, trowel strokes, or slow-motion unfolding of a wall as it seemed to rise from nowhere by magic. And since Bratchi performed every action the same way for each task, again and again, watching him was like watching a lovely and perfected machine, a "machine" that did its work with a dignity that lent the process the air of a liturgical rite.

Bratchi was reverent in the way he treated his tools and materials. Nothing got tossed or dropped. Shovels, hammers, trowels, and mixing buckets were gently picked up and carefully laid aside, to be maintained for decades. Even the nail he kept handy in the pocket of his overalls, from which to hang his plumb line, was always the same nail. His shovel was worn the way a chef's old and favorite knife gets worn by sharpening.

Bratchi's tools seemed to fit his hands, much as a prosthetic limb fits an amputee. To watch Bratchi measure out three wheelbarrows of sand for mortar and mix it with one bag of Portland cement, mix it dry, then add the water and combine it into a damp mound, then add more water until it reached the perfect consistency, was to see something inevitable and right, as if what he did had always been done that way, maybe by God Himself.

Bratchi would let me help him when I wanted to, grabbing a shovel I could barely wield and mixing the dry sand and cement before he added the water. He was very patient when he redid my work, as he almost always did. He never said things like "You idiot" or "Good job." So the few times he expressed an opinion about my work by *not* redoing it, I felt as if I'd been awarded a medal.

Over the years when I'd help out, I did my best to imitate exactly what I'd seen Bratchi do. But no matter how many times I mixed cement or tried to lay a few bricks, my efforts felt embarrassingly awkward. From the way I held a shovel—it didn't nestle in my hands—to the way the mortar would splash when I mixed it in his big, battered square mason's trough, I wasn't even within striking distance of his finesse.

Bratchi's masonry work was so practiced that he never needed to touch the mortar with his hands. I did. When helping him repoint, I just *couldn't* work it between tight bricks or stones without using my fingers. It would slip off the trowel. I'd try and try and then give up and grab a handful. Cement will eventually melt skin. By the end of an hour handling the mortar, fingerprints will be gone. Bratchi let me find out the hard way.

He worked a trowel with perfect dexterity, dipping it into his bucket without even looking and bringing it out with just the right amount of cement, which he would then flick onto a wall when applying stucco, or lay between bricks, or insert into the narrowest seam (a quarter-inch or less) between stone or brick while re-pointing a wall—just the right amount, no more and no less, with no smear stuck to the wall's face and all the mortar wedged at the same depth between the bricks. And Bratchi took his trash with him. It would have bothered him mightily to think there was any taint inside one of his walls. Even abandoning a candy wrapper tucked into some hidden spot that wouldn't be seen again for a hundred years, or a thousand, would have been unthinkable.

The clean, claylike smell of fresh cement always brings Bratchi back. He hovers near if my work gets messy when I'm repairing my old brick house. I see him frown. I'll tear down a bit of wall and start again for him or add a little extra rebar or dig another foot or two below the frost line when pouring a bit of foundation wall. When I rewrite a chapter, I think of Bratchi too. If I could ever write as cleanly as Bratchi built, that would be something.

CHAPTER 15

Much More Miraculous Than a Good Cup of Coffee

If the fact spoken of were a simple historical fact, the accuracy of the historical sources would be of great importance. Here this is not the case, for Faith cannot be distilled from even the nicest accuracy of detail.

Philosophical Fragments, Søren Kierkegaard

I was talking on the phone to Sandra Bazlinton about her husband John. This was a few weeks before he died. John needed prayer. Or maybe he didn't need prayer, but Sandra was comforted by knowing people were praying for him.

I like to think the best of God. When people are dying, I talk to Him as if God too is an innocent bystander and not—as the evangelical/fundamentalists would have it—the author of death just itching to liquidate "non-believers" at Armageddon. My reasonable God is a decent chap, and more like Bratchi than like the tyrannical monster portrayed in the grimmer bits of scripture and "explained" in the classrooms of "civilized" evangelical/fundamentalist seminaries.

"Please help John Bazlinton!" I begged. But I didn't question God too closely about why I was begging for scraps, such as a successful operation for John when, presumably, if the Creator of the universe could give me that wish, He could have just pinched off that ballooning blood vessel or been more like Bratchi—and less like some American "builders" I got to know after Genie and I moved to America—and done a better job building our brains to begin with.

According to the Bible, God has regrets and often repents of the harm he causes. In Genesis we read, "It repented the Lord that he had made man on the earth, and it grieved him at his heart," and in Exodus, "The Lord repented of the evil which he thought to do unto his people." In fact, according to the Bible, God is apologetic so often he gets sick of admitting His faults. "I am weary of repenting," Jeremiah reports the Lord saying.

There are many, many more verses about God repenting, regretting what He does, or changing his mind. Yet other verses say God has no regrets. "The Strength of Israel will not lie nor repent: for he is not a man that he should repent," says Samuel. God contradicts Himself, or rather the Bible's authors contradict themselves, when trying and failing to describe God.

Of course, evangelical/fundamentalists can't stand the Bible's obvious flaws because they worship the Bible, not God. So they try to fix their "inerrant" Bible's reputation by torturous justifications. They even make *rules* for God as if they understand God as some sort of creature trapped in the pages of the Bible, something like a fly caught on flypaper. This also seems to be a problem that plagues Muslims, who say their holy book was actually dictated, so it records the actual words of God. This may explain the apparent paralysis of much Islamic civilization. If the literal last word has been pronounced, what's left to do, say, discover, or invent? How do you change?

Here is one of the leading evangelical/fundamentalist/creationist/intelligent-design gurus, Henry Morris (of the Institute for Creation

Research), telling God what to do. In his 1996 essay "When God Repents," Morris writes,

> There is no contradiction, of course. The words translated "repent" in both Old and New Testaments, are used of actions which indicate outwardly that a "change of mind" has occurred inwardly. It is precisely because God does *not* repent concerning evil, that *His* actions will change toward man when man truly repents (this human "repentance" can go either way; changing from good to evil, or vice versa), and God will respond accordingly, since He cannot change His own mind toward evil.

I'm sure God sat up and took notice! "He *cannot* change His own mind." Got that God? Now *behave!*

Even my mother tacitly admitted that the evangelical/fundamentalist God was trapped in her inerrant Bible. According to this view, God is not the God *of* the Bible but really the God *in* the Bible. God is stuck between a rock and a hard place. The "rock"?—human words by flawed authors. The "hard place"?—the Bible as interpreted by self-interested parties.

My mother seemed to know this was the case, although she never would have said so. But Mom used to work every angle for her henpecked "god" in her prayers. Mom would pray prayers like this: "We pray that You will heal [fill in the name] and that You will also give [his or her] doctor wisdom." Which was it: wisdom for the doctor or healing? If it was only wisdom and the doctor would do the healing, that let God off the hook. And if all God could do was sharpen up the doctor's wit, that wasn't much of a miracle, not much more miraculous than a good cup of coffee. Also, since the basic idea was that healing happened only *if* the person praying had *enough faith*, then that always gave God an out, not to mention the clause in fine print: God might be allowing this "tribulation" for His own mysterious purposes to do the person who wasn't getting healed (or the people praying for that person) some "spiritual good" that couldn't be achieved any other way than by *not* getting their prayers answered or, rather, by God answering "no."

The illness, accident, bankruptcy, divorce, stock loss, missed train, or whatever could then be understood as a "timely chastisement," because of that verse in the Bible that says, "He whom the Lord loveth he chastiseth." That was the silver lining to suffering; it proved God loved you because the trouble He inflicted on you, by either commission or omission, which was the only way to make you into the person you needed to be in order that God would find your character to his liking. A bit circular, but tidy.

The evangelical/fundamentalist "god" trapped in the Bible was covered by more outs than a studio in a movie contract with an unknown director; if you count every "wherefore" and "whereas," it amounts to the studio saying, "Whatever this contract says, here's the bottom line, pal—you have no rights, and we can do anything to you we damn well please!"

Oh, how we Schaeffers used to cling to any scrap of supernatural *proof* of God's power! Oh, how Mom clung to and endlessly repeated the stories of "miracles" that had occurred in China, back in her parents' years there as missionaries in the late nineteenth and early twentieth centuries: the reputed sighting of angels by stranded missionaries or packages of food or money "inexplicably" left on doorsteps just in the nick of time! Oh, how thrilled we were by the signs and wonders of God's provision that made the work of L'Abri possible. Never mind that they could have been mistaken—by the less spiritually "discerning"—as mere coincidences.

Oh, how Mom and Dad abased themselves, and begged God to take all the credit for their hard work! Each gift of money to L'Abri was a miracle and had nothing to do with Mom's wonderful newsletters or Dad's tireless efforts. All the credit must go to the Lord, and details suggesting that we humans might just be the agents of our own destiny were minimized so that nothing might water down a supernatural explanation for any event—from a 100-franc note left on the kitchen table (just when L'Abri had run out of grocery money!)—to my getting Genie pregnant. It was a sin, but, "the Lord used this" so that we might be a witness to many other young people! We did the "right thing"! We got married!

Anything would do as a miracle: an unexpected parking space, a cold that one got over sooner than expected, thus freeing one up to take that all-important exam, a conversation on a train with a "seeking" and "spiritually needy" person who then accepted Christ. That wouldn't have happened *if* it hadn't been for the fact that "the Lord arranged a traffic jam so that we missed the train we'd originally intended to take," and so on.

What strikes me is that this way of praying and hoping for "signs and wonders" misses the point. We tell God our needs, but if we even glance at the reality of human evolution in progress, let alone at the universe, we know that God operates on a different timeline than we do. Bratchi will not be rushed.

My prayers for John Bazlinton didn't work. Sandra called and said he'd died. We talked about John's death. She was calm, stoic, and not bitter, only deeply wounded, empty, and sad beyond description. "So many people were praying for John," she said.

Sandra is a strong woman. There was no self-pity in her voice. There was a healthy skepticism within Sandra too. During a later conversation, she told me that an evangelical friend had called her while John was in a coma and nearing death; he had advised that Sandra call a Pentecostal American healer he had some connection with.

"He wanted me to ring this chap up," Sandra said. "He'd heard that this man had healed someone over the phone. The person he'd healed was about to have some sort of surgery on his ear. This healer prayed for the chap and he 'heard a pop' and was instantly well." Sandra paused and then added dryly, "I explained that John's situation, having been in a coma for six weeks and with three shunts in his head, was a bit more serious."

"The crazies came out of the woodwork when my dad was dying of cancer," I told her. "But if all this healing stuff works, why don't the actuarial tables show that members of Spirit-filled Pentecostal and other 'charismatic' denominations live longer, on average, than, say, Unitarians or United Methodists?"

Sandra laughed. So did I.

Does God suffer because His timetable causes so much human suffering? I don't know, but in the book of Hebrews we read of Jesus, "Who for a little while was made lower than the angels, crowned with glory and honor because of the suffering of death, so that by the grace of God he might taste death for every one." Take it or leave it.

Evagrius captures something of the rule of love trumping theology and "correct" thinking. For instance, in his *Commentary on the Book of Proverbs*, he writes, "There was a time when evil did not exist, and there will be a time when it no longer exists; but there was never a time when virtue did not exist and there will never be a time when it does not exist. For the seeds of virtue are indestructible. And I am convinced by the rich man almost but not completely given over to every evil who was condemned to hell because of his evil, and who felt compassion for his brothers, for to have pity is a very beautiful seed of virtue."

Evagrius is referring to the rich man in Jesus's parable (in Luke) about the man who dies and finds himself in hell because he never helped the poor.

> Now there was a certain rich man, and he was clothed in purple and fine linen, living in luxury every day. A certain beggar, named Lazarus, was laid at his gate, full of sores, and desiring to be fed with the crumbs that fell from the rich man's table. . . . It happened that the beggar died, and that he was carried away by the angels to Abraham's bosom. The rich man also died, and was buried. In Hades, he lifted up his eyes, being in torment, and saw Abraham far off, and Lazarus at his bosom. He cried and said, "Father Abraham, have mercy on me, and send Lazarus, that he may dip the tip of his finger in water, and cool my tongue! For I am in anguish in this flame." But Abraham said, "Son, remember that you, in your lifetime, received your good things, and Lazarus,

in like manner, bad things. But now here he is comforted and you are in anguish. Besides all this, between us and you there is a great gulf fixed, that those who want to pass from here to you are not able, and that none may cross over from there to us." He said, "I ask you therefore, father, that you would send him to my father's house; for I have five brothers, that he may testify to them, so they won't also come into this place of torment."

Evagrius discovers a seed of virtue in the rich man's compassion for his brothers. According to Evagrius, the rich man's situation is not as dire as it might seem. He's dead; he's in Hell, but wait, that's not the end of it. Evagrius writes a postscript. Since the rich man showed pity for his brothers—in other words, he felt and expressed love—there is a way out. Virtue, says Evagrius, will outlast evil. The Law of Love prevails.

Even the rich man who lived his life mired in injustice will find salvation. His hell will turn to paradise because there will come a time when evil "no longer exists," which, given Evagrius's thinking, means that someday Hell will turn into Heaven for the rich man, because if there is suffering anywhere, then evil will still exist and will have outlasted virtue.

The rich man's perception that he is in Hell derives from the gulf between him and God. This gulf was placed there by the rich man's lack of charity, which turned him into someone who cut himself off from love.

I have experienced "Hell" becoming "Heaven." My house was a type of hell when John was at war. It became a type of heaven in an instant. The place didn't change, but the separation from love was ended. It was all a matter of perception. I expressed this in my diary entry about the first time John came home from his first (of several) deployments to war.

July 4, 2003 4:31 A.M. The phone rang. "I'm about a half an hour out," said John. "Check the lawn for mines, Dad! Better yet, pave the garden over!" He laughed. "And while you're at it buy me some body armor and a sidearm! I feel naked!"

5:00 A.M. A tall thin figure slowly unfolds from our old car. I give Genie a head start. Mother embraces son.

"I was so worried," said Genie.

John holds her and she sobs. Her face presses on his olive green T-shirt and leaves a tear stain imprinted as she pulls away to look up. Then it's my turn. He smells like cigarettes and is warm from the car, stretching now from sitting for eight hours. Hard arms hug me. The sharp stones on the driveway cut into my bare feet, reassuring me that I'm awake.

Later . . .

Genie gave me a great gift by allowing me time alone with John. He was bone weary and kept stretching out, then sitting up again to say something. I lay next to him and made sure I was gripping him the whole time, an arm, foot, hand; it didn't matter, I just wanted to be certain that the nightmares were lies. John's eyelids were drooping. He'd speak, fall silent, doze off, rouse himself and then add something else.

"Once we were in a convoy driving through Kabul," said John sleepily. "I was lookout, and I spot this taxi getting between me and our following vehicle, and we don't like it when anyone gets between us. Then I see these tubes on the front seat that look just like RPGs, so I draw a bead on the driver and if he had so much as touched those tubes I would have put one right between the eyes."

John dozed a little and then roused himself and continued.

"We shoot right through the glass in situations like that because at close range the bullets won't deflect. Anyway it turned out those were just cardboard tubes and he was on the way to the post office. I came within a hair of killing him because of cardboard tubes. . . . "

With relief flooding over, under, and around me came an incredible exhaustion. I dozed, soothed into dreamless peace by his beloved voice. I woke and John was asleep next to me, his warm shoulder pressing mine.

Later . . .

John went out for a walk. I offered to go with him but he said he wanted to stroll around the neighborhood alone. "You know, Pop, just to try and get my head in gear."

As the door shut I was overwhelmed by gratitude and also a crushing weight of unexpected sadness. A moment later I was kneeling by my bed. I was praying for Staff Sergeant Shane Kimmett's father Dan, for Corporal Matthew Commons' mother, dad, and stepmother, for Lt. Childers and his parents, and for all the fathers, mothers, sons, daughters, husbands, and wives I knew of those who were not coming home. Before my son went to war, I never would have thought of tears as a sacred duty.

I ask myself why I persist in believing in God when so many smart and decent people tell me I'm crazy for doing so. There are times when I am an atheist. There are times when I am an agnostic. But those moments are always on a theoretical level. I can be in the middle of a period of atheism, but when I wake up at four A.M. to write, I find myself praying, "Lord I offer you this day." I find myself experiencing a presence that I commune with before I think about it. I sense that presence quietly working on His projects just as I'm working on my books and just as Bratchi worked on his walls, getting on with the job at His own pace and doing it His own way.

CHAPTER 16

"First and Last Alike Receive Your Reward"

Even in these relations which we men so beautifully style the most intimate of all, do you remember that you have a still more intimate relation, namely, that in which you as an individual are related to yourself before God?

Purity of Heart Is to Will One Thing, Søren Kierkegaard

The idea that faith consists of signing on to a series of statements, such as "I believe in the Trinity" or "I believe that Jesus died for my sins" or "I believe that selfish genes rule!" and that somehow, by *saying these things as sincerely as possible*, I get "saved" or "enlightened" (the secular version of redemption) is crazy. Saying words is not the same thing as understanding what they mean, let alone living by them.

Because we can never be sure what our motivation for anything is, we don't ever know whether we're sincere enough for those words to count, even if we do happen to be correct in our understanding of what the words mean. Am I saved *enough*? Am I atheist *enough*? I may *say* I believe this or that, but do I believe *enough*? Do I know enough so that I can pass the correct-belief exam? What if I was slightly distracted when I prayed the "sinner's prayer"?

Maybe I got distracted by the nubile breasts of a young, pretty athe-ist while reading the latest "wisdom" from Dawkins on her T-shirt. Now I can't remember. Was it *"The God of the Old Testament is arguably the most unpleasant character in all fiction: jealous and proud of it; a petty, unjust, unforgiving control-freak . . . "*? Or is the *correct* greatest, "most famous" Dawkins line *"The God of the New Testament is arguably the most unpleasant?* . . . Oh crap! Now I'll get tossed out of atheist Sunday school—again!

This is why Pascal's wager, wherein one bets in favor of God rather than risking damnation, is one of the stupidest ideas ever ar-ticulated. If there is a God, He knows you were just a good betting man splitting the odds—insincere but scared. Besides, you'll forget the Most Important Seven Things you *must* always remember, do, or something—and be lost! So belief is not the point. Who is sin-cere enough? And who has a good enough memory?

The point isn't belief, but who we *are*, how we learn to treat the "Higginses" we run across in our lives. The point was to learn from Mr. Parke not to bully, rather than to learn how to *say*, "I'm not a bully" convincingly. The point is to watch Bratchi work and try our best to imitate him.

Some of the earliest writings of the Church's leaders seem to side firmly with the view of an all-redeeming mercy being at the heart of the message of the gospel. In the liturgical tradition, this is expressed at the beginning of Lent (the period of time leading up to Easter). One pre-Lenten service is dedicated to the recollection of the story Jesus told about the Prodigal Son.

The returned Prodigal finds his father's forgiveness and love heavenly, whereas his stay-at-home "good" brother resents the lav-ish welcome his father is giving to his wayward, undeserving brother, who has all those wrong and bad ideas and who has screwed up his life. The older brother's focus is on himself and his good standing with his father. The good son finds his father's non-judgmental forgiveness of his fallen brother hellish. The wayward son didn't even have good motives for coming home! He was just hungry! He wasn't even repenting in some spiritual way! He just wanted lunch!

After the Prodigal's return, both brothers are with the father. Both brothers are *in the same location*, sharing the *same reality*: their father's love. But because of the difference in the content of their characters, one finds the father's love to be Heaven, and the other finds it to be Hell. Hell is a condition of loss. It's not a place. "Hell" and "Heaven" are both experienced as the presence of God: the merciful experience joy, the merciless sorrow.

One of the great sermons of the ancient Church sums up this view beautifully. The fifth-century *Easter Sermon* of St. John Chrysostom is read aloud in every Orthodox Church at midnight Easter service. To understand the sermon, you must remember that many Christians prepare for Easter by fasting, or at least we're supposed to. Yet Chrysostom declares that those who have *not* kept the fast—in other words, people like me—are equally welcome.

How we receive God's love is the issue, not correct ideas, let alone correct rule-keeping. Here's part of Chrysostom's proclamation of hope:

> *Are there any weary with fasting?*
> *Let them now receive their wages!*
> *If any have toiled from the first hour,*
> *let them receive their due reward;*
> *. . . First and last alike receive your reward;*
> *rich and poor, rejoice together!*
> *Sober and slothful, celebrate the day!*
> *You that have kept the fast, and you that have not,*
> *rejoice today for the Table is richly laden!*
> *. . . Let no one go away hungry.*
> *Partake, all, of the cup of faith.*
> *Enjoy all the riches of His goodness . . .*

Chrysostom is not alone in his view of hope for all. For instance, St. Isaac the Syrian writes, "Paradise is the love of God . . . [and] . . . those who are punished in Gehenna [fire] are scourged by the scourge of love." According to this mercy-laden thread of Christian tradition, fire—in other words, Hell—is the love of God, and we experience God's love either as heavenly or as a painful scourge, depending on how we receive it. Basil the Great points out that the "Three Children"—as the three young men in the book of Daniel (Shadrach, Meshach, and Abednego) who were thrown into the fiery furnace are called—were unharmed by the fire, yet the same fire burned and killed the servants at the entrance to the furnace. Basil understood this story as an allegory of Heaven and Hell. Those with loving hearts and forgiveness for all will feel the "fire" as love. And according to St. Gregory the Theologian, God *is* paradise *and* punishment, because each person tastes God's "energies,"—as God's presence is sometimes called—according to the condition of his or her soul. Gregory says the next life will be "light for those whose mind is purified . . . in proportion to their degree of purity" and darkness "to those who have blinded their minds . . . in proportion to their blindness."

Bratchi was the same person to everyone. He built everything well, no matter who his clients were. Fools, good people, and scoundrels alike got the same perfect quality of work. The only people who didn't like Bratchi were the villagers who knew that his honesty and the quality of his work put them to shame. His very existence was a rebuke to them; "Heaven" (and affirmation) for some, and "Hell," a cause of shame, in others.

We make our own destiny. Nichol and I were in Hell standing outside Mr. Parke's door. When we changed from a spirit of fear to relief, from bullying to repentance, Hell became Paradise. What creates gratitude in one person is nursed as jealousy in another. Both receive the same love. According to Jesus's parable, those most convinced that they are saved are the most lost.

I look at my life: marriage, children, grandchildren, my garden, the pictures I paint, the words I write, my dear friends both living and dead, debts, fears, failures, sins, illness, and disappointments, and I remember the whole journey as an experience of God's love. My belief in what Bill Maher would call my "imaginary friend" contains all the superstition and/or faith and/or insanity accumulated over my lifetime. It has nothing to do with any guarantee that things will work out to my liking. It, like Bratchi, is what it is. It is also inscrutable. Bratchi never did say much. If you wanted to know anything about him, you could learn it only from what he'd built or by remembering the experience of sitting quietly with him.

At its best, faith in God is about thanksgiving, shared suffering, loss, pain, generosity, and love. The best religious people and best secular people learn to ignore their chosen (or inherited) religions' nastier teachings in order to preserve the *spirit* of their faith, be that faith in secular humanism, science, or in God. It's the tediously consistent fundamentalists—religious or atheist—who become monsters. They are *so sure* they have *the* truth that they dare claim that only the members of "my" religion will be saved. This is the road to my aunt Janet's madness, and her clutching a phone while speaking not one word to her sister, alone in her "purity" and utterly cut off from those who loved her.

Because holy books—this includes books on science or political theory that are regarded as holy by so many atheists—are written by people just like you and me, they contain all facets of the human experience: love, compassion, *and* calls for the murder of the "infidel," or perhaps, as in the case of people like Singer, calls for "defective" children to be killed. They are also, inevitably, full of mistakes. The question is what to follow and what to ignore, in the same way one ignores a village idiot but knows the value of the village where both the idiot and the rest of us all live.

Every religious and every scientific/secular tradition has a "village idiot" or two lurking in its scriptures, be they in the Bible, the

Koran, or scientific texts. The good news is that most of the scriptures of the world also provide a reason to override our village idiots: the Law of Love.

Groups and individuals who are at various stages of "recruit
training" coexist. In one part of the globe, a thirteen-year-old
child is buried up to her neck in sand and then stoned to death
because she was raped. In another part of the world, a thirteen-
year-old is punched by her stepfather and is then removed from
the stepfather's home, under the protection of the law, and put in
foster care. In yet another household, a stepfather who *feels like*
punching his thirteen-year-old stepdaughter *sits down and reads
her a story* instead, because he has evolved to a place of greater
spiritual enlightenment.

Atheists, agnostics, Jews, Muslims, Eastern Orthodox, Hindus,
Mormons, Roman Catholics, Protestants, et al. we are all on a journey. That journey is happening to us with or without our approval.
It's called evolution. Some of us say we believe "every word of the
Bible" or "every word of the Koran" or "what science says" or
whatever other scripture we hold dear, but we're all slowly learning
discernment because we are evolving in spiritual sensibilities as well
as physically. This is why today, there are fewer religions that de-
mand blood sacrifices than there used to be. This is why Christianity is less anti-Semitic than it used to be. This is why I believe that
in the contest between extremism and moderation, enlightened Muslims will eventually win the hearts and minds of most Muslims, who,
like almost everyone, want to love their families in peace.

I think that most people are better than their official theology
and/or ideology. There are wars aplenty in the world and hatred
abounds, but there is also peace aplenty and love abounds as well.
There are extremists in all our camps—religious and secular—who'd
kill the rest of us just to prove a point. They have the anger, or worse
yet the blind certainty of their correctness, but the rest of us have
the numbers. The future belongs to the peacemakers.

In the Gospel of John, Jesus showed us the way to get beyond "boot camp" to the deeper meaning of faith in God:

> Jesus went unto the Mount of Olives. . . . And the scribes and Pharisees brought unto him a woman taken in adultery; and when they had set her in the midst, they said unto him, "Master, this woman was taken in adultery, in the very act. Now Moses in the law commanded us, that such should be stoned: but what sayest thou?" [Jesus answered] "He that is without sin among you, let him first cast a stone at her." . . . And they which heard *it*, being convicted by *their own* conscience, went out one by one, beginning at the eldest, *even* unto the last: and Jesus was left alone, and the woman standing in the midst. When Jesus . . . saw none but the woman, he said unto her, "Woman, where are those thine accusers? Hath no man condemned thee?" She said, "No man, Lord." And Jesus said unto her, "Neither do I condemn thee: go, and sin no more." Then spake Jesus again unto them, saying, "I am the light of the world: he that followeth me shall not walk in darkness, but shall have the light of life."

What is the light? How do we follow it? Jesus demonstrated the essence of this light to the woman taken in adultery. He put the Law of Love *above* the rules of "boot camp." She had been faithless, but Jesus didn't rebuke her. Rather he *set a better example* of what faithfulness is. Jesus broke the Old Testament law by not condemning her to death. He demonstrated loyalty to a higher call; "Neither do I condemn thee," Jesus said. He returned faithfulness to a faithless stranger.

The divine catalyst of love makes trying to follow "the Lord, the Creator of life"—as God is called in the Nicene Creed—a worthwhile if quixotic quest. I am privileged to stand up in my chosen community of faith and say that creed, even with complete incomprehension. I thus identify with others on my little part of the path to God who (like me) are struggling to find the words to express the paradoxical longing we all have to connect with something greater than ourselves.

Some days I *know* that life has no ultimate meaning. Other days I *know* that every breath I take has eternal meaning. I also *know* that I'm crazy to believe these two opposites simultaneously. I'd feel even crazier denying them. I believe that both statements are true. Like that particle in a physics experiment, I am in two places at once.

So I continue to "look for the resurrection of the dead, and the life of the age to come," as the Creed beautifully describes the ultimate human quest. Since I believe that God's revelation is the gift of love, the gift of eternal life seems possible too. Because if I had the power to do so, that's exactly what I'd give to my darling Lucy.

ACKNOWLEDGMENTS

Family members and friends read this book at various stages and made helpful suggestions. I thank my wife Genie, my son Francis, my daughter-in-law Becky, my old friend Frank Gruber, professor of the history of science at Princeton University Angela Creager, and professor of philosophy and theology at Harvard Divinity School David Lamberth. Father Antony Hughes, of St. Mary's Antiochian Orthodox Church in Cambridge, Massachusetts, also read the book and commented. I thank them all for their wonderful generosity. (I let my son John off the hook on this book! He was at his new job and enduring very long days, not to mention needing every moment with Lucy.)

I want to thank my friend, my editor, and the publisher of this book, John Radziewicz. His editorial suggestions inspired me. John nurtured this project from the beginning and guided me patiently. Thanks to Lissa Warren, my indefatigable publicist, for her efforts on behalf of all my books. Others at Da Capo Press also go to bat for my work. Sean Maher and Jonathan Crowe are among them. Connie Day did a lovely job copyediting this book, and Collin Tracy was kind as she took the book through the production process. Thank you all.

My agent Jennifer Lyons is my dear friend and champion, and I thank her as always. My brother-in-law Jim Walsh showed up on the right day at the right time to fix a menacing computer problem when the deadline crunch was on and saved my peace of mind. Thank you! And I want thank the several thousand people whose emails (whether kind or rude) prompted me to write this book as they reacted to my memoir *Crazy For God* with questions such as "Well, what do you believe now?"

I found Wikipedia helped refresh my memory regarding certain facts. I borrowed some wording from their page on apophatic theology.

My wife Genie is the bedrock upon which every project of mine rests. My children Jessica, Francis, and John are my light. My grandchildren Amanda, Benjamin, and Lucy make life sweet. My son-in-law Dani and my daughter-in-law Becky are so patient and kind. Thank you all for providing me with a good life and thus making writing about that life seem worthwhile.